The Lord's Supper
in the Reformed
Church in America

american
university
studies

Series VII
Theology and Religion

Vol. 264

PETER LANG
New York • Washington, D.C./Baltimore • Bern
Frankfurt am Main • Berlin • Brussels • Vienna • Oxford

Christopher Dorn

The Lord's Supper in the Reformed Church in America

Tradition in Transformation

PETER LANG
New York • Washington, D.C./Baltimore • Bern
Frankfurt am Main • Berlin • Brussels • Vienna • Oxford

Library of Congress Cataloging-in-Publication Data

Dorn, Christopher.
The Lord's Supper in the Reformed
Church in America: tradition in transformation /
Christopher Dorn.
p. cm. — (American university studies. Series VII,
Theology and religion; v. 264)
Includes bibliographical references and index.
1. Lord's Supper—Reformed Church in America.
2. Reformed Church in America—Liturgy. I. Title.
BX9525.L67D67   264'.05732036—dc22   2007006864
ISBN 978-1-4331-0001-7
ISSN 0740-0446

Bibliographic information published by **Die Deutsche Bibliothek**.
Die Deutsche Bibliothek lists this publication in the "Deutsche
Nationalbibliografie"; detailed bibliographic data is available
on the Internet at http://dnb.ddb.de/.

The paper in this book meets the guidelines for permanence and durability
of the Committee on Production Guidelines for Book Longevity
of the Council of Library Resources.

To John D. Laurance, S.J.
Scholar, Mentor, Friend

Table of Contents

Tables

Acknowledgments

I gratefully acknowledge a debt of gratitude to several people, without whose dedicated friendship and unflagging encouragement this project would never have seen its completion. Among those deserving of special mention include Terrence Crowe, Edward P. Anderson, Arun Iyer, Deirdre Dempsey, Mark and Margaret McDonough, Roger Burns, Andrei Orlov, Derek DeJager, and Bruce and Jean Mulder. Last but not least are my parents, Steven and Rosemary Dorn, who provided steadfast emotional and financial support from the very beginning.

For their technical assistance and general guidance, I am grateful to Karen Krueger and Gale Prusinski. Nor can I fail to mention in this regard the competent members of the Interlibrary Loan Department at Marquette University. Mike Murawski, Joan Sommer, John Lent, Vicki Meinecke, and Christopher Stephenson facilitated my research by expeditiously processing frequent requests for material.

Gregg Mast, president of New Brunswick Theological Seminary, graciously consented to read three chapters of the manuscript. For their critical and constructive input into the arduous undertaking of conceiving, constructing, and sustaining a book-length argument, I would also like to express my gratitude to Joseph Mueller, S.J. and William Kurz, S.J. These men through the years have exemplified to me and no doubt to many the ideals of careful and exacting theological scholarship.

Finally, I would also like to mention Donald Bruggink and I. John Hesselink, professors emeritii of Western Theological Seminary, whose example both in teaching and writing inspired in me a *studium* for the liturgical and theological integrity of the Dutch Reformed tradition in America. With keen theological acumen and ecumenical sensitivity, John Laurance, S.J. patiently helped me to see this tradition in the wider scope of the *una sancta catholica et apostolica ecclesia*. It is to him that this book is respectfully dedicated.

Portions of the material in the chapters and appendices of this book have appeared in other published works. Grateful acknowledgment is hereby made to copyright holders for permission to use the following copyrighted material:

A slightly revised and condensed version of chapter three was previously published as "The Lord's Supper in Reformed Churches in an Age of Liturgical and Ecumenical Renewal: 1900-1968," *New Horizons in Faith and Order* 1, no. 1 (2007), http//www.ncccusa.org/faithandorder/journals/newhorizons/010105.pdf. Reprinted by permission of the Faith and Order Commission of the National Council of Churches of Christ in the USA.

Material from chapters one, two, three, and five appear in "The Liturgy for the Lord's Day and the Lord's Supper: Critical Turning Points" in James Hart Brumm, ed. *Liturgy among the Thorns* (Grand Rapids: Wm. B. Eerdmans Publishing Co. © 2007). Used by permission of the publisher.

Several liturgical texts have been reprinted from *The Liturgy of the Reformed Church in America, together with the Psalter Selected and arranged for responsive reading*, ed. by Gerrit T. VanderLugt (New York: The Board of Education, 1968). Copyright Reformed Church Press. All rights reserved. Used with permission.

Introduction

In 1968 the Reformed Church in America (RCA) completed almost two decades of liturgical study and revision with the publication of *Liturgy and Psalms*, the most recent revision of its liturgy to date.[1] The most noteworthy contribution to this latest revision, as well as the focal point of this present investigation, is "The Order for the Sacrament of the Lord's Supper."[2] A consideration of the structure of this order reveals the aim of the RCA to compose a liturgy of the Lord's Supper on the basis of the classic eucharistic prayers of the early Church, an aim common to the Roman Catholic Church and many Protestant churches during this period. The "Communion Prayer," with which the liturgy of the Lord's Supper proper begins, proceeds in the following manner.

Let us lift up our hearts unto the Lord!

Holy and right it is and our joyful duty to give thanks to thee at all times and in all places, O Lord, holy Father, almighty and everlasting God. Thou didst create the heaven with all its hosts and the earth with all its plenty. Thou hast given us life and being and dost preserve us by thy providence. But thou hast shown us the fullness of thy love in sending into the world thy eternal Word, even Jesus Christ our Lord, who became man for us men and for our salvation. For the precious gift of this mighty Savior who has reconciled us to thee we praise and bless thee, O God. Therefore with thy whole Church on earth and with all the company of heaven we worship and adore thy glorious name.

Holy, holy, holy, Lord God of Hosts. Heaven and earth are full of thy glory. Hosanna in the highest! Blessed is he that cometh in the name of the Lord. Hosanna in the highest.

Holy and righteous Father, as we commemorate in this Supper that perfect sacrifice once offered on the cross by our Lord Jesus Christ for the sin of the whole world, in the joy of his resurrection and in expectation of his coming again, we offer to thee ourselves as holy and living sacrifices. Send thy Holy Spirit upon us, we pray thee, that the bread which we break may be to us the communion of the body of Christ and the cup which we bless the communion of his blood. Grant that being joined together in him we may attain to the unity of the faith and grow up in all things into him who is the Head, even Christ our Lord.

And as this grain has been gathered from many fields into one loaf and these grapes from many hills into one cup, grant, O Lord, that thy whole Church may soon be gathered from the ends of the earth into thy kingdom. Even so, come, Lord Jesus.

And now, as our Savior Christ has taught us, we are bold to say:

Our Father, who art in heaven, hallowed be thy name. Thy kingdom come. Thy will be done on earth as it is heaven. Give us this day our daily bread. And forgive us our debts, as we forgive our debtors. And lead us not into temptation, but deliver us from evil; for thine is the kingdom, and the power, and the glory, forever. Amen.

The Lord Jesus, the same night in which he was betrayed, took bread; and when he had given thanks, he broke it and gave it to them, saying, "Take, eat; this is my body which is broken for you: this do in remembrance of me." After the same manner also, he took the cup, when they had supped, saying, "This cup is the new testament in my blood: this do ye, as oft as ye shall drink of it, in remembrance of me."

The bread which we break is the communion of the body of Christ.

The cup of blessing which we bless is the communion of the blood of Christ.[3]

This celebration of the sacrament of the Lord's Supper commences with praise and thanksgiving to God for the gifts of creation and for the redemption accomplished by Jesus Christ, "who became man for us and for our salvation."[4] The liturgical community then joins its praise with that of the hosts of heaven by reciting the *sanctus* ("Holy, Holy, Holy, Lord God of Sabaoth"), which concludes with an acclamation in the words of a royal messianic Psalm ("Blessed is he that cometh in the name of the Lord. Hosanna in the Highest"), the words that the people of Jerusalem used to herald Jesus' entry into the city (Matt. 21:9).[5] Following the command of Jesus that the meal be celebrated in memory (*anamnesis*) of him, the prayer continues with a brief statement in which the community commemorates Christ's perfect sacrifice offered once on the cross for the sin of the whole world. Immediately following this the members of the community offer themselves as living sacrifices in view of the joy of Christ's resurrection and the expectation of his coming again. The prayer then moves to the *epiclesis*, which calls upon God to send the Holy Spirit upon the community so that the symbolic actions of breaking the bread and blessing the cup may become for its members a sharing in the body and blood of Christ. This is followed by a corporate recitation of the Lord's Prayer. After the presider intones the institution narrative (which, while tied to the prayer, is not properly a part of it), he or she distributes the bread and the cup to the worshippers with words adapted from the Apostle Paul's First Letter to the Corinthians (10:16).

The Committee on the Revision of The Liturgy appointed by the RCA reported that it decided to adopt the form of this prayer on the basis of a close reading of the apostolic faith attested in the accounts of the Last Supper that Christ shared with his disciples (Matt. 26:26–29; Mark 14:22–25; Luke 22:15–20; 1 Cor. 11:23–26), which constitute the foundation of the Christian churches' practice of the Eucharist or Lord's Supper.[6] In this decision the committee followed the lead of the Anglican Benedictine liturgical scholar Gregory Dix, who in his monumental study, *The Shape of the Liturgy*, analyzed the Last Supper of Jesus into four basic actions:

1. Jesus took bread, then a cup of wine
2. He gave thanks, or pronounced the blessing
3. He broke the bread
4. He gave the bread and the cup to his disciples.

According to Dix, the liturgical tradition that developed from this four-action shape was certainly not uniform in every respect, but in general maintained the same four-fold structure:

1. The Presentation of the Gifts, in which the offerings are "taken" and laid on the table.
2. The Eucharistic Prayer, into which the institution narrative is embedded as a component part.

3. The Breaking of the Consecrated Bread.
4. The Communion Rite.[7]

That this four-fold structure determines the manner in which the Lord's Supper subsequently was to unfold in the congregations of the RCA marks a significant shift in the history of Reformed celebrations of the Supper. For the form for the Supper that the RCA itself inherited from the sixteenth century, as we will see, does not even remotely resemble this structure. Indeed there is a certain irony that the Reformers did not heed their own call to return to the sources in regard to the liturgical reforms they proposed for the celebration of the Lord's Supper. On the contrary, they did not interpret the words of Christ to his disciples "do this" to mean to "take bread and wine, give thanks over them, break the bread, and give the bread and the cup." Nor did they discern this four-fold structure in the Roman Canon, the eucharistic prayer used in the Roman Catholic Church at the time of the Reformation.

The abandonment of the Roman Canon in the Reformation churches, however, was not accidental. Martin Luther (1483–1546) determined that the offering up of the bread and wine as "holy unspotted sacrifices" (*Post-sanctus*) at the celebration of Mass contradicted the meaning of the gospel. Through his reading of the gospel Luther discovered a God who condescends as savior to meet sinners in their need and gives himself for them. The character of God revealed through the self-offering of Jesus Christ consists in free and unbounded giving. For Luther this God desires nothing in return for the gifts of creation and redemption: the only appropriate response is thanksgiving; in the expression of thanks the community at worship acknowledges that God is the merciful giver of every temporal and spiritual gift.

Luther initially did not see a need to change the structure of the Mass to express this concept of worship, but only a need to eliminate from the Canon the formulae that contained sacrificial ideas. Consequently, the *Formula Missae* that he outlined in 1523 consisted only in a brief preface, the institution narrative, and the *sanctus*. But by 1526, in his *Deutsche Messe*, the institution narrative appears apart from the context of the prayer, and is preceded by a paraphrase of the Lord's Prayer and a brief admonition.[8] In the form of the *Deutsche Messe* especially we see reflected the idea of Luther that the power of the Mass is found solely in the institution narrative. The narrative is not merely to be understood as containing the words of consecration; it consists at the same time of the words of promise Christ addresses to the liturgical community, words by which the worshippers are enabled to receive through faith the gifts of Christ's body and blood under the elements of bread and wine. In sum, there is no place in the celebration of the Supper for an offering by the worshippers; the focus is exclusively on what the worshippers receive, namely, the word and the gift of Christ.

Thus the attempt to reshape the Roman Canon in accord with Reformation principles gradually led to its total elimination. This development is most evident in the Reformed communion orders. The forms for the Supper used in the Reformed churches derived in most cases from a vernacular paraliturgical service popular in the territories of Southwest Germany and the Swiss city states. In the form for the Supper found in the *Forme des Prieres* that John Calvin (1509–1564) provided for Geneva in 1542 the institution narrative (drawn from 1 Cor. 11:23–29) serves as a scriptural warrant for the celebration and, after a brief prayer for worthy reception, introduces the entire order.[9] Just as the biblical text precedes the sermon, so that there is no question that the minister proclaims the word under the authority of the Lord, so too the institution narrative precedes the entire celebration, so that there is no doubt that this same Lord authorizes the words and actions associated with it.[10] To extend the parallel between the sermon and the Supper, we can view the admonitions, exhortations, and doctrinal statements that follow the institution narrative as constituting an extensive exegesis of the Pauline passage. The form concludes with the words of distribution, communion, and a post-communion thanksgiving. The outcome is that the Eucharist became a paranetic and didactic exhortation addressed to the community in the name of God instead of a eucharistic prayer addressed to God in the name of the community.

From this brief overview, it is clear that the Communion Prayer represents a significant departure from the typical sixteenth century Reformation forms of the Lord's Supper. Howard G. Hageman, an important catalyst in this momentous change in the worship life of the RCA, realized this when he said that, because the new order for the sacrament of the Lord's Supper differs radically from the traditional forms, it ought to invite serious theological study.[11] The present work is our attempt to respond to this invitation. Our aim is to show that this departure involves not merely a change in the shape of the celebration, but, more importantly, a change in the expression of its meaning. But before we can do this, we must naturally turn first to the traditional forms in order to determine the shape and meaning of the celebration embodied and expressed in them.

The traditional forms to which Hageman referred are designated in *Liturgy and Psalms* as the "unabridged" and "abridged" forms for the sacrament of the Lord's Supper. In the 1968 revision both are relegated to the status of alternate orders.[12] In the first chapter we examine the unabridged form, its historical context, structure and content in order to find our liturgical and theological bearings at the origins of the RCA tradition of the Lord's Supper. In chapter two we continue the historical investigation into this tradition by tracing in the life of the RCA those changes which led to the destabilization of the first form, resulting in the composition of the abridged form during the later nineteenth and early twentieth centuries. We complete this investigation in the third chapter, where we survey the influence of the twentieth century liturgical and ecumenical movements on the committee's decisions that were critical for the formation and adoption of the Communion Prayer in 1968. In the last two chapters we shift our focus from historical to critical and constructive concerns. In the fourth chapter we attempt to assess critically whether and how far the RCA succeeded in modeling its new order for the sacrament of the Lord's Supper on the eucharistic faith and practice of the earliest Christian communities, as they are attested in the New Testament and other ancient documents. In the fifth chapter we apply the insights gained from our analysis of the structure and dynamic of eucharistic praying at the origins of the Christian tradition to the Communion Prayer itself. On the basis of these insights, we attempt to demonstrate that the celebration of the Lord's Supper within the framework of the Communion Prayer entails a modification of the traditional Reformed meaning of this sacrament precisely because and as it is expressed through this framework. We hope that the results of the following investigation might stimulate the RCA to review critically and constructively its own liturgical and doctrinal traditions, in order to ask how these traditions can be received and integrated more accurately and adequately into the life of that denomination today.

PART ONE

Historical Background

The Lord's Supper in a Century of Reform: The German Palatinate and the Dutch Reformed Tradition in the Sixteenth Century

What *Liturgy and Psalms* designates as the "unabridged" form originated out of the form for the celebration of the Holy Supper contained in a Dutch service book published by Petrus Dathenus (1531–1588) at Heidelberg in 1566.[1] Having begun his vocation as a Carmelite friar, Petrus Dathenus embraced the Reformed faith in 1550, and became a preacher of the new doctrine. He traveled to London during the reign of Edward VI (r. 1547–1553), and became familiar with a congregation of Dutch refugees there, one of the many "Stranger Churches" under the superintendence of the Polish reformer, John à Lasco.[2] After Edward's death, his sister Mary acceded to the throne and launched a violent campaign to restore the Roman Catholic faith to England. Consequently, many Protestants were forced to flee to the Continent to escape persecution. Dathenus fled to Germany, and became pastor of a Flemish congregation in Frankfurt from 1555 to 1562. When increasing opposition from the Lutherans there finally forced him out, Dathenus and sixty families under his care moved to Frankenthal, a city in the territory of the Rhine Palatinate. Here the elector Frederic III (1515–1576) offered to the beleaguered refugees the use of a former monastery for their worship services. Out of respect for the elector's desire for political and religious stability in his territory, Dathenus diplomatically translated into Dutch many of the liturgical forms and prayers contained in the Church Order of the Palatinate (*Kirchenordnung der Kurpfalz*), which the elector had commissioned and published in Heidelberg in 1563.[3] Because Dathenus' form for the celebration of the Holy Supper is an almost exact translation of that contained in this church order, the Palatinate form became the prototype of the celebrations of the Lord's Supper in the Reformed Church in the Netherlands and later in America through the centuries even to the present day.

In order to determine how the Lord's Supper was understood at the origin of the Dutch Reformed tradition in the Netherlands and America, it is necessary to situate this form in its proper historical context. We begin, accordingly, by considering the emergence of the Church Order of the Palatinate. This is central to our purpose because what we can learn about the political and theological climate in which this church order was composed will significantly influence how we ought to understand the celebration of the Supper in the churches of the territory. As we will see, our historical survey will reveal that the final edition of the church order included a new catechism. The Heidelberg Catechism was intended by the drafters of the church order not only to be a compendium of private instruction, but also the standard for the doctrine, discipline, and worship of the churches.[4] The structure and content of the form for the Lord's Supper, consequently, cannot be understood apart from an appreciation of the role envisaged for this catechism in the regulation of the ecclesial life of the Palatinate. It will therefore be necessary for us to indicate this role before we proceed to our proper subject matter. We will then analyze the form for the Holy Supper by giving a description of its general shape while at the same time offering commentary on the content of the rite. This chapter will conclude with a brief overview of the reception of the form in the Netherlands and in America during the seventeenth and eighteenth centuries.

Emergence of the 1563
Church Order of the Palatinate

The German territory of the Rhine Palatinate was one of the seven great electoral principalities into which the Holy Roman Empire had been divided around the middle of the fourteenth century. While the members of the Hapsburg dynasty, the emperor Charles V (r. 1519–1556) and his brother Archduke Ferdinand, controlled the system of imperial governance at the time of the Reformation, the seven princes nonetheless shared important responsibilities in the imperial administration and exercised considerable autonomy over the affairs of their own territories. The jealousy of the princes for their territorial independence at least partly contributed to the success of the broad scale religious reforms which Martin Luther introduced in Saxony in the early 1520s with the support of prince Frederick the Wise (1463–1525). In fact, it was the support and protection of the princes and their allies that helped make the spread of Protestantism throughout Germany possible.[5] The Rhine Palatinate cautiously adopted the Lutheran Reformation under the reign of its prince Frederic II (r. 1544–1556), but did not unreservedly embrace the new movement until Frederic II's successor, Otto Henry (r. 1556–1559), acceded to the principate. The Palatinate then began to move away from Lutheranism in a Calvinist direction about 1560 under the leadership of Frederic III (r.1559–1576).

Among the causes for this turn of events in the Palatinate was the conflict that erupted in the confessional life of the German churches claimed by Luther's reform. With Luther's death in 1546 the theological tensions that had existed between the great reformer and his trusted colleague and adviser Philipp Melanchthon (1497–1560) produced a sharp division of parties. A crucial point of doctrine on which the two parties diverged concerned the modality of Christ's presence in the Lord's Supper. Underlying this controversy was the broader question about which edition of the Augsburg Confession (*Confessio Augustana*) was to be received as authentic.[6] This authoritative statement of the Lutheran faith, which Melanchthon drew up to present to the emperor at the Diet of Augsburg in 1530, existed in two versions. In the "unaltered" Latin text of 1531 (*Invariata*) Melanchthon appeared to make common cause with Luther on the manner in which Christ is present in the Supper. Article 10 reads: "the body and blood of Christ are truly present [the German text adds: under the form of bread and wine] and communicated (*distribuantur*) to those who eat the Lord's Supper." Later, however, Melanchthon gave expression to his mature position on this subject. In his revised edition of the Augsburg Confession, published in 1540, he deleted the words *vere adsint* (truly present), substituted the word *exhibeantur* (presented) for the word *distribuantur* (communicated), and added the phrase *cum pane* (with the bread). In this "altered" text (*Variata*) the amended article now reads: "with the bread and wine, the body and blood of Christ are presented to those who eat in the Lord's Supper." The "Philippist" Lutherans, and even Calvin himself, endorsed this amended article.[7]

If at first Melanchthon's revised text of the Augsburg Confession was accepted as the latest and improved edition in the churches and schools of the Lutheran territories, its status was later to change as a result of the catastrophic events in Germany during the years 1546 to 1548. In 1546 Charles V declared an imperial ban against the Lutheran princes John Frederick of Saxony and Philip Landgrave of Hesse, and prepared to settle the religious difficulties in Germany by force of arms.[8] The Smalcald League mustered its forces in response to the threat, but in spite of its military superiority, it did not overcome the emperor's armies. With the support of Duke Maurice of ducal Saxony, Charles defeated John Frederick of Saxony at Mühlberg on 25 April 1547. In return for helping him defeat the Lutheran princes of the League, the emperor awarded the office of elector of Saxony to Maurice, and brought John Frederick into imperial custody. At the instigation of his son-in-law, Maurice, and the elector of Brandenburg, Philip, too, surrendered himself to Charles. With the two major protectors of the German Reformation in captivity, Charles now had control over the Smalcald League and sought once again to reassert his power over all Europe.[9]

The outcome of the Smalcald War seemed to threaten the achievements of Luther's reforms in the German territories, but it soon became clear that the emperor was politically unable to realize his ambition of reclaiming the empire for the one Church. At the Diet convened at Augsburg between 2 September, 1547 and 30 June, 1548, Charles had a unity formula drafted, called the Augsburg Interim, which he intended to serve as a temporary settlement until the religious breach between the Lutherans and the Roman Catholics could be healed by a general council.[10] The formula affirmed Catholic doctrines and mandated the restoration of Catholic practices in the churches, but it also made several important concessions to the Lutherans, including clerical marriages without papal dispensation, communion under both kinds, a statement on the doctrine of justification by faith, and an acknowledgment of the need for reform.[11] These concessions, however, failed to satisfy the theological interests of most Lutherans, and many from both the southern and northern territories preferred exile to living under the new regime.[12] Fearing the civil unrest, the electors Maurice of Saxony and Joachim of Brandenburg appealed to Melanchthon to revise the Augsburg Interim to conciliate the disaffected Lutherans in the empire.[13]

Melanchthon responded by drawing up and promulgating a new document called the "Leipzig Interim" on 17 December, 1548. It contained an unambiguous statement on the Lutheran doctrine of justification by faith, but at the same time conceded to the Roman Catholics the validity of the seven sacraments, thereby acquiescing to the desire of Charles to reimpose Catholic practices on the churches.[14] Melanchthon defended his initiative by arguing that concessions to Roman Catholics on worship and ceremonies were *adiaphora* [indifferent matters], and posed no threat to pure doctrine. His willingness to compromise, however, invited fierce criticism from fellow Wittenberg theologians Matthias Flacius Illyricus (1520–1575) and Nicholas von Amsdorf (1483–1565). These men and their followers were no longer confident about the direction in which Melanchthon was leading Luther's reform; they began to distance themselves from Melanchthon, and eventually began to identify themselves in opposition to him as the "genuine Lutherans" (Gnesio-Lutherans). The bitter antagonism between the two parties would later have fateful consequences for the political stability of the territory of the Rhine Palatinate.

The conviction of Melanchthon about the *adiaphora* was not to be tested. The opportunistic Maurice later entered into an alliance with Charles's enemy, King Henry II of France, seized control of the Smalcald League, and turned against the emperor.[15] With the combined forces of France and the League, Maurice defeated the imperial armies at Innsbruck in the spring of 1552, and forced Charles to negotiate for peace at Passau. John Frederick and Phillip of Hesse were subsequently released, and the Treaty of Passau, signed in August of the same year, restored religious rights to the Protestants. The Diet of Augsburg in 1555 ratified the terms of this treaty, and issued the Religious Peace of Augsburg. This political solution to the religious conflict provided that the princes who had adopted the Augsburg Confession were afforded the same legal protections as the Catholic princes, and decreed that every prince had the right to decide the religion of his territory (*cuius religio, eius regio*). Citizens who did not agree with the religion of their prince were free to move rather than face heresy charges. The Religious Peace also stipulated that all church lands in the possession of Lutherans before the Treaty of Passau were to be retained by them. And, finally, it required that every ecclesiastical prince—archbishop, bishop, abbot—forfeit his title, land, and privileges in the event of his conversion to Protestantism.[16] It is significant, however, that the provisions of the Religious Peace did not extend to those Protestants—including Calvinists—who did not subscribe to the Augsburg Confession.

The new situation in the German territories certainly gave security to the Lutheran princes who were zealous for advancing the evangelical cause. When Otto Henry acceded to the principate of the Rhine Palatinate in 1556, he began aggressively to carry out the same Reformation policies as he had done in his duchy of Neuberg, for which he had provided a church order in 1554. As soon as Otto Henry had assumed his electoral responsibilities, he commissioned his court preacher Michael Diller, former Augustinian friar, Henry Stoll, professor at the University of Heidelberg, and Johannes Marburg, Protestant preacher from Strassbourg, to draft a new church order for the territory. This committee drew on the existing church orders of Neuberg, Württemberg, and Strassbourg as their sources, and incorporated in their composition the Small Catechism of Württemberg theologian Johannes Brenz (1499–1570). Otto Henry introduced the Palatinate Church Order of 1556 with a mandate "concerning the abolition of Catholic worship and a provisional order of worship in the evangelical manner (*Sinne*), dated 16 April, 1556." In it the new elector appealed to the desire of his predecessor Frederic II to advance the Reformation in the Palatinate, as well as to his own jurisdiction in the territory and to the reforms that he had already successfully carried out in Neuburg. Otto Henry proscribed the celebration of the Mass and the Catholic ceremonies that still predominated in many churches in the territory, and stipulated that only biblical preaching, German hymns, absolution, baptism without Catholic ceremonial, and the Lord's Supper under both kinds, be observed in all the churches of the territory.[17] In December of 1557 he reissued the mandate against Roman Catholic practices, ordering all Palatinate civil officials to provide for the removal of images, side altars, ciboria, and other decorations in the churches.[18]

Most significant, however, for the later momentous developments in the Palatinate were the university reforms that Otto Henry introduced in 1557 and 1558. Relying on the counsel of Melanchthon, the elector appointed several important Protestant scholars to influential positions at the University of Heidelberg. He succeeded in enlisting the services of the French Reformed scholar Petrus Boquinus, who was to have a distinguished career as professor of New Testament in the faculty of divinity until 1577. Boquinus was soon joined by the Gnesio-Lutheran Tilman Hesshus, whom the elector appointed to serve as the dean of the faculty of divinity, general superintendent of the churches, and minister of the Church of the Holy Spirit. In 1558 Otto Henry called to Heidelberg the Swiss Reformed scholar Thomas Erastus, who was to serve as both the court physician, professor of medicine, and later rector of the university. Erastus had been trained in theology as well as medicine, and would exercise a considerable influence in the political and ecclesial affairs of the territory.[19] Curiously, the divergent confessional traditions represented by these and other men did not seem to be a concern to Otto Henry. Whether he deliberately sought to make the University of Heidelberg a flagship of confessional unity by these appointments is unclear. In any case, he was naïve to assume that men of diverse theological opinion could work together without conflict.[20] As a result of his predecessor's policies, Frederic III found in key political and ecclesiastical positions officials representing all the major Protestant traditions—Gnesio-Lutherans, Philippists, Zwinglians, and Calvinists—when he assumed electoral office in 1559. This volatile state of affairs was bound to lead to trouble, and it later exploded in a public controversy involving Hesshus and the Calvinist William Klebitz, a young student at the university and deacon at the Church of the Holy Spirit.

The academic disputations that Boquinus had scheduled for two theology students, Klebitz and Stephen Sylvanius from Groningen, served as the lightning rod of this controversy. As the general superintendent and dean of the theological faculty, Hesshus strenuously objected to the examination of these two students, whose confessional commitments placed them outside the acceptable bounds of the type of Lutheranism that he represented. Hesshus' persistent opposition brought him into his first conflict with the rector—now Thomas Erastus—and the university senate, which responded to the belligerent zealot by summarily excluding him from its meetings. Thus the bold stand of the leaders of the Reformed party, Boquinus and Erastus, against their theological adversary succeeded in winning their university's support in this conflict.[21]

In early April 1559 Hesshus left Heidelberg for his hometown of Wesel to attend to family matters. During his absense the University conferred on Klebitz a degree in theology, for which the young student defended the following seven theses on the Lord's Supper:

1. To take Christ's words of institution: "This is my body," simply (that is, literally) is not permitted by the rule of faith.
2. The Lord's Supper consists of two distinguishable parts, one earthly and one heavenly, as the pious have agreed.
3. The earthly is the bread and wine; the heavenly is the communication with the body and blood of Christ.
4. The earthly is eaten with the bodily mouth; the heavenly is eaten with the mouth of the soul, that is with faith.
5. That the word of Christ in the first place, as men are wont to say, applies to the sacrament itself but that the second refers to the enjoyment (profit) or working of it, is as the Apostle teaches, not a correct distinction of the truthful speech (word).
6. The instructing power is inseparable from the communication of (with) the body and blood.
7. Concerning other purposes this holy meal does not appear to raise any strife in the churches.[22]

Klebitz's theses exposed an open target for Hesshus' attack. Hesshus had insisted on a strict interpretation of Luther's doctrine of the Lord's Supper, and demanded a view of the real presence according to which the body and blood of Christ are corporeally present in the elements of the bread and wine, as Article 10 of the 1530 Augsburg Confession (*Invariata*) unambiguously taught. The slightest deviation from this position was inadmissable, according to the superintendent, in a territory claimed by Luther's reforms. And so when Hesshus returned from Wesel, he began denouncing the young deacon from the pulpit, vilifying him as a Zwinglian, a sacramentarian fanatic, and an Arian.[23] Klebitz pressed the counter attack, and soon the controversy was raging among the students and townspeople in Heidelberg.

Because Frederic had been away at the Diet during this turmoil in Heidelberg, his brother-in-law the Count Georg of Erbach attempted to intervene by urging Hesshus and Klebitz to desist from their polemicizing until the elector returned to settle the issue. The two men ignored the pleas of the court official, and continued to revile each other from the pulpits. When Frederic did finally return to Heidelberg, he summoned the two agitators before him, and enjoined silence on them for the sake of public morale. Hesshus refused to obey the order, and promptly re-engaged his enemy. When Klebitz retaliated, the Lutheran theologian placed him under a church ban. On 9 September, 1559 the elector intervened a second time, demanded that Hesshus lift the ban, and ordered both parties to adhere to Article 10 in the 1540 Augsburg Confession (*Variata*) as the norm for teaching and preaching.[24]

At worship in the Church of the Holy Spirit the next day, the court preacher Michael Diller and William Klebitz distributed the Lord's Supper to the elector and his court, thereby signalling that the peace and unity in the territory had been restored. But the Gnesio-Lutheran supporters of Hesshus, and a few days later Hesshus himself, once again fomented public discord by resuming their persecution of Klebitz. The young deacon was now so provoked that he resorted to physical violence. Frederic despaired of reconciling the two parties, and on 16 September summarily dismissed their two ringleaders, Hesshus and Klebitz. He then sent his private secretary Stephen Cirler to Wittenberg with a request to Melanchthon for counsel on the vexed problem of the proper understanding of the Lord's Supper. In his response Melanchthon approved of the measures Frederic had taken, condemned Hesshus' doctrine of the Supper, and proposed as a formula of union the words of the Apostle Paul in 1 Corinthians 10:16: "The bread which we break is a communion [*koinonia*] in the body of Christ."[25] The heart of Melanchthon's *Responsio*, dated 1 November, 1559, is found in the following excerpt:

> The word *koinonia* needs to be explained. It does not mean that the nature of the bread is changed, as the papists say. It does not mean that the bread is the substantial body of Christ, as the theologians of Bremen say. It does not mean that the bread is the true body of Christ, as Hesshus says. But it means *koinonia*, that is, a communion by which union takes place with the body of

Christ—a union which takes place in the use, and not without our cognizance, as when mice nibble at bread...The Son of God is truly present in the service of the Gospel, and is truly effectual in those who believe. And he is present not for the sake of bread, but for the sake of men, as indeed he says: "Abide in me, and I in you." And again: "I am in the Father, and you are in me, and I in you." And in this true comfort he makes us members of himself and certifies that he will vivify our bodies.[26]

Frederic was profoundly impressed by this statement of Melanchthon, but had not yet devised a plan to settle the dispute in his territory. Meanwhile the pressure from the Gnesio-Lutherans mounted. While still in Heidelberg, Hesshus had sent out a statement of his doctrine of the Supper to the theologians at the University of Jena, who gave to it their unqualified stamp of approval. Since the beginning of the conflict, Frederic's son-in-law John Frederick of Saxony-Gotha warned him not to succumb to the temptation of the devil by abandoning pure Lutheranism.[27] The force of these circumstances prompted Frederic to investigate the matter further. Consequently, he seized the opportunity afforded by the marriage of his daughter Dorothy Susanna to John Frederic's brother John Wilhelm of Saxony-Weimar on 3 June through 7 June, 1560, to schedule a public debate on the Lord's Supper. The Heidelberg "wedding debates" were conducted in the new philosophy auditorium of the university and featured two prominent theologians from Saxony, John Stössel and Maximillian Mörlin, who represented the Gnesio-Lutheran camp, and Boquinus, Erastus, and Paul Einkorn, professor of Old Testament at the University, the leaders of the Reformed camp at Heidelberg.

The debates succeeded only in heightening the tension between the two parties.[28] Boquinus presented the theses that his student Klebitz defended the year before. The extent to which the positions reflected in the theses were irreconcilable with those espoused by the Gnesio-Lutherans is revealed especially in three of the twenty-four theses advanced by Stössel and Mörlin:

1. That the true body and blood of our Lord Jesus Christ is truly and substantially present, dispensed, and exhibited, in, with, or under the bread and wine...

4. That...[Christ] is thus received and eaten not merely in a spiritual fashion by faith, but also bodily by mouth, according to the sacramental conjunction of body and blood with bread and wine...

7. That...the body and blood are received not alone by the pious and worthy, but also by the godless, the hypocrites, and unworthy; yet with this distinction: that to the pious such eating is salvific, while to the godless it contributes to greater damnation and judgment.[29]

Frederic, for his part, seems not to have been very impressed with the arguments of the Saxon theologians, for in August of 1560 he decided to remove a number of Gnesio-Lutheran pastors from their posts. The remaining pastors in the territory were required now to subscribe to the conception of the Supper outlined in Melanchthon's *Responsio*, which the elector published for this purpose. The Reformed camp in the territory undoubtedly interpreted these measures as favorable to their cause, since they viewed the Melanchthonian doctrine of the Lord's Supper as entirely congenial with their own.

To Frederic's opponents, on the other hand, these developments in the Rhine Palatinate furnished incontrovertible evidence that the elector was defecting from the Lutheran faith. From Bremen, Hesshus pronounced judgment on the apostasy of the elector, published a rebuttal of Melanchthon's *Responsio*, and reasserted his own position in a tract called "Concerning the Presence of Christ in the Lord's Supper."[30] The Gnesio-Lutheran theologians Johannes Brenz and Joachim Westphal agreed with Hesshus that Frederic was no longer a loyal adherent to the Augsburg Confession.

Whether or not Frederic was faithful to the Augsburg Confession was more than a matter of mere theological interest. The provisions of the Religious Peace of Augsburg, as we have already seen, extended only to those German Protestant territories whose religion was determined by that confession. If the charges of his opponents were legitimate, Frederic stood in risk of losing his electoral privileges and even his territory itself.[31] But the problem of which edition of the Augsburg Confession was official and binding had still not been resolved. Aware of the internal divisions in the Lutheran territories this problem was causing, the Lutheran princes called a convention at Naumburg to meet in January of 1561. The confessional unity of the Lutheran territories was an urgent concern in the face of renewed opposition to their cause by the German emperor and by a resurgent Roman Catholic Church, which was then putting its own house in order at the Council of Trent. The princes convened at twenty-one sessions between 20 January and 8 February to discuss three major concerns: the signing of the Augsburg Confession, negotiations concerning the Council of Trent, and united evangelical action.[32] The outcome of the first issue on the agenda was obviously of paramount importance to Frederic and the Rhine Palatinate.

Frederic prepared well for the occasion, and argued forcefully that the later *Variata* ought to be adopted as the authoritative and binding confession. Moreover, he demonstrated that his own views on the Lord's Supper were wholly consistent with Article 10 in the *Variata*, thereby answering his opponents' accusations that he was defecting from the Lutheran faith. Even though the elector's competent presentation impressed his hearers, the Gnesio-Lutherans remained staunchly opposed to the *Variata*, pointing out the "heresies" of Melanchthon in this revised confession. They were unyielding in their demand that only the *Invariata*, together with the Smalcald Articles, serve as the basis of confessional unity among the Lutheran territories in the empire.

Finally, the princes could only settle on a compromise. They endorsed the *Invariata* of 1531 as the basis of their unity but, on the recommendation of the elector Augustus of Saxony, acknowledged in a preface that the *Variata* was an acceptable interpretation of the Augsburg faith.[33] The precarious nature of this compromise, however, became apparent only a few brief months later. Having withdrawn from Naumburg in protest, Frederic's son-in-law, John Frederic of Saxony-Gotha, organized opposition to the settlement achieved there, and succeeded in drawing many Lutheran princes over to his side. In July of 1560 leading Lutheran theologians from Lübeck, Bremen, Hamburg, Rostock, Magdeburg, and Brunswick convened at Lünenberg to condemn the Naumburg preface, and to encourage ongoing resistance to all heresies.[34] In the last analysis, then, Naumburg contributed only towards driving a deeper wedge between the contending Lutheran camps, and cast the die for an enduring division between the "genuine" Lutherans and the Philippists.

No doubt disillusioned over the failure of the followers of Luther and Melanchthon to surmount their doctrinal divisions, Frederic became increasingly amenable to the moderate Reformed influence in his own territory. When he returned to Heidelberg, he began to appoint more Calvinists to positions at the university until eventually they made up the entire faculty of divinity. He called Petrus Dathenus, the pastor of the Dutch refugee congregation at Frankenthal, to serve as his court preacher. He also invited Immanuel Tremellius to be the hebraist at the university, and Zacharius Ursinus (1534–1583) to be the professor of dogmatics. Ursinus was a man of massive learning whose intellectual and spiritual odyssey coincided with the confessional vicissitudes of the Church of the Palatinate. He had studied with Melanchthon for seven years, and then spent time at Zurich and Geneva, the two great centers of the Reformed movement, before assuming the chair of dogmatics.[35] Ursinus, together with the Calvinist Caspar Olevianus (1536–1587), to whose chair of dogmatics he was succeeding, would play leading roles in the composition of the new catechism that was already in the planning stages.

Frederic himself steadfastly disavowed confessional allegiance to the Calvinism that he seemed so openly to promote, but by these appointments he clearly indicated the course in which he was directing the churches in his territory. A decisive point in this course was an order that he issued in December of 1561 to the churches in Heidelberg to introduce the Reformed rite of the "breaking of the bread" (*fractio panis*) before the distribution of Communion.[36] Since this gesture embodied the Melanchthonian-Calvinist conception that the presence of the Lord at the Supper is located in the use or action of the distribution rather than in the bread and wine, it symbolized a definitive break with the Gnesio-Lutherans. This mandate coincided with the elector's determination to continue the purgations of the churches introduced by his predecessor Otto Henry. He replaced Lutheran altars with communion tables, the Host with ordinary bread, golden communion ware with ordinary utensils. He continued to remove religious art, cover statues, and close organs. He abolished Latin choral music and deleted from the church year all saint days, reducing the number of Christian feast days to Christmas and the day after, New Year's, Easter and the day after, Ascension and Pentecost and the day after.[37]

In early 1562 Frederic commissioned the drafting of the Heidelberg Catechism to promote and consolidate the reforms that he envisaged for his territory. On the one hand, he needed a doctrinal statement that located the church of the Palatinate securely within the boundaries prescribed by the *Variata*; on the other hand, he needed a statement on which the Philippists, Calvinists, and Zwinglians in his territory could agree. For this reason he desired the catechism to be a committee project. Among the prominent theologians, superintendents, and church officers who comprised the committee, there was one Zwinglian (Erastus), one Philippist (Diller), and several Calvinists (Tremelius, Olevianus, Ursinus, et al).[38] Finding common ground between these divergent parties proved trying, but the elector regarded it as indispensable to the unity of his reform and to prevent the identification of the document with any one theological party.[39] The first edition appeared on 19 January, 1563, soon to be followed by two more editions. Then on 15 November, 1563 the fourth edition of the Heidelberg Catechism appeared in the new Church Order of the Palatinate, which contained a form for the Lord's Supper. Before turning to the form, however, we need to provide a broader framework within which to situate the role of the Heidelberg Catechism in public worship generally.

The Heidelberg Catechism and Public Worship in the Palatinate

Public worship in the churches of the Palatinate cannot be properly understood apart from an appreciation of the role the Heidelberg Catechism was designed to play in the regulation of this worship. The liturgical forms bear the stamp of the catechism in their structure, theological content, and even in their wording. The documentary evidence suggesting that this was deliberate is a letter dated 25 October, 1563, from Caspar Olevianus to Heinrich Bullinger (1504–1575), successor to the great Swiss Reformer Ulrich Zwingli. Olevianus wrote that the new church order was not intended simply as a revision of the older Church Order of 1556, but was composed in compliance with the wish of Frederic that the praxis of the churches "approach as closely as possible the method and purity of the Catechism."[40]

That the Heidelberg Catechism was intended to serve as the norm for the expression of the faith of the churches at worship is reflected in the plan and organization of its material. Like most traditional catechisms, the Heidelberg Catechism provides instruction in the Christian faith by explaining the Apostles' Creed, the Ten Commandments, the Lord's Prayer, and the sacraments. But the distinguishing feature of this catechism consists in its arrangement of the material according to a threefold *ordo salutis* scheme: "misery" (*elend*), "deliverance," and "gratitude." Accordingly, the subject matter of the first section is human sin, which is revealed by the Ten Commandments (qq. 3-11); the second section treats the redemption and freedom of human beings through Jesus Christ, as taught by the Creed and the sacraments (qq.12-85); the concluding section addresses the topics of thankfulness and obedience, which are explicated by the Lord's Prayer and the Ten Commandments (qq. 86-129). Since, according to a rubric at the head of the section on doctrine and preaching, the word of God itself, "tends to arrange doctrine" according to this threefold scheme, ministers are to "attend diligently to these themes in treating their texts."[41] To ensure that their program of preaching was organized on the basis of the dogmatic outline supplied by the Heidelberg Catechism, the church order stipulates the following for its use in public worship: first, it directs the minister to read out several questions prior to the sermon on Sunday morning, according to a set schedule that enabled him to cover the entire catechism in nine weeks; second, it mandates that every Sunday afternoon throughout the year a preaching service was to be held for the purpose of catechetical instruction. To aid the preacher in this task, the 129 questions and answers were further divided into 52 Lord's Days. Finally, to adapt their preaching to the "limited understanding of the common people"[42] ministers were to cite the questions in the catechism that related to the themes of their sermons.[43]

A further consideration is the place that the Heidelberg Catechism occupies in the church order. It is inserted between the forms for baptism and the Holy Supper, which suggests that an important purpose of the catechism was to prepare young people for full participation in the worshipping community at the Lord's table. Young people who desired admission to the Lord's table for first communion were required to appear before the congregation at a special service of preparation.[44] This was held on the Saturday afternoon before the Sunday on which the Supper was to be celebrated. After preaching on the meaning of the sacrament, the minister moved to the front of the table and invited the young people to stand with him. He then asked them to recite the Creed, the Lord's Prayer, and the Decalogue, as well as to give the prescribed answers to questions from the catechism concerning the Lord's Supper. Afterward, the minister turned to the congregation and began his charge: "the word of God ascribes to us three points: first our sins; second, our redemption; third, the gratitude which we owe God in return."[45] Each of these themes is developed in the form of an examination question, to which the members of the congregation were to respond with the words, "we do" or "it is."

The content of the three questions betrays a close dependence on the Heidelberg Catechism.[46] In the first the faithful learn how to come to an awareness of their sin. The will of God is understood to be expressed in the sum of God's commandments, namely, to love God with all one's soul, mind, and strength, and one's neighbor as oneself. But since none has kept these commandments, the law functions as a mirror, in which the sin and misery of the faithful are reflected back to them. In the second question, however, the sure promise of the Gospel of redemption is explained: the Father in his mercy sent into this world his only Son who made satisfaction for sin and fulfilled for sinners all righteousness, which God ascribes to them in spite of their unworthiness. This redemption, promised and granted to individuals in their baptism, is to be confirmed for them by means of the Holy Supper, as with "true warrants and seals and through the action of the Holy Spirit in [their] hearts."[47] The Supper for this reason is a consolation to the faithful, because in it they are assured that the passion and death of Christ are their own. They are, accordingly, to celebrate it with joy and gratitude until their Lord returns to deliver them from the cross that they have had patiently to bear in this vale of tears, and to receive them into the kingdom of the Father. Appropriately, then, the third question exhorts the faithful to search their hearts to see whether they desire to live in gratitude to Christ for the rest of their

lives, renouncing sin, and extending to their neighbors the same forgiveness that they have received from Christ.

After this rather protracted examination, the minister gave to the
congregation the assurance of pardon, and then brought the service to
an end with the Lord's Prayer and the benediction. After the service,
the minister remained for private confession and absolution if necessary. Thus the congregation was prepared to celebrate the Holy Supper on the following day.

The Lord's Supper in the Palatinate: "The Liturgy of the Heidelberg Catechism"

The form for the Supper was to be used once a month in the cities,
once every two months in the villages, and in both places on Easter,
Pentecost, and Christmas. On the day of the celebration the minister
was to deliver a brief sermon on the death of the Lord and the purpose for which the Supper was instituted. A rubric directed the minister, after the sermon and the Sunday prayers, to move to the table to
read the form aloud to the congregation. It proceeds in the following
order.

1. Institution Narrative from 1 Corinthians 11: 23-29
2. Self-Examination in Three Parts:
    a. Sinfulness and God's wrath
    b. Faith in God's Promise
    c. Thankfulness and the Life of Love
3. Excommunication
4. Comfortable Words
5. Exposition in Three Parts:
    a. Homily on the Atonement
    b. Interpretation of the Institution Narrative
    c. Exhortation to Unity in the Holy Spirit
6. Prayer for Worthy Reception and Lord's Prayer
7. Apostles' Creed
8. Reformed *Sursum Corda*
9. Distribution accompanied by a Song or Scripture Readings
10. Post-communion Psalm or Prayer of Thanksgiving (two forms) [48]

The drafters of the form did not introduce any significant changes
in the general structure of the Reformed celebration of the Lord's
Supper as it had come down to them; in the order in which it unfolds

the form betrays a close dependence on the liturgical scheme that John Calvin had drawn up in his *La Forme des Prieres*, published in Geneva in 1542.[49] In Calvin's Geneva the Supper commenced with the singing of the Creed and the prayer of worthy reception. Then the minister recited the institution narrative from 1 Corinthians 11:23–29. The following penitential sections, consisting in the excommunication, the self-examination, and the comfortable words, comprised the response to the Pauline admonition to everyone "to examine himself" lest he "eat and drink condemnation to himself" (vs. 27–29). Then came a long exposition of the promises that relate to the institution of the Supper, culminating in the "Reformed" *Sursum corda*. The distribution followed, accompanied either by the singing of a Psalm or biblical verses read by the minister. The post-communion thanksgiving concluded the service, and the people were dismissed with a blessing.

The general structural affinities, as well as the similiarity in ideas and language, between the two forms furnishes evidence that the drafters of the Palatinate form had Calvin's Genevan *Forme des Prieres* before them. Indeed it would be difficult to imagine otherwise when we see that the language the drafters used for the "comfortable words" borrows extensively from the corresponding section in Calvin's rite.[50] But this does not mean that the Palatinate form is merely a slavish copy of the Genevan liturgy. In the first place, the excommunication in Calvin's order precedes the self-examination; in the Palatinate form this sequence is reversed. In the second place, the prayer for worthy reception, with which Calvin's order opens, occurs much later in the Palatinate form, before the *Sursum corda* and the distribution. It is apparent that in these features at least the drafters preferred to follow the order of the 1556 form.[51]

But what constitutes above all the distinguishing feature of the form is its close dependence on the Heidelberg Catechism. If, as we have already seen, the liturgical forms generally bear the stamp of the structure, theological content, and even the wording of this catechism, this is no less true in the case of the form for the Lord's Supper. This impress is certainly conspicuous in the section on self-examination. Adopting the familiar threefold scheme of the catechism, the material in this section also corresponds closely to the examination questions addressed to the congregation at the service of preparation on the previous evening.[52] The homily on the atonement, which carries out the command "to proclaim the Lord's death until he comes" (1 Corinthians 11:26), consists in a restatement of the teaching of the catechism on the satisfaction made by Christ through his perfect obedience to the Law and substitutionary death on the cross.[53] Similarly, the interpretation of the institution narrative teaches in the language of the catechism how the faithful are reminded and assured of Christ's love and faithfulness to them through the sacrament.[54]

Since the drafters of the Church Order of the Palatinate intended the Heidelberg Catechism to serve as the standard for the doctrine, discipline, and worship of the churches, it is not surprising to find the form for the Lord's Supper deeply imbued with it. Consequently, Sunday worship, especially on those Sundays when the Supper is celebrated, ought to be understood as a ritual enactment of what it means to live and die in the comfort of the Christian faith—precisely as the Heidelberg Catechism expounds it. The first question of the catechism reads:

> Question 1: What is your only comfort in life and in death?
> That I belong—body and soul, in life and in death—not to myself but to my faithful Savior Jesus Christ, who at the cost of his own blood has fully paid for all my sins and has completely freed me from the dominion of the devil; that he protects me so well that without the will of my Father in heaven not a hair can fall from my head; indeed, that everything must fit his purpose for my salvation. Therefore, by his Holy Spirit, he also assures me of eternal life, and makes me wholeheartedly willing and ready from now on to live for him.[55]

The second question explains what the faithful must know to rest secure in this comfort:

> Question 2: How many things must you know that you may live and die in the blessedness of this comfort?
> Three. First, the greatness of my sin and wretchedness. Second, how I am freed from all my sins and their wretched consequences. Third, what gratitude I owe to God for such redemption.[56]

The threefold content of the answer to the second question, which the rest of the catechism elaborates, serves as the pattern according to which the order of worship for the regular Sunday service in the Palatinate unfolds. This service opens with the words from 1 Tim 1:2 to convey that God approaches the worshippers as he is — their only comfort. This is to be impressed on the congregation in the words of judgment and grace in the sermon. But in order to be prepared for the reception of these words, the congregation is led in a prayer of confession, which reminds the faithful of the greatness of their sin and wretchedness and need for grace. Then follows the sermon, which may now expound more extensively the judgment and grace indicated in the simple prayer. After the sermon comes another prayer of confession, to which the "comfortable" words (i.e. scriptural promise of redemption) and the absolution are appropriately added. The faithful can now offer the intercessions in confidence, because they have been freed from their sins. For this reason the service can conclude with praise and gratitude.[57]

On the Sundays when the Holy Supper continues this service, the same moments of this divine-human confrontation are developed along another line. In the Supper the faithful pledge in more concentrated expression to adhere to the threefold pattern of misery, deliverance, and gratitude, as they had learned in the catechism and heard in the preceding prayers and sermon. From this perspective we can see the Supper rite as an intensification of what has already preceded: by objects, ritual gestures, and especially words, it reinforces precisely the understanding of the Christian faith imparted by the catechism, as well as by the prayers and sermon.

Here, however, we must add parenthetically that in his Dutch rendering Dathenus did not succeed in preserving the symmetry between the two parts of the service. For reasons not entirely clear, he introduced substitutes for the regular Sunday morning prayers provided in the Palatinate Church Order. While his opening prayer of confession conforms structurally with the Palatinate original it replaces, the prayer after the sermon is not so clearly marked by an acknowledgment of the deliverance from sin proclaimed in the sermon. Confession and supplication for pardon predominate throughout, unrelieved by the comfortable words and the absolution. The intercessions are not preceded by a thanksgiving for God's gifts of preservation and forgiveness of sins, as in the Palatinate original. The faithful then can hardly approach God in prayer in any other attitude than that of dejection thanks to their own unworthiness. The cumulative result of such a service could only be an increased awareness of sin, obscuring from view the themes of deliverance and gratitude essential to the Palatinate Reformers' understanding of the gospel.[58] Those responsible for the twentieth century revisions of the liturgy of the RCA did not ignore these structural deficiencies in Dathenus' order of worship.[59]

Returning to the form, we see that the Pauline exhortation to self-examination is expressed exactly in terms of the answer to the second question ("true self-examination consists of these three parts"). If participation in the Lord's Supper is the outstanding expression of the desire of the faithful to live and die in the comfort of the Christian faith, then they must test themselves to discern whether their desire is sincere. Accordingly, the function of the self-examination is to establish criteria upon which membership in the body of Christ is based, for in the view of the Reformers to judge oneself on the basis of the divine judgment is the condition of the divine pardon through the freely given grace of God (cf. 1 Corinthians 11:31). If the worshipper is confident that she stands in this grace, she can then in good conscience enter into the rite to hear and accept the terms of the covenant through which this grace is mediated: perfect trust in the vicarious suffering of Jesus Christ, judged for sin. The content of these terms is developed once in the homily on the atonement and again in the interpretation of the institution narrative. The purpose of the exposition, accordingly, is to confirm and deepen the faithful in this trust. It concludes with the declaration that by eating and drinking the faithful are reminded and assured of Christ's "hearty love and faithfulness" to them. The absolute guarantee of this love and faithfulness is the cross, on which Christ gave up his body and shed his own blood for the forgiveness of sins. And so it is to the cross that the bread and the cup direct the community. Since this covenant of grace includes not only the forgiveness of sins but also the Spirit of sanctification, the community is also reminded that by this death Christ obtained the "quickening Spirit" so that its members may enjoy communion with Christ their head and with one another.

If we are to read the form to this point as a simple commentary on an action with which it is only extrinsically related, then are we to understand the sacrament as no more than a symbolic action in which the faithful acknowledge that the covenant between God and the Church has been concluded through the atoning sacrifice of Jesus Christ for the forgiveness of sins? If this is the case, then the rite of eating and drinking to follow can only be a visual analogy of the grace of the covenant communicated independently of the sacrament. That is, in the strict sense there is no sacramental gift. This is the conclusion of the critic Howard Hageman, who has observed that the "hungry and thirsty souls" are not satisfied by the communion of the body and blood of the Lord through the reception of the bread and wine. Rather they are satisfied by directing their faith to the sacrifice the Lord made once on the cross, "where he took away the cause of our perpetual hunger and grief—sin." The verdict that Hageman has pronounced on the rite is that it merely gives the participants at the table a closer view of Christ's death and passion.[60]

What Hageman has regarded as decisive for this "memorialistic" conception of the rite is the section that interprets the institution narrative. Just as in the second part of the service of preparation on the evening before, the section that expounds the atoning sacrifice of Christ is followed by a section that teaches the Supper to be understood as a certain sign and pledge that the faithful share in the benefits of the saving death of Christ. But Hageman has complained that the form is not consistent here with the Melanchthonian-Calvinist view on the relation between the sign and the signified in the Supper. He has called attention to the sources on which the drafters of the Palatinate form relied for the section on the institution narrative, and noted the alterations they made. In the Supper forms in the Württemberg Church Order (1553) and the Palatinate Church Order (1556), the corresponding section affirms that the bread and wine are a certain sign and pledge that Christ has given his body to [the faithful] for food.[61] The biblical background of this statement is John 6:53–58, in which Christ refers to himself as the heavenly bread given for the true nourishment of the believer to eternal life. According to Hageman, the omission of this direct language in the 1563 form is due to a "Zwinglian" influence. The "basic idea of Zwinglianism" according to Hageman, is "that the only value in the Supper is making us remember the atoning death of Christ on Calvary."[62] The doctrine of the Reformed churches, on the other hand, teaches that the Supper is an event made effective by the Holy Spirit, through whom Christ's broken body and shed blood is really communicated to the faithful for their spiritual nourishment by means of the bread and the wine.[63]

What the doctrine of the Reformed churches has to teach about the manner in which the body and blood of the Lord is communicated through the Supper, however, is a more complicated subject than Hageman seems to have suggested.[64] In the first place, the explanation for the alteration in this section is that the drafters wanted it to express more clearly the teaching of the Heidelberg Catechism, as we have come to expect:

> ...and [he] will as certainly feed and nourish our hungry and thirsty souls with his crucified body and shed blood to everlasting life, as this bread is broken before our eyes, and this cup is given to us, and we eat and drink in remembrance of him.

> Question 75: How are reminded and assured in the holy Supper that you participate in the sacrifice of Christ on the cross and in all benefits?
> In this way: Christ has commanded me and all believers to eat of this broken bread, and to drink of this cup in remembrance of him. He has thereby promised that his body was offered and broken on the cross for me, and his blood was shed for me, as surely as I see with my eyes that the bread of the Lord is broken for me, and that the cup is shared with me. Second, he has promised that he himself as certainly feeds and nourishes my soul to everlasting life with his crucified body and shed blood as I receive from the hand of the minister and actually taste the bread and the cup of the Lord which are given to me as sure signs of the body and blood of Christ.[65]

The construal of the relation between the sign and the signified in the Palatinate Lord's Supper represents a branch in the Reformed tradition that has coexisted with the one that Hageman has claimed to be most authentic. On these two branches of the Reformed doctrine of the Lord's Supper, Paul Rorem has remarked:

> The two views of the Lord's Supper have managed to live side by side within the Reformed tradition for centuries. Does a given Reformed statement consider the Lord's Supper as a testimony, an analogy, a parallel, even a simultaneous parallel to the internal working of God's grace in granting communion with Christ? If so, the actual ancestor may be Heinrich Bullinger, Zwingli's successor in Zurich. Or does it explicitly identify the Supper

as the very instrument or means through which God offers and confers the grace of full communion with Christ's body? The lineage would then go back to John Calvin (and Martin Bucer)...[66]

Whether or not we can accept the view of Bullinger as compatible with that of Calvin, we can at least see that the form is consistent here with an important aspect of the teaching of Calvin:

In the Supper the sacrifice of Christ is so shown to us there as almost to set the spectacle of the Cross before our eyes—just as the apostle says that Christ was crucified before the eyes of the Galatians when the cross was set before them.[67]

According to Calvin, Christ has instituted the use of the sacrament so that the faithful, directed to it by the word, can see in the form of the action and in the use of the elements the very promises of the word set forth visibly.[68] This is reaffirmed in the Heidelberg Catechism: "The Lord's Supper testifies to us that we have complete forgiveness through the one sacrifice of Jesus Christ which he himself has accomplished on the cross once for all" (q. 80).[69] The Supper is a *verbum visibile* of God displayed before the assembly.

In the second place, the prayer to the Father for the Holy Spirit that follows suggests that the meaning of the Supper cannot be unambiguously reduced to a memorialistic understanding if indeed that is how we ought to read the preceding sections. The Father is asked to "act upon the hearts [of the faithful] by the Holy Spirit *in this Supper*" (emphasis added). The object of the petition appears to be twofold: first, that the Spirit may work in the hearts of the faithful, to the end that they may be conformed in obedience to Christ and in perfect trust in the Father; and second, that the faithful may be fed and comforted with "the true body and blood" of Christ, to the end that they may participate in the "new and eternal testament and covenant of grace." Participation in this covenant of grace depends on the mystical union of the faithful with the glorified Christ. Since the Holy Spirit, who lives both in Christ and in his Church, is the bond of this union, the assembly must pray to the Father for the Spirit to accomplish the goal of the the Supper. Nor does the Catechism neglect to support the intention of this prayer:

Question 76: What does it mean to eat the crucified body of Christ and to drink his shed blood?

It is not only to embrace with a trusting heart the whole passion and death of Christ, and by it to receive the forgiveness of sins and eternal life. In addition, it is to be so united more and more to his blessed body by the Holy Spirit dwelling both in Christ and in us that, although he is in heaven and we are on earth, we are nevertheless flesh of his flesh and bone of his bone, always living and being governed by one Spirit, as the members of our bodies are governed by one soul.[70]

The twofold answer corresponds structurally to the two principal parts of the form, the exposition and the prayer for worthy reception. But Hageman has pointed out in his historical research that in the Reformed churches the former — the embracing with a trusting heart — was almost invariably stressed at the expense of the latter — our being united with the blessed body of Christ.[71] The tension between the *fruitio dei* (the sanctification of sinners), and the *mirabilia dei* (the saving actions of God recalled and celebrated in the Supper), has not come to a final resolution in the tradition of the Reformed Lord's Supper celebrations. To this problem we will return when we explore in the third chapter the concerns that prompted the revisions that the RCA introduced into its order for the sacrament of the Lord's Supper.

The Lord's Prayer gathers the intentions of the people expressed in the preceding prayer; in this respect it may be seen as a collect which concludes the prayer for worthy reception. The position of the Creed at the conclusion of the didactic part of the rite accords with the Reformation insistence that the Supper cannot be celebrated properly unless the members of the assembly are prepared to approach it intelligently. The final admonition, the "Reformed *Sursum corda*," is meant to express this same concern. The people are not to find Christ in the bread and the wine, but rather to "lift up their hearts" to contemplate him in his glory at the right hand of the Father. While removed from the assembly, he nevertheless imparts to its members his body and blood through the power of his Spirit. In this it is clear that the admonition also serves to recapitulate the content of the prayer for worthy reception.

The distribution of the elements immediately follows the final admonition and is accompanied by words drawn from 1 Corinthians 10:16. The distribution formula no doubt is dictated by the advice of

Philip Melanchthon to Frederic III occasioned by the disputes of the theologians over the corporeal presence in the eucharistic elements of the body and blood of Christ, as we have already seen. It is important here to mention also that, in the Dutch churches, before the distribution the faithful were invited in successive groups to sit around long tables. This was the practice in the Dutch "stranger" churches in London, over which the reformers John à Lasco and Martin Micron presided. According to the London Church Order, sitting at the Lord's table was a public witness of the love and unity of the assembly, whose members sat together in convivial fellowship to enjoy the spiritual food and drink.[72] But the practice was also a sign of the assembly's eschatological peace with God the Father through Christ; to be seated portrayed an image of the faithful's future inheritance in the Kingdom of Christ, where Christ's own will feast at his table. That this practice was meant to point to the eschatological character of the Supper is suggested in the preface to the post-communion thanksgiving provided in Micron's order.

> I also hope that all of you who have sat here at the Table of the Lord have with the eyes of faith seen the future sitting with Abraham, Isaac, and Jacob in the kingdom of God and that you are certain of it because you trust in the righteousness, merit, and victory of Christ the Lord...[73]

In the Palatinate form the post-communion thanksgiving was simply preceded by the minister's invitation to praise the name of the Lord with thanksgiving. The sacrifice of thanksgiving in the traditional Reformed rites always is the fruit of communion received rather than an act integrally bound up in the remembering of Christ's atoning death. In the Palatinate form it consists of various biblical texts in the following order: Psalm 103:1–4, 8, 10–13; Romans 8:32; Romans 5:8–10. A second prayer of thanksgiving follows, but a rubric indicates it as a second option. Dathenus' Dutch translation omits the rubric, and inserts between the two prayers the words: "so may everyone speak with open heart and receptive mind," indicating that the two prayers were to be read successively. With this the rite is ended. Assured in the Supper that they have been freed from their sins, the assembly concludes its worship with praise and gratitude.

Conclusion: The Historical Transmission of Dathenus' Form for the Holy Supper

The Dutch Reformed Church in the Netherlands and in America introduced very few changes to the form for the Holy Supper that it had inherited in 1566 from Petrus Dathenus. At the provincial synod of Holland and Zeeland convened at Dordrecht (Dort) in 1574, church leaders passed resolutions to adopt the prayers and forms for the sacraments that Dathenus compiled for his own congregation at Frankenthal.[74] The only modification to the form for the Supper was the required use of the words of distribution based on Martin Micron's London rite:

Neemt, eet, ghedenckt ende ghelooft dat het lichaem Iesu Christi ghebroocken is tot een volcomen versoeninghe aller onser sonden.
Neemt, drinkt alle daer wt, ghedenckt ende gheloouet dat her dierbaer bloet Iesu Christi vergoten is tot versoeninghe al onser sonden.

[Take, eat, remember, and believe, that the body of Jesus Christ has been broken for the full forgiveness of all our sins.
Take, drink all of it, remember and believe that the precious blood of Jesus Christ has been poured out for the forgiveness of all our sins.][75]

At the national Synod convened at the Hague in 1586, the Reformed Church in the Netherlands mandated that their congregations were to adhere strictly to Dathenus' form for the Supper, which the minister was to read at the table on those Sundays when the sacrament was celebrated.[76] In 1618–1619 the national Synod of Dort officially ratified the prayers and forms for the sacraments provided by Dathenus, and directed that they be added to the public documents of the church. By this synodical resolution these liturgical texts (designated now as the Netherlands Liturgy[77]) acquired the same authority as that of the doctrinal standards of the Church in the Netherlands, which consisted in the Heidelberg Catechism (1563), the Belgic Confession (1561), and the Canons promulgated at the Synod of Dort.[78]

Along with these doctrinal standards the Netherlands Liturgy accompanied the colonists who settled on Manhattan Island (New Amsterdam) less than a decade after the Synod of Dort concluded its sessions. The churches the immigrants planted in the soil of the new world were subject to the authority of the governing body of the Reformed Church of Amsterdam in the Netherlands, the Classis of Amsterdam. A classis in the Reformed Church in the Netherlands was composed of pastors and elders who represented their local congregations within its boundaries. The classis stood under the higher authority of the Synod, but retained the authority to ordain candidates to the ministry. Because of their subordinate relationship to the Classis of Amsterdam, the fledging congregations in the new world became as Dutch Reformed in doctrine and in worship as those in the Netherlands itself.[79] The distinctive character of these colonial churches survived the annexation of New Amsterdam by the English in 1664; the new English government prescribed laws that guaranteed to the Dutch the rights to freedom of conscience and to worship publicly in accord with their own customs and church discipline.[80] As a result, Dutch language and culture flourished under English rule for more than a century: even French and German immigrants who later arrived in the older colonial settlements in the Hudson valley and on Long Island adopted Dutch as their language rather than English.[81]

Over time the use of the Dutch language among the growing urban populations of the renamed English colonies of New York and New Jersey eroded. To adapt to the forces of social change in America during the mid-eighteenth century, the consistory of the Dutch Reformed Church of the city of New York issued in 1763 a formal request to the Classis of Amsterdam for a pastor able to preach and to catechize in English.[82] The classis responded by recommending the Reverend Archibald Laidlie, a Scotsman who had been serving an English church in Vlissingen (Flushing), a seaport town in the southern region of the Netherlands. The consistory extended the call, and after some deliberation the Scottish pastor set out on the voyage across the Atlantic to assume his new post. In spite of opposition from the pro-Dutch party, Laidlie successfully introduced English preaching in the Dutch congregation of New York in April 1764.

Now that it had a minister who conducted worship in the English language, the church in New York would have to provide an English translation of the Netherlands Liturgy, including the doctrinal standards. Before Laidlie accepted the call, the consistory of the church had already decided to appoint a committee to begin a translation of the Dutch Psalter. Three years after Laidlie began his preaching ministry, the consistory presented its completed project in the form of the *New-York Liturgy*, which included not only a complete metrical Psalter for congregational singing, but also translations of the Heidelberg Catechism, the Belgic Confession, and the public prayers and forms from the Netherlands Liturgy.[83] The appearance at this time of a service book in English was emblematic for the changes soon to come, because in 1772 the Classis of Amsterdam approved a plan by which the Dutch Reformed Church in the American colonies was to establish independence from the mother Church in the Netherlands. In 1788 the General Synod of the Reformed Dutch Church in the United States of America (or the Dutch Reformed Church in North America)[84] appointed a committee to translate and revise the entire Church Order of Dort, as well as the doctrinal standards and liturgy. In 1793 these documents were published together as the new church's official "Constitution," consisting from this time until the present day in the threefold "Doctrine, Liturgy, and Government." While it made modifications and additions to the documents to adapt to the changed political circumstances in a now independent United States of America, the committee did not alter the form for the Lord's Supper. Until the proposals for liturgical reform in the twentieth century were implemented, the traditional form continued its official life in the transplanted Dutch Reformed churches in America as an English translation of Dathenus' Dutch translation of the Palatinate prototype.

The Lord's Supper in a Century of Transition: The German and the Dutch Reformed Churches in America in the Nineteenth Century

In view of the long fidelity of the Dutch Reformed churches to the Palatinate form for the Holy Supper, it is remarkable that the Committee on the Revision of The Liturgy appointed by the General Synod of the RCA in 1950 did not address itself to that form when it began to reconsider the structure of its traditional Lord's Supper celebration. Instead the committee turned to an alternate order for this sacrament, which appeared in the *Liturgy and Psalms* published in 1906, the most recent revision of the liturgy up to that time.[1] The "abridged" form, as the alternate order was known, was a composite of formulae drawn from the Palatinate Supper form and a prayer that appeared in a selection of occasional prayers in an earlier revision of *Liturgy and Psalms*, which was presented to the General Synod in 1873.[2] Approved for provisional use the following year, this revision of *Liturgy and Psalms* was later published as the denomination's official service book in 1882.[3] The rubric above the prayer designates it as a "Eucharistic Prayer," a term apparently not used by the denomination before that time.[4]

In their historical researches Reformed scholars Howard Hageman, Jack Martin Maxwell, and more recently Gregg Alan Mast have located the sources of this eucharistic prayer in the liturgical productions that came out of the worship renewal movements in Reformed circles in the nineteenth century.[5] During this time the Catholic Apostolic Church in Albury, England, the German Reformed Church in the United States, and the Church of Scotland published eucharistic liturgies that were the product of careful research into the liturgical traditions of the Eastern Orthodox, Roman Catholic, Anglican, and Reformed communions. These scholars have shown how the liturgies that issued from these renewal movements influenced the liturgical development in the Reformed Church in America in the later nineteenth century; their research provides important clues about how this influence extended to the more radical and far-reaching liturgical reforms that the RCA launched in 1950.

Our more limited task in this chapter will be to focus on one of these movements, one that was destined to play a significant role in these later reforms. In the mid 1840s a sophisticated program of theological and liturgical renewal known as the Mercersburg theology emerged in the German Reformed Church in the United States of America (GRC). During the course of the next several years, the two progenitors of this theology, John Williamson Nevin (1803–1886) and Philip Schaff (1819–1893), produced a voluminous body of literature in which they argued forcefully for an inclusive, ecumenical vision of an "evangelical and catholic" Church. They emphasized in their writings the historical, visible, and catholic nature of the Church and a corresponding form of liturgical worship centered on altar, Eucharist, and the sacramental mediation of grace. The Mercersburg theology generated one of the most protracted and intense ecclesiastical conflicts in American church history, and opponents in both German and Dutch Reformed circles denounced it for its "Romanizing tendencies." Yet this theology had important consequences for the conception of liturgy and worship not only in the GRC, but also in the RCA in the later nineteenth and especially mid-twentieth centuries. In an unpublished essay Hageman avowed that at his ordination he was a complete convert to Mercersburg, and already determined to flesh out his convictions in his own church. This influence on Hageman, and by extension the liturgical committee on which he played a leading role, provides the main apologia for devoting the present chapter to an exploration of Mercersburg.

We begin this chapter by tracing the origins of the German Reformed Church in the United States of America. We will see that there existed a close relationship between the GRC and the Reformed Church in the Netherlands and in America from the very inception of the first. Next, we will show how this close relationship was ruptured with the onset of the Mercersburg theology beginning in 1844. Our overview of the causes of the division between these two Reformed communions will serve as our point of access into the liturgical movement in the GRC, which we divide into two phases (1849–1857) and (1858–1866). After we have surveyed the most significant events of this movement, we will return to the RCA to consider how it responded to the changing approaches to liturgy and worship adopted in other Reformed communions. We will see that by as early as 1873 this denomination was on the way toward reclaiming for itself a eucharistic liturgy.

The Dutch and German Reformed Correspondence during the Colonial Era

Swiss German and Palatinate Reformed immigrants arrived in the American colonies almost one hundred years after their Dutch coreligionists. Determined to escape a desperate cycle of poverty, war, and oppression in the Palatinate, early groups began to settle in the American colonies about 1710. They came at first to the Carolinas, Virginia, Maryland, as well as to New Jersey and New York where they made contact with the Dutch colonists. Some of these new settlers found better living conditions in William Penn's woods; and when they reported to their fatherland about the reception they enjoyed there, an almost continuous stream of German immigrants through the port of Philadelphia soon followed.[6] Over time the territory extending from that city to the lands of the frontiers became the home of increasing numbers of people from the Palatinate region.

The fraternal bonds between the German and Dutch colonists were forged not long after the first groups of the German people began to establish their new lives in America. These people were devout, and sought to maintain in their family worship the beliefs and practices of the Reformed faith as defined in the Heidelberg Catechism. Many of the new settlements, however, did not have an adequate supply of ordained German clergy, and consequently were without the benefit of an organized congregational life. In many instances, Dutch Reformed ministers intervened to meet the religious needs of the people, especially in the new German settlements in states adjacent to their own; there is even record of a Dutch Reformed pastor who preached and baptized children in the Pennsylvania territories of Neshaminy, Skippack, White Marsh, and Germantown between 1710 and 1715.[7]

In 1725 the histories of the Dutch and German Reformed settlers in America became even more closely intertwined. On 15 October of that year John Philip Boehm, schoolmaster and lay preacher who had organized the first German Reformed congregations in Pennsylvania, presided over the first German Reformed Lord's Supper in America at Falkner Swamp, Pennsylvania. Aware that church order and sacramental discipline of the Reformed churches in Europe required a duly ordained minister for this practice, Boehm applied for ordination through the Reformed Church in the Netherlands. Three years later the Classis of Amsterdam authorized a group of Dutch Reformed clergyman to ordain Boehm to the ministry.[8] By this action the Reformed Church in the Netherlands entered into a close relationship with the German Reformed in America that continued for over sixty years. During this period the Church in the Netherlands exercised faithful oversight over its adopted daughter. Not only did the Classis of Amsterdam continue to supervise the ordination of ministers, but it also maintained an ongoing correspondence with the fledgling congregations, providing money, Bibles, and religious tracts as needed.

The responsibility the Reformed Church in the Netherlands assumed for regularizing the ordination of ministers proved to be most instrumental in the formation of the GRC as an independent denomination. In 1746 the Classis of Amsterdam appealed to the Consistory of the Palatinate to send a German minister to America. In cooperation with that governing body, the classis deputized the Reverend Michael Schlatter to Pennsylvania to supervise the German congregations and to "organize the ministers and congregations into a coetus."[9] Schlatter discharged his commission within the same year by creating the Coetus of the Reformed Ministerium of Congregations in Pennsylvania. Analogous to a synod, a coetus is a governing body composed of ministers and elders from all local churches. The Coetus convened once a year, usually in Philadelphia or Lancaster, to report on the conditions of the local congregations, as well as to decide on a *censura morum* for errant ministers. When the sessions of the Coetus adjourned, that body sent the minutes of the proceedings to the Church in the Netherlands, which reserved the prerogative to review and approve them.[10]

This new organizational structure provided the emergent GRC with a greater measure of self-determination, but it still did not possess the authority to ordain candidates to the ministry. That caused problems when delays in communications across the Atlantic impeded the ability of the GRC to provide congregations with urgently needed ministers. In fact, it was largely owing to those breaches of correspondence that in 1791 the Coetus voted to affirm the right of the church to examine and ordain candidates for the ministry without waiting for permission from the Netherlands.[11] In 1792 the church drew up a new constitution, and in the following year the new *Der Synod der Reformierten Hoch Deutschen Kirch in den Vereinigten Staaten von America* (Synod of the German Reformed Church in the United States of America) convened at Lancaster, where it adopted its own *Synodalordnung* (synod order).[12] With this action the GRC embraced the challenge to define its own place in an American Protestant landscape that was becoming increasingly pluralized.

The Dutch and German Reformed Correspondence during the Mercersburg Era

Still uncertain about its own identity and mission and limited by a chronic shortage of ordained ministers, the GRC was open to cooperation with various Protestant denominations in the early nineteenth century. Because of their shared history, the GRC was especially close to the Dutch Reformed Church in North America (DRC).[13] Nurtured by the same mother, the two bodies discussed already in 1794 the prospect of a merger, but the desire of the GRC to promote and maintain the German language frustrated the plan.[14] In spite of this failed attempt, the relations between the two remained amicable, and in 1804 they began a regular correspondence by letter. From 1813 this relationship became even closer when the synods of the two denominations began exchanging fraternal delegates.[15]

In 1834 a fraternal delegate from the German Synod presented to the DRC a request for missionary assistance for the impoverished German immigrants in the West, especially in the Alleghenies. The Dutch granted the request, and from their own congregations began to select and train missionaries adept at the German language.[16] Evidently this action served as a catalyst to renew interest in plans for a merger, because in 1842 the two denominations appointed a joint committee to work towards this end. Although this committee concluded that the conditions at the time did not warrant an "entire amalgamation" of the two bodies into one, they did propose a "Triennial Convention," to which twelve delegates each from the Synod of the DRC and the Eastern and Western Synods of the GRC should be sent.[17] The proposal was approved, and the delegates were instructed to prepare reports for the convention on the general conditions and needs of the respective church bodies. The first convention met at Harrisburg, Pennsylvania on 8 August, 1844.

John Nevin and "Catholic Unity"

The leading theologian in the GRC, John W. Nevin, was chosen to open the proceedings of the joint convention. The theme of the keynote sermon he was to deliver was that of Christian unity. The DRC no doubt was already familiar with the animus of this theologian against the divisive individualism rampant in the Protestant churches. In the preceding year Nevin had addressed this problem in *The Anxious Bench*, which created a significant sensation in the American Protestant world.[18] In this polemical tract he charged the revivalistic techniques made popular by evangelist Charles Finney (1792–1875) as responsible for the growing sectarianism in America. Among the objectionable "new measures," as these techniques were called, can be counted invitational hymns, pleas addressed to sinners by name, and the use of an "anxious seat" or bench to which the preacher summoned the "convicted" for admonitions and prayers.[19] In a revised and enlarged edition of this tract, Nevin complained that the dramatic conversions these techniques were calculated to induce depended on "sudden and violent experiences belonging to the individual separately taken, and holding little or no connection with his relations to the Church previously."[20] The "system of the bench" thus betrayed, *inter alia*, a false ecclesiology, which presumed that the "Church is to be enlarged by additions mechanically brought into connection with it from without rather than by the extension of its own organic life from within."[21] Against this Nevin objected that it was rather the forms of church life, embodied in the traditional disciplines and institutions of the (sc.Heidelberg) Catechism, that mediated this "organic life" to individuals. If the Church continued faithfully in sound preaching, patient instruction, pastoral visitation, and church discipline, revivals would happen as a matter of course. "In this view the Church is truly the *mother* of all her children. They do not impart life to her, but she imparts life to them."[22]

In arguing for the "system of the catechism" against the "system of the bench" Nevin already adumbrated the ecclesiological and sacramental principles that were to constitute the foundation of the Mercersburg theology. In his keynote sermon "Catholic Unity," Nevin developed these principles in the form of a programmatic statement of that theology. He chose for his text Ephesians 4:4–6, and divided the sermon into two parts. In the first he treated the "nature and constitution of this Holy Catholic Church"; and in the second he addressed the "duty of Christians as it regards the unity, by which it is declared to be thus Catholic, and Holy, and True."[23] It will be helpful to sketch a detailed summary of the content of this sermon in order to facilitate a grasp of the major themes of the Mercersburg theology at the outset.

According to Nevin, the "principle or root" from which the life of the Church stems is the incarnate person of Jesus Christ. By the power of the Holy Spirit, the Church's members are united to Christ and live in the power of a common life grounded in his very person. In this connection Nevin appealed to the eucharistic images in the Bread of Life discourse in the Gospel of John: "Except ye eat the flesh of the Son of Man, Christ himself has said, and drink his blood, ye have no life in you...[H]e that eateth my flesh and drinketh my blood, dwelleth in me, and I in him...(John 6:53–57)." From this it follows that union with Christ cannot be conceived as merely "moral," involving a "harmony of purpose, thought, and feeling," but is "substantial and real" entailing a "oneness of nature." With reference to Ephesians 5:30, Nevin asserted that the Church is comprised of persons who constitute the "members of [Christ's] body, of his flesh, and of his bones."[24]

Concerned that this startling image might seem mysterious to his hearers, Nevin clarified his argument by developing the Pauline themes of human solidarity with the first and second Adam (Romans 5:12-19). In virtue of their natural descent, human beings participate in the very nature of Adam: "his humanity, soul and body, has passed over into our persons."[25] Following the Apostle Paul, Nevin then used analogous language to represent how Christians are related to Christ, the second Adam. By faith, in the power of the Holy Spirit, Christians are inserted into his life, and thereby participate in this new life as fully as they did before in the corrupt life that they inherited from the first Adam.[26] This participation in the life of Christ, moreover, constitutes the very basis of the Christian's hope in the resurrection, for in the end the "glorified body, no less than the glorified soul" of the Christian is only the "natural and necessary product" of the life of the incarnate Lord, in which "he has thus been made to participate."[27]

Since redemption depends in this way on the "inward union on the part of the believer with the entire humanity of Christ," it is understandable that the mystery of the sacrament of the Lord's Supper has "entered deeply into the consciousness of the Church" during the course of history. This is because the communion of Christians in the Supper is really with the flesh and blood of the incarnate Lord. But in insisting on this Nevin was careful to point out that he was only following the lead of the Reformers themselves. Since they knew that the life of the Christian involves a "real communion with the flesh and blood, as well as with the spirit" of Christ, the Reformers maintained the doctrine of the "Real Presence" of Christ in the Supper.[28] To impress this point, Nevin reminded the two denominations of what their common doctrinal standard, the Heidelberg Catechism, taught on this subject:

> [T]o eat the crucified body and drink the shed blood of Christ is "not only to embrace with a believing heart all the sufferings and death of Christ, and thereby to obtain the pardon of sin and life eternal; but also besides that, to become more and more united to his sacred body, by the Holy Ghost, who dwells both in Christ and in us; so that we, though Christ is in heaven and we on earth, are not withstanding, flesh of his flesh, and bone of his bone; and that we live and are governed forever by one Spirit, as members of the same body are by one soul.[29]

Participating in one and the same life of Christ, especially through the sacrament of the Lord's Supper, Christians are vitally related to one another. The catholic unity of the Church therefore is bound up with the very economy of salvation itself, since the members of the body of Christ are properly united to their head only insofar as they belong to the body. Extending the metaphor of the body of Christ, Nevin argued that the unity of the Church is organic in nature. "The whole is greater than its parts, and these last spring perpetually from the presence of the first." Conversely, "the parts in the end are only a revelation of what was previously included in the whole." Since Christ comprises in his own person "the new creation, or humanity recovered and redeemed as a whole," then "whatever the Church becomes in the way of development, it can never be more in fact than it was in him from the beginning." Failing to see this is to reduce the Church to a "mere aggregation or collection of different individuals, drawn together by similarity of interests..."[30] Because of this failure, the "one body" is not a reality in the present, but the "one Spirit" nevertheless reigns through all communions, and "binds them together in one great spiritual whole."[31]

From this organic conception of the Church it follows that catholic unity cannot be engineered by "stratagem or force," but can only emerge in history as a manifestation of the unity proper to the Church's inner life. The process, however, is neither blind nor unconscious. For church unity to be authentic, it must be the "free and spontaneous product of Christian knowledge and love."[32] Accordingly, in the second part of the sermon Nevin appealed to the churches to "consider and lay to heart" the evil in the disunity and division present in the "catholic Church." Nevin expressed the hope that heartfelt conviction of the "deep and radical defect" in the present state of affairs would move concerned Christians to seize opportunities to advance the cause of catholic unity. In a passage infused with the ecumenical zeal for church unity later distinguished as the hallmark of the Mercersburg theology, Nevin challenged his hearers:

All Christians, then, in their various denominational capacities, are required, as they love the Church and seek the salvation of the world, to encourage with all their might a closer visible connection between the different parts of Christ's body, in every case in which the way is found to be open for the purpose. It is terrible to be concerned, however remotely, in dividing the Church, but a glorious and high privilege to take part, even to the smallest extent, in the work of restoring these divisions where they already exist.[33]

Nevin did not neglect to add in this sermon some encouraging remarks about the efforts made by the DRC and the GRC to promote a closer union. But it is clear that the unity he contemplated had less to do with sectarian mergers than with a transformed understanding of what it meant to be a member of the body of Christ. Some Dutch ministers even at the convention stood opposed to Nevin's conception of the Church, complaining that his use of organic metaphors gave evidence of the dangerous influences of "Hegelianism" in his theology.[34] Nevertheless, the delegates participated in an open dialogue about the issues facing the two denominations, formed a "Committee on Action," and appointed Nevin as chairman. The committee drafted five proposals, which were unanimously approved by both denominations.[35] Encouraged by this outcome, the GRC and the DRC enthusiastically planned for a second convention for 1847.

Philip Schaff and the "Principle of Protestantism"

Meanwhile Nevin was joined on the faculty at Mercersburg by the young German church historian, Philip Schaaf (later Schaff).[36] After a brief career on the faculty at the University of Berlin, Schaff had accepted an invitation in the fall of 1843 to replace a professor and become Nevin's sole colleague there. The young professor arrived in America in time to be present for Nevin's address in Harrisburg, and was gratified to find that Nevin's conception of the Church revealed a theological orientation compatible with his own. In his inaugural address to the German Reformed Synod convened at Reading on 25 October, 1844, Schaff applied the concept of organic development to the history of the Church.

Schaff made two major points in an address on his chosen theme, "The Principle of Protestantism."[37] In the first place he attempted to show that the Reformation did not spring *de novo* from Luther's ninety-five theses, but developed out of the preceding centuries. Medieval Catholicism, as the bearer of Christian faith and life, pressed ineluctably toward the Reformation. "The mortification of the flesh and...legal wrestlings after righteousness with God by the noblest spirits of the Middle Ages"[38] were the birth pangs in the Catholic Church, induced by what was to issue later in the Protestant Reformation. As the legitimate offspring of the Catholic Church, the Protestant Reformation, therefore, could claim catholicity for itself in the genuine sense of the term. On the basis of this organic relationship between Medieval and Reformation Christianity, Schaff proceeded in the second part of the address to diagnose rationalism and sectarianism as the great diseases of contemporary Protestantism. He concluded by arguing that the way forward was to realize an "evangelical catholicism." In language that most clearly revealed his own dependence on the ideas of German idealism, Schaff envisioned a new synthesis of what is true in both traditions.

> Protestantism cannot be consummated without Catholicism; not in the way of falling back to the past, but as coming into reconciliation with it finally in a higher position, in which all past errors shall be left behind whether Protestant or Catholic, and the truth of both tendencies be actualized, as the power of one and the same life, in the full revelation of the kingdom of God. The consummation of both will be at the same time their union.[39]

Schaff's theory of organic development informed an interpretation of the Church according to which the successive periods of its history made a positive contribution to the progressive realization of the ideal of the one holy, catholic, and apostolic Church. On this view, the aim of the Protestant Reformation was not so much to dismantle and reconstruct the entire Church as to carry forward and complete a process that had its origins in a tradition to which it was rightful heir.[40] At least at this early stage Nevin too came to adopt the position that the legitimacy of Protestantism could not be based on a thoughtless rejection of Roman Catholicism as the "Great Apostasy," but only on the historical role of Protestantism as a transition to a higher and better catholic universality.[41] Nevin publicly endorsed Schaff's views by translating an enlarged version of the address, adding an introduction, and publishing it with his "Catholic Unity" in June 1845.[42]

In this new context, however, Nevin's vision of church unity appeared suspiciously to betray the cause of Protestantism, and almost immediately heresy hunters rushed to the denominational presses to condemn the views of the Mercersburg professors. The adverse reaction that the writings of Nevin and Schaff provoked can be most clearly seen against the background of the virulent anti-Catholic ethos that had pervaded the Eastern seaboard region since the early colonial period. The massive influx of Roman Catholic immigrants to this region in the mid-nineteenth century only increased the tensions between Protestants and Catholics. In May 1844 these tensions erupted into violence when riots in Philadelphia broke out after the public school board granted to the Roman Catholic bishop Francis Kenrick his request to permit Catholic children to use their own version of the Bible in public school religious exercises. When the riots were finally suppressed thirteen Philadelphians had been killed and more than fifty others wounded.[43]

Joseph F. Berg, minister of the prominent Race Street Reformed Church in Philadelphia, distinguished himself as the most ferocious crusader in the cause of "Protestant truth." Berg considered it his solemn vocation to combat "Romish" error wherever he found it, and by the time Schaff arrived to America he had already published five anti-Catholic tracts, with such titles as *The Great Apostasy Identified with Papal Rome* and *Oral Controversy with a Catholic Priest*.[44] It is not surprising then to find that Berg launched the first attacks against Nevin and Schaff with articles in the *Protestant Banner* and in his own *Protestant Quarterly*, an organ devoted exclusively to the vindication of Protestant "truth" against Catholic "error." The *Lutheran Observer* published criticisms of Nevin's sermon and his application of the phrase "spiritual real presence" to the sacrament of the Lord's Supper.[45] The *Christian Intelligencer*, the leading paper of Dutch Reformed circles, warned that Schaff's sympathy with hierarchical forms of church government threatened to seduce the Reformed churches away from historic Calvinism toward Anglicanism or Roman Catholicism.[46] Elbert S. Porter, its editor, also found fault in the Mercersburg professors for stressing the Church and sacraments at the expense of personal conversion and individual piety.[47] Porter was later to become one of the severest critics of Nevin and Schaff, and under his editorship the *Christian Intelligencer* offered its pages freely to the heresy hunters who labored to maintain the Protestant fortress against the encroachments of "Popery."[48]

Beginning in August 1845, Nevin answered his critics in a series of articles published in the *Weekly Messenger*, the official organ of the GRC. In the first he issued the countercharge that the opinions held by his opponents did not represent a true Protestantism but a "Pseudo-Protestantism." In carelessly "unchurching" the Roman

Catholic Church, they failed to make the important distinction between a true church and a pure church. Protestantism defines a true church as one with a regular ministry commissioned to preach the word and administer the sacraments. According to this definition, the Roman Catholic Church was a true church, whatever the corruption in its teachings and institutions. To the second charge that he taught a "spiritual real presence" in the Lord's Supper, Nevin freely confessed in an article published in October.[49] But he denied that he derived this teaching from Roman Catholicism; on the contrary, this was a doctrine unambiguously taught in the Reformed confessions, and on this doctrine he was unwilling to compromise:

> To my own mind, all that is great and precious in the gospel may be said to center in this doctrine. Without it, I must feel that the whole Christian salvation should be shorn of its glory and its force. I have no hope, save on the ground of a living union with the nature of Christ as the resurrection and the life. Both for my understanding and my heart, theology finds here all its interest and attraction. For no truth am I more willing to suffer contradiction and reproach, if such be the will of God…[than that] the Christian life holds in an actual communication with the humanity of Christ, and that this, in particular, forms the soul of the Lord's Supper…[50]

Berg and the anti-Mercersburg party were not convinced. The suspicion that Romanizers were infiltrating the ranks of the Protestants galvanized the crusader and a small faction in the German Reformed congregations of Philadelphia to press for a heresy trial. For the meeting of the Philadelphia Classis on 16 September, 1845, Berg and his committee prepared six resolutions, four of which were in the form of doctrinal statements concerning the proper understanding of the sacraments and their efficacy.[51] The resolutions were adopted by the Philadelphia Classis, and referred to the Synod to convene at York the following month.

At the hearing Nevin and Schaff were exonerated of all the charges, but the vote of confidence from the York Synod did not succeed in allaying the suspicions of their detractors. The controversy continued to rage in the church papers, prompting Nevin and Schaff to develop and fortify their positions in two apolegetical tracts that appeared in April 1846. The first was *What is Church History? A Vindication of Historical Development* by Schaff; the other was the *Mystical*

Presence:. A Vindication of the Reformed or Calvinistic Doctrine of the Holy Eucharist by Nevin. "Arguably one of the most significant works of historical theology in the history of American thought," [52] the *Mystical Presence* offered an historical defense on the basis of a close reading of Calvin's writings and the Reformed confessions of the major themes programatically stated in "Catholic Unity." At this stage in the debate Nevin evidently perceived more clearly that the church question was inseparable from the question of the Eucharist:

> As the Eucharist forms the very heart of the whole Christian worship, so it is clear that the entire question of the Church, which all are compelled to acknowledge the great life-problem of the age, centers ultimately in the sacramental question as its inmost heart and core. Our view of the Lord's Supper must ever condition and rule in the end our view of Christ's person and the conception we form of the Church. It must influence at the same time, very materially, our whole system of theology, as well as all our ideas of ecclesiastical history.[53]

Herman Harmelink claims that the DRC's rejection of the high sacramental theology that Nevin championed in *The Mystical Presence* "simply revealed that church's misunderstanding of its own Calvinistic heritage."[54] This assertion must be qualified, for it is not exactly the case that the DRC misunderstood its own heritage. Rather it tended historically to align itself with the strong predestinarian strain in the Calvinism enshrined in its own Canons of Dort, as Nevin himself was well aware. In this strain God's eternal decree is seen as the absolute principle of salvation, a salvation consequently realized in the elect in virtue of this decree. But critics of this tradition—including Nevin himself—have charged that an exaggerated emphasis on the doctrine of the decrees empties salvation of any real meaning as an event fulfilled in history. If salvation for the elect is a foregone conclusion in the mind of God from eternity, then the charge seems inescapable that the written and proclaimed word of God, the sacraments, the Church, even the incarnation itself, are superfluous. Whether or not Calvin's doctrine of election is really incompatible with his doctrine of the sacraments is debatable. In any case, we must see at least that where the former is the central concern of theology, the latter does not receive the attention that it merits. Consistent with the interests of the Mercersburg agenda, Nevin argued that the doctrine of the decrees as such never entered into the constitution of the Reformed Church in the Palatinate, but the sacramental doctrine determined its character as a distinctive confession.[55]

Whatever the deeper theological issues at stake, the agitation that the pamphleteering wars caused was enough to provoke the Classis of Bergen of the DRC to vote for the abrogation of the correspondence between the two denominations. When the overture of that classis came before the Synod of the DRC in June 1846, the committee appointed to review this correspondence, however, urged the denomination not to "rupture the bonds of Christian fellowship between the two portions of Christ's Church so nearly allied by a common origin and common standards."[56] Instead it recommended that the DRC charitably present her difficulties to her sister church in an attempt "to bring her back to the paths" from which she may have strayed.[57]

But to the DRC the difficulties soon appeared insurmountable. At the Synod of 1847, the committee on correspondence reported that the dissent in the DRC from the views expressed in the Mercersburg professors' writings was serious enough to recommend the dissolution of the ties between the two denominations. Another reason to consider this action was that none of the Dutch ministers interested in serving in German congregations had found pulpits there, and none of the other aims proposed at the first Triennial Convention had been achieved.[58] For all these reasons the committee recommended to the DRC aborting plans for a future convention. Delegates were appointed, and the second convention opened at Reading on 11 August 1847, but the die was already cast: the following year the Synod voted to discontinue the convention. From 1848 to 1852 — the year in which the DRC lodged its final protest against the "Romanizing tendencies" of the Mercersburg theology by suspending all correspondence with the GRC — relations between the two denominations reverted to the earlier custom of exchanging fraternal delegates between one another's synods.

Worship and Liturgy in the Dutch and German Reformed Churches

One of the aims proposed by the Committee on Action at the 1844 Triennial Convention directed "that there should be as near an agreement as possible in the liturgy and form of worship in the churches of the different bodies represented."[59] In principle this should have been the least complicated of the proposals to implement, since the two ecclesial bodies freely acknowledged the Palatinate liturgy as the source of their common worship tradition. But in reality there was little continuity with this source in the worship life of the Dutch and German Reformed churches in the first half of the nineteenth century. In a typical service the sermon was central, prayers were mostly or entirely extemporaneous, and corporate participation was limited to hymn or psalm singing and in some places financial contributions. The Lord's Supper was celebrated at most four times a year in the Dutch congregations and twice a year in the German congregations; although it was celebrated in a spirit of solemn reverence, it remained peripheral to the conventional worship life of both communions.[60]

Critical remarks from an address delivered in 1835 by a renowned Dutch Reformed minister named George Washington Bethune reflect the state of affairs in the DRC:

> The Reformed Dutch Church has a liturgy adapted to all the offices and occasions of worship. It is perhaps to be regretted that its disuse has become so common among us, perhaps from a weak desire to conform to the habits of other denominations. Certainly there are occasions when the forms of prayer are at least as edifying as many extemporaneous effusions we hear from the desk [sc. pulpit], and it is evident that the wise fathers of the church did not intend that they should remain a dead letter in our [sc. liturgical] books.[61]

A layman in the DRC corroborated these observations. He reported to the *Christian Intelligencer* that he had participated in many Dutch Reformed congregations in New York and New Jersey during the second quarter of the nineteenth century. But their disregard of the order of worship prescribed in the Netherlands Liturgy led him to conclude ironically that the Dutch have no liturgical forms of prayer of their own. He expressed regret that he had not heard the form for the Lord's Supper read in its entirety for many years.[62]

Evidently this correspondent's reaction to this state of affairs was widespread enough to provoke an official response, because in 1846 the Dutch Synod appointed a "Committee on the State of the Church" to investigate such matters. In a long report presented to the DRC the following year, this committee deplored the "unseemly diversity" that prevailed in the congregations in regard to the use of its liturgy. The committee regarded the neglect of the forms for baptism and the Lord's Supper as a particularly grave matter, since as carefully worded ordinances intended to seal the promises of the faith to the believer, they had to be read in their entirety in order to guard against doctrinal error.[63] Accordingly, this committee recommended that the Synod appoint another committee to "find means to secure greater uniformity in the use of the liturgical forms contained in our books."[64] This the DRC did in 1848, but the committee disbanded the following year. The DRC eventually succeeded in making its liturgy the object of study and revision in 1853, but the liturgical committee correctly judged that anything more than stylistic changes would not have received the official sanction of the denomination. A new revision was approved and published in 1857, but apart from a relatively insignificant grammatical correction, the form for the Lord's Supper remained substantially unchanged.

The situation in the GRC was no more promising. The problem of diversity in worship practices was compounded by the ongoing difficulties that plagued the attempts of the new American denomination to establish and train an indigenous ministry. The missionary fathers of the eighteenth century brought to the new world the liturgies then used in those regions of Germany, Switzerland, and the Netherlands from which they came. But none of these were to obtain the exclusive endorsement of the Synod. Despite this profusion of different liturgies, the Palatinate liturgy perhaps enjoyed more extensive use than any other. But when it was superseded in Germany, it did not receive a reprinting in America, and only a few manuscript copies survived into the early nineteenth century. In its place ministers in the German speaking congregations adopted variously Swiss liturgies from Berne, Basle, Coire, and forms from the sixteenth century Reformation liturgies compiled in August Ebrard's *Reformiertes Kirchenbuch*.[65]

In the early nineteenth century the influences coming from the surrounding denominations only added to this liturgical diversity. Some ministers in English speaking congregations resorted to the Anglican *Book of Common Prayer*, while others used the New York translations of the forms from the Netherlands Liturgy appended to the Dutch Reformed hymnals. Still others preferred to draw on their own resources, sometimes borrowing from sources of unknown origin forms for the celebration of the sacraments.[66] But by far the cause for most serious concern among such influential church leaders as Nevin and Schaff was the disintegrating effects of the revivalistic "new measures," as we have already seen. Set forms precluded public prayer spontaneously inspired by the Spirit, so the proponents of the new measures argued. But to their critics the arbitrary freedom of the minister led to excesses that were undesirable. Attempts to impose a measure of uniformity in worship were made by the denomination as early as 1820, when the Classis of Maryland made a request to the Synod to "improve" (*verbessern*) the church's liturgy. After a long delay, a committee entrusted with the task presented to the Synod in 1837 a series of forms for occasional services (marriage, baptism, Lord's Supper, ordination, burial, church dedication). The Mayer Liturgy, as it was called, was published in German and English in 1841, but it did not gain widespread popularity among the congregations. Among the reasons for its poor reception was that it contained no order of worship for ordinary Lord's Day services; it was too dull and didactic; it diverged too far from the structure of the historic Reformed liturgies; and it was "uncongenial to the spirit of the Heidelberg Catechism."[67] The Mayer form for the Lord's Supper in particular compromised the doctrinal heritage of the Palatinate, as Bard Thompson has elaborated. The term "ordinance" substituted for the term "sacrament;" "symbol" and "emblem" for "true signs and seals." The exposition following the institution narrative proclaimed to the congregation that Jesus had instituted the Lord's Supper because "an absent friend is easily forgotten."[68] This strict memorialistic interpretation of the Supper was manifestly inconsistent with the teaching of the Heidelberg Catechism, but it was agreeable to the American Protestant habit of mind predominant in sections of the German (and Dutch) Reformed Church, as we have already seen.

The Liturgical Movement in the German
Reformed Church (1849–1857): Auspicious Beginnings

Nevin's early essays on the Heidelberg Catechism and especially his tract *The Anxious Bench* served to invigorate confessional identity in the GRC, and subsequently to stimulate in it a desire for a liturgy that expressed the genius of that catechism.[69] In 1847 the Classis of East Pennsylvania made a request to the Synod of Lancaster either to re-print the Palatinate liturgy or to commission the preparation of an-other that harmonized with it. When the Synod convened the following year in Hagerstown, Maryland, the GRC referred the mat-ter to a committee, of which the Reverend John H.A. Bomberger (1817-1890), pastor of a prominent congregation in Philadelphia, was made chairman. In the early stages of the liturgical movement Bomberger was to play an instrumental role in reintroducing to his denomination its liturgical heritage, as we will see later. In the report that he presented on behalf of the committee to the Synod at Norris-town in 1849, he advocated a return to the "liturgical forms...as rec-ognized by our forefathers," especially to those of the Palatinate.[70]

Bomberger's report generated a lively debate that continued through several sessions, and the exchange of opinion already re-vealed the tensions that would eventually lead to crisis both in the committee and in the denomination. One member expressed his op-position to all set forms, repeating the charge that these interfered with the "freedom and fervor" in the expression of public devotion. Another opponent raised the question: "if I read another man's prayer, is it I who pray, or the one who wrote it?" Nevin for his part confessed that as a result of his intensive study of the sacramental theology and liturgical practices of the early Church, his mind had undergone a "complete theological revolution." He then presented to the committee his understanding of the relation of "liturgical worship with the idea of the Church as the body of Christ, of the communion of the saints as a present reality in the public devotions, of the sacra-ments as means of grace, and of the nature of true worship as a united act of the whole congregation." After the debates, a general consensus was reached and the Synod decided to adopt Bomberger's report. It then appointed a committee to research the liturgical productions of the Reformed churches, and instructed its members to prepare an outline of a new liturgy, providing specimens, old or new, at their discretion. Nevin was to assume chairmanship of this new committee.[71]

In response to the charge of the Synod, Bomberger translated into English the forms from a 1684 edition of the Church Order of the Palatinate, and published them in the *Mercersburg Review*, the organ that Nevin and Schaff had established in 1849 for the dissemination of the ideas of the Mercersburg theology.[72] Parenthetically, we should review two of these forms in order to understand more clearly the issues at stake in the later controversy. As we have already seen, the order of worship for the ordinary Sunday morning service opens with an invocation from 1 Timothy 1:2 ("Grace, mercy, and peace..."). Then comes the prayer of confession, which includes a petition for the saving apprehension of the word, and concludes with the Lord's Prayer. After the sermon, the service continues with another prayer of confession, to which the "comfortable words" (i.e. scriptural promise of redemption) and absolution are added. Then follow the thanksgiving and intercessions, to which is appended yet another Lord's Prayer. A Psalm is sung, and the minister pronounces the Aaronic benediction to dismiss the assembly.[73]

We will also remember that on those Sundays when the Lord's Supper was celebrated, the minister, following the intercessions, moved from the pulpit to the table to read aloud to the congregation the form for the Supper. This form consists in the institution narrative as drawn from 1 Corinthians 11:23-29, to which the self-examination, excommunication, comfortable words, and exposition on the meaning of the atoning death of Christ and his Supper constitute, as it were, a response of obedience to the injunctions contained in the Pauline text. Then follows the prayer for worthy reception, the Apostles' Creed, the Reformed *Sursum corda*, the fraction accompanied by the words of distribution, and communion. The rite concludes with a post-communion thanksgiving.

Already in 1850 Nevin revealed that he himself did not consider a repristination of the Palatinate forms as the course for the movement to pursue; on the basis of his study of the early Church, he became convinced that it would not be enough simply to reproduce the liturgies of the Reformation era. On the other hand, he was equally convinced that his denomination had not yet attained a mature conception of the Church that required a liturgy in the proper sense of the term. Consequently, he reported to the Synod in 1850 that until the denomination settled the church question, it would not be advisable to progress any farther along the course. But if the GRC insisted on going forward, he made the concession that it should simply reprint the old Palatinate forms.

In 1851 Nevin suffered a crisis of conscience, and no longer felt able to continue serving the denomination in his current capacity while the whole church question was undergoing a radical revision in his own mind. He resigned as chairman from the liturgical committee, as well as from his professorship at the seminary, so that he could devote himself undistractedly to what had become for him a profoundly existential concern. Increasingly harrassed by the adversaries of the Mercersburg theology, Nevin despaired about the viability of an "evangelical catholicism," and considered seriously whether the Roman Catholic Church was after all the true home for the contemporary Christian. Nevin's inner struggle found expression in a remarkable series of scholarly articles, "Anglican Crisis," "Cyprian," and "Early Christianity," which he published in the *Mercersburg Review* in 1851 and 1852.[74] In these sharply polemical writings, Nevin contrasted the essentially catholic character of the early Church with the unhistorical character of contemporary American Protestantism and Anglicanism. The critical question with which Nevin was now engaged was the very validity of Protestantism itself: "Has it been possible at all to maintain a true succession of the ancient life, under this form?"[75]

Despite his defeatist attitude, Nevin remained obedient to the appointment of the Synod by continuing to serve as a member of the committee. But he now yielded the reins to the indomitable Schaff, who energetically carried forward the enterprise by convening the committee for frequent meetings during the summer of 1852. To the members Schaff delegated the responsibilities of drawing up a general plan of the proposed liturgy, as well as preparing several specimen forms for services. At the meeting of the Synod at Baltimore in 1852, the committee submitted forms for regular services on the Lord's Day (four), adult baptism, infant baptism, and marriage. These accompanied a remarkable report which revealed that the committee

had departed dramatically from the agenda that Bomberger had outlined at Norristown. The seven methodological principles that the
committee formulated to guide the composition of the new liturgy are
of particular interest. Since the program for liturgical reform in the
RCA a century later will have, in effect, embraced most of these principles to undergird the revision of its own liturgy, it will be instructive for our purposes to enumerate here those proposed to the
Baltimore Synod:

1. The basis of the new liturgy would be the Greek and Latin liturgies of
   the third and fourth centuries.
2. Elements from the Reformed liturgies of the sixteenth century and from
   the Palatinate liturgy would be given special attention.
3. The liturgies both of the ancient Catholic and the Reformed churches
   would not be copied slavishly, but adapted in a "free evangelical spirit"
   to the needs of the contemporary German Reformed Church.
4. Several different forms for the ordinary Lord's Day service and the
   Lord's Supper would be prepared to provide sufficient latitude to
   churches with varying liturgical sensibilities and expectations.
5. The liturgy would be devotional rather than didactic in style and language.
6. The liturgy would be a people's prayer book rather than a manual of
   forms for the minister alone. It would include forms for private and
   family devotion to prepare the people for intelligent participation in
   Lord's Day worship.
7. Although ordinary Lord's Day worship would be conducted by means
   of set forms, sufficient room would be afforded for the exercise of free,
   extemporaneous prayer in all other worship settings.[76]

The report continued that if the new liturgy were to be constructed on
the foundation of these principles, the result would be a "bond of union both with the ancient Catholic Church and the Reformation, and
yet be the product of the religious life of our denomination in its present state."

It is clear from this *desideratum* that the Baltimore proposals embodied Schaff's theory of organic development and the historical continuity of the one holy catholic Church through the centuries. Perhaps
even more significantly, they provided wide scope for a "working out
in an art form of the ideas and faith of the Mercersburg theology,"[77]
as we will see later. In view of the intransigent opposition maintained

by key leaders against the tendencies of this theology, it is astonishing that the Synod adopted this report without closer scrutiny of the implications of the principles. But even if the Synod did not understand fully the consequences of its action, it is apparent that Schaff and his committee certainly did. With the approval of the Synod, Schaff continued to guide the movement along the trajectory now firmly established. After the Synod's adoption of the Baltimore proposals, he directed the members of the committee to familiarize themselves with the Roman Catholic scholar Renaudot's *Liturgiarum Orientalium Collectio* and the fourth volume of Bunsen's *Hippolytus and His Age*, both of which contained the eucharistic liturgies of the early Church. Schaff did not neglect to mention that these were to be consulted together with the liturgies of the sixteenth century.[78]

In 1853 the Synod granted Schaff a leave of absence to reward him for the diligent service he had been rendering the denomination.[79] He exploited this opportunity for a sorely needed rest by boarding a ship bound for Europe. His travels in England and Scotland and throughout the continent brought him into contact with leading churchmen, theologians, and scholars with whose thought he and Nevin had been engaging at Mercersburg. In England he visited with such prominent figures as Pusey, Wilberforce, and Maurice; and in Germany with F.W. Krummacher, pastor of the largest Reformed congregation in Germany, and the renowned philosopher F.W.J. Schelling. In almost every German university town he visited, Schaff delivered public lectures to Germans interested in hearing his interpretations of Church and culture in America.

But it was on his return through England that an event decisive for the liturgical movement in his own denomination occurred. In a letter to his wife dated 5 February, 1854, Schaff described his experience of a liturgical celebration in the Central Church of the Irvingite or Catholic Apostolic Church:[80]

> Sunday I spent the greater part of the day with the Irvingites. In the morning I found their beautiful Gothic church in Gordon Square, the first of the seven churches of London, thronged with devout worshippers. The Lord's Supper was administered with great solemnity, an imposing ceremonial, many hundreds communing. They observed the best of order, passing up one aisle, then kneeling and passing down the other aisle. The liturgy is

> very beautiful...The service this morning, I believe, was the most beautiful
> and perfect liturgical service I have yet attended.[81]

The eucharistic liturgy celebrated in the large cathedral church in
Gordon Square that day was an elaborate rite patterned closely after
early Greek liturgies, such as those of St. John Chrysostom and St.
James. Schaff returned from Europe with a copy of the eucharistic liturgy used in this service to suggest it to the committee as a model for
their own order for the Lord's Supper. In fact it was to be this liturgy
that enabled Schaff to realize the Baltimore proposal for a liturgy
based on those of the ancient catholic Church of the third and fourth
centuries.

When Schaff resumed the chairmanship of the committee upon
his return, he made a request to Nevin late in 1855 to submit his own
liturgical contributions. Nevin was coming out of his retirement to enter into public life once again, but his pessimistic attitude towards the
cause of the movement had not changed, as revealed in his sullen re-
ply:

> I will try to furnish the family prayers you request for the Liturgy. But I
> must decline the task of the other services you mention. I have no helps here
> at hand, no access to the ancient Liturgies...But what is worse I have no
> heart, no faith, no proper courage for any such work. A leitourgia (commun-
> ion service) in the old sense demands a sort of faith in the real presence,
> which I am afraid goes beyond all that is possible to engraft on Protestant-
> ism, even in our G.R. version of it. And without this, I feel that it is for me at
> least a species of mockery to pretend to use of the like words and forms. I
> cannot bear the sense of unreality which comes over me when I think of
> manufacturing on any such plan for public use a form of worship, into
> which our faith is not allowed to breathe the same mysterious soul.[82]

As it turned out, Nevin was not the only discouraged member of
the liturgical committee. During the preceding two years the members had become overwhelmed by the enormity of the project. The
more they studied, read, and conferred, the more they came to realize
that the composition of a liturgy on the scale they had conceived
proved no easy undertaking. Nevin remarked later that the "work
seemed continually to unsettle and destroy itself."[83] Accordingly, the
members requested permission from the Synod of Chambersburg
(1855) to limit temporarily the scope of the project to the preparation

and publication of a provisional liturgy only. This liturgy would carry no binding authority in the GRC, but simply introduce forms to ministers and congregations for use on a trial basis. After an extended trial, the GRC would be in a position to decide on the practicablity of the new liturgy.

The Synod's adoption of the report infused the liturgical committee members, including even Nevin, with new energy. At the meeting of the Synod in Allentown (1857), Nevin enthusiastically announced on behalf of the committee that at last they had brought their labors to completion. He reported that a volume of about 400 pages in length containing forms for a wide range of worship services and dedications, including family prayers, a lectionary, and a selection of hymns and psalms, was now at the presses.[84] The contrast between the orders of worship in what the committee simply designated as the Provisional Liturgy and the comparatively simple services of prayers and sermon contained in the Church Order of the Palatinate is significant, as an examination of two representative orders from the former will make apparent:

Table 1: Provisional Liturgy

Regular Service on the Lord's Day (1)	**The Holy Communion**
Invocation	Invocation
Confession	Prayer for Purity
Assurance of Pardon	Scripture Sentences
Profession of Faith (Apostles' Creed)	*Gloria* (*Te Deum*, Canticle, or Hymn)
Thanksgiving and Praise (Psalm, *Te Deum* or the *Gloria*)	Gospel
Scripture Lessions	Epistle
Collect	Sermon or Lesson
General Petition	Nicene Creed
Hymn	Offering
Sermon	(Exposition of the Elements)
Prayer	Exhortation
Hymn	Confession
Offering	Assurance of Pardon
Benediction[85]	Introductory Dialogue
	Sursum Corda
	Preface
	Sanctus
Continued on next page	Institution Narrative

Table 1–Continued   Epiclesis
                                             Anamnesis and Self-Oblation
                                             Intercessions
                                             Lord's Prayer
                                             Benediction
                                             Peace
                                             Words of Distribution
                                             Post-Communion Prayer
                                             Benediction[86]

We must defer a detailed analysis of the structure and meaning of the eucharistic prayer to a later point in our study. Here we want only to highlight briefly how these representative orders of worship fulfilled the proposals outlined at Baltimore, as well as provided a vehicle by which to convey the faith and ideas of the Mercersburg theology. First, the structure of the rite for Holy Communion is clearly modeled on the eucharistic liturgies of the third and fourth centuries rather than the Reformation liturgies. An analysis of the sources of the eucharistic prayer in particular reveal Schaff's dependence on the Liturgy of St. James, which was mediated to him through the eucharistic liturgy of the Catholic Apostolic Church.[87] In this structure, every element in the rite is dynamically oriented to the Lord's Supper as the climactic liturgical event. It is significant that this orientation is retained even when the form for Holy Communion is not used. The first form for the "Regular Service on the Lord's Day," specified by the committee as the order to be used on the mornings when the sacrament was not celebrated, concludes with the offertory. By this placement the committee intended to impress on the worshipping community that the service is an "ante-communion," that is, a service normally to be completed by the celebration of the Supper. In this connection, the rubrics for the Holy Communion rite, as well as for the regular service on the Lord's Day, prescribe that ministers are to lead worship from the altar, ascending to the pulpit only at the sermon. The altar and not the pulpit is thereby liturgically represented as the focal point in the sanctuary, since, as Nevin was to affirm later, the "root and foundation of all Christian worship is the mystical presence of Christ in the sacrament of the Holy Supper."[88] The *epiclesis*, probably from the pen of Nevin himself,[89] is a liturgical transcript of the sacramental theology that he had been strenuously insisting was proper to Calvin and the Reformed confessions ever since his sermon on "Catholic Unity:"

> ALMIGHTY GOD, our heavenly Father, send down, we beseech Thee, the powerful benediction of Thy Holy Spirit upon these elements of bread, that being set apart now from a common to a sacred and mystical use, they may exhibit and represent to us with true effect the Body and Blood of Thy Son, Jesus Christ; so that in the use of them we may be made, through the power of the Holy Ghost, to partake really and truly of his blessed life, whereby only we can be saved from death, and raised to immortality at the last day.[90]

Finally, to facilitate the corporate action through which this mystical union between Christ and his people can properly take place, both orders provide for the active participation of the worshipping community. The versicles and responses, the corporate recitation of the Creed, as well as the rubrics signalling the places in the orders in which to stand and to kneel, clearly show that the new liturgy was designed for the participation of the whole people of God and not for the minister alone.

The Liturgical Movement in the German Reformed Church (1858–1866): Conflict and Controversy

The liturgical experiment in the GRC, which at this time appeared so promising, almost immediately encountered formidable obstacles. The first was the uneven reception of the Provisional Liturgy among the congregations to which the committee recommended it for trial use. The scheme of liturgical worship represented in the new forms inspired relatively few of them, and most of the ministers who actually did accept the new liturgy preferred only the forms for occasional services—especially those for church consecrations and dedications, ordinations and installations.[91] Nevin for his part had harbored few illusions that the Provisional Liturgy would be generally accepted. The departure of the set forms from the free prayer that predominated in public worship was too drastic. Moreover, the very status of the liturgy as provisional suggested that it was going to be superseded, thereby discouraging any serious consideration of its long term practicability. Yet Nevin was far from despairing that the labors of the previous ten years had gone to waste. On the contrary, he was convinced that the Provisional Liturgy was already serving as a means to educate the congregations, propagating sound ideas on Christian worship among the people. Even if the congregations were not yet prepared to incorporate the whole liturgy into their public worship, it was at least apparent that they were no longer satisfied with what they had previously. Nevin seemed unusually confident that the Provisional Liturgy was promoting in his denomination the cause of the liturgical movement from which it issued.

The problem of the incorporation of the Provisional Liturgy into the public worship of the German Reformed churches, however, was precisely the second obstacle. Rules for public worship in the GRC (as well as in the DRC) were part of the constitution of the denomination, and could not be modified apart from a synodical resolution. Moreover, a synod could only authorize the modifications after submitting them for approval to the several classes. On the question of whether the new forms — or indeed the new scheme of liturgical worship — committed to the congregations for trial use were compatible with the rules there was no consensus. The complications that this problem added to the discussion about the Provisional Liturgy forced the Synod of 1860 to rescind its earlier decision to grant to it a ten year trial period in the congregations. At the Synod of 1861 the GRC decided to reconstitute the original committee, and charged it to prepare a final revision that would meet with the approval of the Classes.

The growing realization among the more conservative members in the GRC that the Provisional Liturgy did indeed introduce a decisive break with the traditional pattern of worship prescribed in the Palatinate liturgy was by far the most serious obstacle. The most militant critic in the ensuing controversy was the former champion of the Mercersburg theology and staunch supporter of the Provisional Liturgy, John H.A. Bomberger.[92] For reasons that are not entirely clear, Bomberger broke ranks with the Mercersburg men and turned against the liturgical movement they had inspired.[93] In his estimation the Provisional Liturgy did not enjoy widespread acceptance in the congregations because it imported features alien to the genius, history, and practices of the Reformed churches. Among those features Bomberger singled out for criticism included the responses and the sacramental forms. According to Bomberger, the responses had no precedent in historic Reformed worship, which was decidedly not "ritualistic," and the forms, which were in any case too long and didactic, contained doctrines of the Church and sacraments that were theologically objectionable.

It comes as no surprise that the critical issue that came more clearly to the fore in the course of the debates was the precise place of the traditional Reformed cultus itself in the Provisional Liturgy. Bomberger capitalized on the occasion afforded by the new commission of the Synod of 1861, and called for a reversal of the first and second methodological principles the committee proposed at the Synod of Baltimore in 1852: in the final revision the Reformation liturgies should serve as the basis of the Provisional Liturgy, with secondary reference to those of the third and fourth centuries. Curiously enough, Bomberger and his supporters did not believe that the radical alterations they were recommending need violate the integrity of the Provisional Liturgy as it already stood. Nevin and his supporters, however, were perceptive enough to see that merely eliminating the responses from the forms hardly penetrated to the crux of the matter. The core of the problem really consisted in two mutually opposed conceptions of the function and meaning of a liturgy. Nevin now was forced to "affirm the breach" and to offer his denomination nothing more than an "either-or choice."[94]

In a report drawn up to clarify for the Synod of Chambersburg (1862) the issues now at stake, Nevin attempted to distinguish the two competing conceptions of a liturgy.[95] According to the first, a liturgy is a compilation of forms to guide the minister in conducting various worship services as the occasion demanded. On this view, a liturgy is merely "a service book, a book of examples and forms, a mere collection of prayers" for use in the pulpit alone.[96] Nevin conceded that a liturgy in this sense is certainly to be preferred to no liturgy at all. At least the forms safeguarded the expression of the faith of the worshipping community against the vagaries of extemporaneous prayer. On the other hand, a liturgy conceived merely as a "book of examples and forms" was not adequate to the true idea of Christian worship. The true idea was embodied in the second conception, according to which a liturgy is

...a whole order or scheme rather of public worship, in which all the parts are inwardly bound together by their having a common relation to the idea of the Christian altar, and by their referring themselves through this always to what must be considered the last ground of all true Christian worship, the mystical presence of Christ in the Holy Eucharist.[97]

But Nevin had to admit to his opponents that the conception that he advocated in these terms did not harmonize with the pattern of worship in the majority of the Reformation liturgies, which indeed were "liturgies of the pulpit." In these the "office" of the Lord's Supper was only one among several, relegated to the status of an occasional service. So too in his own GRC, there had always only been infrequent celebrations of the sacrament, to which the ordinary Sunday services were thematically unrelated. But Nevin's studies of the early Church convinced him that authentic Christian worship demanded that the significance of the Lord's Supper remain central, whatever the worship practices of his own denomination. To accommodate to these less than ideal practices, at least the "*idea* of the Christian altar" [emphasis added] should predominate in the ordinary Sunday services, so that even these "shall be felt to be still part and parcel always of what is transacted, at certain seasons, in the celebration of the Eucharist."[98] The structure of the regular service of the Lord's Day, as we have already seen, was designed to ensure this continual relation to the altar.

Later in the report Nevin expressed his opinion that the liturgies produced by the churches of the Reformation were deficient as models for the Provisional Liturgy. According to Nevin, the Reformers were too absorbed in more urgent concerns to attend carefully to the subject of the liturgy (which they at any rate regarded as *adiaphora*). But even if they had, they would have been too hampered by the general ignorance of the history of liturgy characteristic of their age. Perhaps more fundamentally, they were unable to reconcile the imperatives of evangelical freedom with the constraints imposed by rites and ceremonies. The exaggerations to which this freedom tended, combined with the protests against the perceived worship abuses in the Roman Catholic Church, prevented the Reformation churches from realizing a liturgical worship in the proper sense.[99] In this criticism of the Reformation Nevin of course was exposing an open flank to the attacks of his opponents. But he nonetheless insisted that the GRC should not be bound to the sixteenth century: "must the past liturgical practice of the church, so far as there has been any such practice control our worship now?"[100]

> Admittedly, the Provisional Liturgy is not after the pattern strictly of any system of worship which has prevailed hitherto in the German Reformed Church either in this country or in Europe...It aims to be an improvement upon this whole past cultus, by which it is to be made more throughly liturgical than ever before...The new liturgy is for us as a church, in many respects, a new scheme of worship. It is not the pattern according to which our fathers worshipped either in these United States or elsewhere.[101]

In the face of the opposition, Nevin and his supporters in the liturgical committee continued to hold firm to the liturgical ideal enshrined in the Provisional Liturgy. At the request of the Synod of 1863, the liturgical committee was charged to bring to completion the final revision. In 1866 the committee presented to the Eastern Synod of York its completed project in the form of *An Order of Worship*, which that regional governing body agreed to approve for publication in the event that the Synod to convene at Dayton six weeks later acted on it. *An Order of Worship* was subsequently adopted by the Synod of Dayton, published, and offered to the congregations for another trial period.[102] With relatively insignificant exceptions, this liturgy maintained the structure and substance of the Provisional Liturgy. The controversy over the Mercersburg theology and the liturgy continued to plague the denomination until a truce was called in the 1884.[103] But the serious theological and liturgical studies that found practical expression in the Provisional Liturgy and *An Order of Worship* would exert a profound influence in Reformed circles for decades to come, not least in the RCA in the late nineteenth and mid-twentieth centuries.

Liturgical Renewal and the
Dutch Reformed Church: Early Stirrings

Hageman has argued that the influence of Mercersburg on worship in the Reformed churches was for the most part indirect: "Sometimes there were direct borrowings from the *Order of Worship*; more often the influence of the movement in other churches was seen in the stimulation of liturgical study and publication."[104] The evidence of this influence is seen as early as 1857 in *Presbyterian Liturgies with Specimen Forms for Public Worship*, whose compiler A. Bonar referred to the Provisional Liturgy just then published in the United States.[105] In 1867 the Church Service Society of the Church of Scotland published an unofficial service book under the title *Euchologion*.[106] In the introduction to the communion services appear outlines of several historic liturgies as well as modern services. The eucharistic liturgies of the Catholic Apostolic Church and the GRC are included among the latter. Later George Sprott, one of the authors of the *Euchologion*, acknowledged that the eucharistic prayer in the service book derived largely from the prayers of these two denominations.[107] As we will see later, the eucharistic prayer contained in the *Euchologion* was destined to play a pivotal role in the evolution of the order for the Lord's Supper in the DRC.

In 1868 the DRC (by this time renamed the Reformed Church in America=RCA) appointed a liturgical committee, to which it called Elbert S. Porter, the former editor of the *Chrisitan Intelligencer* and opponent of the Mercersburg theology, to serve as chairman. In 1870 Porter, however, asked to be relieved from his responsibilities. The Synod nominated in his place Mancius Smedes Hutton, minister of the Washington Square Church in New York; with this appointment, in the judgment of Hageman, a very crucial chapter in the history of the liturgy of the Reformed Church in America was opened.[108]

Hutton wished to restore to the RCA its character as a liturgical church. In the report that he presented on behalf of the committee to the Synod of 1871, Hutton outlined three principles to guide the study and revision of the liturgy. The first provided for greater corporate participation in public worship. For Hutton "the Gospel minister is not by virtue of his office a priest, but the people themselves are a royal Priesthood, with all the power and privilege of prayer."[109] The second simply served to remind the RCA that it should distinguish itself from other Presbyterian churches by acknowledging its tradition as a liturgical church. The third suggested that the RCA possessed in Calvin's Strassbourg Liturgy an exemplary model with which to guide its own revisions.

After only two years the liturgical committee was prepared to submit to the Synod of 1873 a Revised Liturgy.[110] But what transpired in the committee in the brief period between the first report it presented and this liturgy is unfortunately lost to posterity, because the minutes of the Synod of that year oddly do not contain the report. Hageman and Mast have relied on Edwin Corwin, a respected historian of the nineteenth century RCA, as a source for the topics that were treated in this lost report. According to Corwin, an elaborate liturgical service based on that of the Anglican Church was discussed in the committee, but in the end not presented to the Synod. In this connection, the committee seemed also to have deliberated on the question whether to recommend to Synod the use of the Anglican *Book of Common Prayer* as the liturgy of the denomination. Finally, Corwin claimed that the report contained a long discussion of the history of the form for the Lord's Supper. This history was apparently accompanied by a modified form for this sacrament, but in the end the committee also decided against proposing this to the Synod.[111] The content of this lost report would have been invaluable for gaining deeper insight into the mind of the RCA concerning the liturgy and the Lord's Supper at this stage in its history.

The content itself of the Revised Liturgy of 1873, however, remains as a reliable testimony to the direction in which the liturgical committee wished to proceed. We restrict our considerations here to the revisions suggested for the form for the Supper. The committee proposed to divide the two most extensive sections in the traditional form, namely, the self-examination and the exposition on the meaning of the atonement and of the institution narrative, into two parts. It recommended that the first part be incorporated into a service of preparation, that is, a special service to be held before the Sunday on which the sacrament was to be celebrated. Whether the service of preparation was an institution in the RCA as it was in the Palatinate and in the GRC, it is difficult to ascertain with absolute certainty. For no order for the service of preparation appears in the translation of the Netherlands Liturgy included in the Constitution of the Church (1793). A second modification the committee introduced was the insertion of a rubric before the Apostles' Creed prescribing that both the minister and the congregation recite that Creed corporately. In addition, the post-communion thanksgiving (Psalm 103) was set to be read responsively, and the Romans text omitted. Apart from these relatively minor alterations, the form underwent no substantive change at the hands of the committee. The corporate recitations suggest that committee sought to adhere to the principle that the whole people of God — minister and congregation — comprise the royal priesthood before God and offer together the sacrifice of praise in worship. But, it must be admitted, the compression of the form seems determined more by pragmatic considerations than anything else. In the judgment of the committee the traditional form for the Supper was simply too long, and needed to be adapted to the limited capacities of the worshippers.

Eucharistic Prayer of 1873

The committee's considerations of the order of the Lord's Supper, however, were not limited to these modifications to the traditional form. The single most significant contribution to the Revised Liturgy of 1873 is a prayer designated as a "Eucharistic Prayer," which appeared in an appendix named "Prayers for Special Occasions."[112] An analysis of the sources of this prayer reveal again the influence of the eucharistic liturgy of the Catholic Apostolic Church. It was not, however, the liturgical productions of the GRC, but rather the *Euchologion* that directly mediated this influence to the RCA. With few exceptions, the liturgical committee appointed by the RCA adopted for their own use the eucharistic prayer found in the *Euchologion*. The Eucharistic Prayer of the Revised Liturgy of 1873 has the following structure:

> Preface
> *Sanctus*
> *Epiclesis*
> Self-Oblation
> Thanksgiving for the Church Triumphant
> Statement of Eschatological Hope

The prayer commences with praise and thanksgiving to God for the gifts of creation and for the redemption accomplished by Jesus Christ "who being Very and Eternal God, became Man for us men and for our salvation." In this vein the preface continues with a rather extensive catalogue of the events constitutive of this salvation. Not only the incarnation of Jesus Christ, his life, sufferings, and death, his resurrection from the dead, and his ascension to the right hand of God are recounted as cause to bless God. The preface also contains a section on the work of the Holy Spirit, which includes an account of the work of the Church, in its sacramental life, as it awaits the Second Coming of Christ. The community then joins its praise with that of the hosts of heaven by reciting the *sanctus* ("Holy, Holy, Holy, Lord God of Sabaoth"), which concludes with an acclamation in the words of a royal messianic Psalm ("Blessed is he who comes in the name of the Lord"), the words the people of Jerusalem used to herald Jesus' entry into the city (Matt. 21:9). The text of these formulae appears in capital letters, indicating that the whole community was to recite them. The prayer continues with the *epiclesis*, which asks God to "bless and sanctify with [his] Word and Spirit" the "gifts of the bread and wine," in order that in receiving them the assembly may "through the power of the Holy Ghost, be very partakers of the [Saviour's] body and blood." The prayer then moves to the self-oblation, in which the worshippers offer themselves, "souls and bodies, to be a reasonable, holy, and living sacrifice unto [God}." The concluding section gives thanks to God for the "Church Triumphant," that is, for the "servants who have departed in the faith." This section is completed by a statement of eschatological hope, which petitions God to empower the people to "follow [the] faith and good example [of the departed]" so that the worshipping community, with all the Church, may be "presented with exceeding joy before the presence of [God's] glory."

We will return to this remarkable prayer when it re-emerges in connection with the 1906 revision and again with the revisions introduced in 1950. Let us simply say here that the prayer has presented something of a puzzle to the historian of the denomination. In the first place, since no report accompanied the Revised Liturgy of 1873, there is also no explanation why the committee decided to introduce a liturgical prayer that until then had no precedent in the denomination. In the second place, it is difficult to know with any certainty what role the prayer was supposed to play in the Lord's Supper celebrations in RCA congregations. As we have already seen, the traditional form already contained a "prayer for worthy reception." Did the committee intend the "Eucharistic Prayer" to serve as a substitute for this prayer, to be chosen at the discretion of the minister? But if so, would it not have seen that the interpolation of the prayer in the form would have violated the integrity of that form? Hageman has suggested that the rubric beneath the title offers a possible clue.

> The constitution of the Church directs that in the administration of the Lord's Supper, "after the Sermon and usual prayers are ended, the Form for the administration of the Lord's Supper shall be read, and a prayer suited to the occasion shall be offered, before the members participate of the ordinance.[113]

Hageman has read into this rubric a custom in the Supper celebrations in which both the traditional form and a prayer were used. The absence of permanent communion tables or altars in the church buildings of the RCA during this era meant that the minister read the entire form from the pulpit. When he finished reading the form, the minister descended from the pulpit to stand at the long tables that were provisionally set up for the communicants. But Hageman has surmised that for many this must have been an awkward transition. To maintain an uninterrupted flow in the rite, the minister offered another prayer as he presided at the table. The custom thus emerged that two "communion prayers" were offered at the celebration of the Supper: the prayer for worthy reception the minister read from the pulpit and another prayer he offered at the table. The committee seized the opportunity afforded by this custom to suggest as an option for the table prayer the "Eucharistic Prayer." There is no documentary evidence that suggests how many churches used the Eucharistic Prayer in this manner. But this prayer was retained unaltered when the Revised Liturgy of 1873 was adopted and issued in 1882 as the official service book of the denomination. In the 1882 revision, the Eucharistic Prayer appears closer to the beginning of the book in a section designated "Special Prayers."

In 1902 another liturgical committee was appointed to respond to the demands of the congregations for abbreviated forms, especially those for the sacraments. Mancius Holmes Hutton, son of the chairman of the committee responsible for the 1882 revision, was appointed chairman. Interestingly, the report and the revised forms that the committee presented to the Synod of 1903 reveal a curious attempt to conflate the traditional form for the Supper with the 1873 Eucharistic Prayer. The committee substituted the *epiclesis* in that prayer for the Pauline version of the institution narrative with which the traditional form commences. The rationale that the committee offered was that it had been receiving requests from the churches to introduce the form with a prayer instead of the Scripture reading. The committee further pointed out that reading the institution narrative at the beginning of the form was redundant since much of the text recurred in the section on the meaning of the Supper in the exposition. Following this line of reasoning, the committee also eliminated the Lord's Prayer at the end of the prayer for worthy reception, since it is offered again after the post-communion thanksgiving. One more significant change was the decision to move the self-oblation from the 1873 Eucharistic Prayer to a place before the prayer for worthy reception, with a rubric indicating the traditional prayer as an alternate.

The upshot is that the traditional form now contained two parts of the 1873 Eucharistic Prayer, separated from that prayer and relocated in what can only be seen as arbitrary places in that form. Holmes Hutton refers to the 1873 Eucharistic Prayer in his report: the prayer the committee had proposed "consisted of the richer parts of a communion prayer [sc.Eucharistic Prayer] already in the earlier part of the liturgy [sc. 1882 revision] among the special prayers." The suspicion that Holmes Hutton had neither the liturgical scholarship nor even the basic knowledge of the conventions necessary for an acceptable eucharistic celebration hardly needs justification. To remove the *epiclesis* and the self-oblation from the Eucharistic Prayer, refer to them as the "richer parts," and then arbitrarily relocate them in the traditional form, is to reduce the celebration to incoherence.[114] We will return to the problem of the basic requirements of the form and structure of the eucharistic prayer in the fourth chapter.

The recommendations in the 1903 report failed to gain the approval of the majority of the Classes, and the RCA was bound to take up again the project of revision the following year. The Synod of 1904 appointed a new committee, and instructed it to continue the work of its immediate predecessor. This committee endorsed the decision to introduce the celebration of the Lord's Supper with a prayer. But interestingly the committee was determined to use even more of the 1873 Eucharistic Prayer within the traditional form. The proposed form was now to begin with the preface and *epiclesis*. The self-oblation, however, remained in the place immediately preceding the prayer for worthy reception. The formulae omitted from the Eucharistic Prayer include the *sanctus*, thanksgiving for the Church triumphant, and the statement on the eschatological hope. The one other significant change was the restoration of the institution narrative to its original place at the beginning of the traditional form. The simple elimination of the narrative from the second part of the exposition effectively solved the problem of its redundancy: it now occurs only once, but appears after the preface and *epiclesis* from the transposed 1873 Eucharistic Prayer.

Now that we have demonstrated how the "abridged form" to which we referred at the outset of this chapter is a composite of formulae drawn from the Eucharistic Prayer of 1873 and the Palatinate Supper form, we are now prepared to outline its structure. ("EP" before the liturgical unit designates the Eucharistic Prayer of 1873 as the source of that unit):

1. EP. Preface
2. EP. *Epiclesis*
1. Institution Narrative from 1 Corinthians 11:23-26
2. Self-Examination (abridged—Excommunication omitted)
3. Comfortable Words (slightly abridged)
4. Exposition in Three Parts
    a. The Homily on the Atonement (abridged)
    b. Interpretation of the Institution Narrative (Narrative omitted)
    c. The Exhortation to Unity in the Holy Spirit (abridged)
3. EP. Prayer of Self-Oblation or,
5. Prayer for Worthy Reception (Lord's Prayer omitted)
6. Apostles' Creed
7. Reformed *Sursum corda*
8. Distribution
9. Post-Communion Psalm and Prayer of Thanksgiving (concluded with Lord's Prayer)[115]

This form was successfully introduced into the 1906 *Liturgy and Psalms,* but only after the Synod reached a compromise with the dissenting midwestern Classes. If for the liturgical committee, comprised mostly of leaders of the older congregations in New York and New Jersey, the term "liturgy" denoted the entire pattern of worship, for the more conservative leaders of the midwestern congregations, tied to the emigration of the *Gereformeerde* people that came to America in 1847, the term still retained the traditional meaning of the "historic formulations of classic Reformed theology."[116] To the latter then the attempt to alter these formulations threatened the integrity of that theology. In order to avert the rupture that it had witnessed in the GRC, the Synod agreed to publish the traditional (Palatinate) form for the Supper alongside the revised one in the 1906 service book. Designated by the RCA as the "unabridged" and "abridged" forms respectively, these were reprinted in the 1968 *Liturgy and Psalms* as alternatives to the Order for the Sacrament of the Lord's Supper, as we have already mentioned.

Conclusion: Mercersburg and its Aftermath

We have sought to narrate in this chapter the changes in approach to liturgy in the histories of the German and Dutch Reformed communions in America, changes that contributed to the destabilization of the Palatinate pattern of worship to which both were heir. These two ecclesial bodies traced their origins from the Reformation in the Palatinate, and were confessionally defined by their formal adherence to the Heidelberg Catechism as norm for doctrine, discipline, and worship. Because of these strong affinities in polity, doctrine, and worship, the two bodies naturally wanted to move toward merger. The plans for closer cooperation between them, however, came to ruin with the rise of the Mercersburg theology in the GRC, which the DRC, among others, condemned for theological tendencies that it could not reconcile with its own understanding of the Reformed faith.

When we turned to consider briefly the themes of the Mercersburg theology itself, we found that the concern of its proponents to determine the soteriological significance of the incarnation, the Church, and the sacraments resulted in a demand for a liturgy that expressed precisely the role of the Church in mediating the mystical union between Christ and his people through the action of the sacraments. Our analysis of the guiding principles that informed the liturgical research and composition of the German Reformed liturgical committee revealed a strategy to meet this demand: by adopting a scheme of worship modeled on the classic eucharistic liturgies of the third and fourth centuries rather than one on the sixteenth century Reformed liturgies, the liturgical committee sought to return the congregations of the GRC to a pattern of worship in which the Eucharist constituted the nucleus of each Lord's Day worship service.

The misgivings that Nevin had over contributing to the cause of the movement arose from his awareness that the new scheme of worship that the committee sought to introduce to the congregations departed too drastically from the non-eucharistic pattern of worship to which they were accustomed. Nevin realized that the mentality of most of these congregations did not allow a conception of worship in which the encounter between God and his people is mediated by grace-bearing sacraments; according to their mentality, this encounter rather occurred by means of an experience of the Spirit in the relatively free sphere of praying, singing, and hearing the word preached.

In spite of the resistance to their movement, Nevin, Schaff, and their supporters did not consider the enterprise they launched a total loss. The service books were published and sold; people read them and thereby became more educated about the liturgy and the principles of Christian worship. More importantly, their publication sowed seeds that very soon germinated in other movements also intent at this time to introduce a liturgical form of worship in their own Reformed churches. Among these churches we singled out for consideration were the Church of Scotland and the RCA, which adopted a eucharistic prayer from a service book published by the Church Service Society of the Church of Scotland. We saw that this prayer, however, succeeded neither in serving as a new form for the Lord's Supper nor even in providing a new framework within which the celebration could be reconceived. In the interest of preserving as much of the Palatinate heritage as possible, the committee arbitrarily combined elements from the eucharistic prayer with the traditional form for the Supper to create a strange hybrid that amounted to a confused aggregate of unrelated parts surrounding the institution narrative. After we surveyed the curious fate of the prayer as it suffered this dismemberment at the hands of the committee, we were forced to conclude that the committee had insufficient knowledge of the broader liturgical tradition and of the principles and conventions necessary for an adequate celebration of the Eucharist.

We will see that the new committee that the RCA appointed in 1950 to revise its liturgy was far more qualified to reconstruct the order of the Lord's Supper on the basis of sound liturgical principles. The liturgical and ecumenical movements of the twentieth century, and the enormous amount of biblical, liturgical, historical, and theological scholarship they generated, created a climate for liturgical study and reform as never before seen in the history of the Christian churches. Consequently, the members of the committee were able to carry out their assignments informed by a knowledge of both the history and principles of liturgy and the theologies of Christian worship that simply was not available to their predecessors. What they learned, and how they applied this learning to their composition of the elements that were to constitute the new Order for the Sacrament of the Lord's Supper, will form the subject of the next chapter.

The Lord's Supper in a Century of Ecumenism: The Reformed Church in America in an Age of Liturgical Catholicity

We have already noted that the Reformed Church in America appointed a new committee in 1950 to assume once again the task of the revision of the liturgy. Almost two decades later this liturgical committee concluded that never before in the history of its organized life had the denomination attempted as thoroughgoing a reform of its liturgy as it had just then completed.[1] The protracted drama played out on the relatively small stage of the RCA must be seen against the wider backdrop of the global changes that impacted the worship life not only of Reformed churches, but also of Roman Catholic, Anglican, Lutheran, and free churches worldwide. There are several factors that account for the astonishing developments in the sphere of the liturgy before and after the time the new liturgical committee of the RCA was formed in 1950. In this chapter we will examine the most important among these factors before we retrace the steps in the liturgical reconstruction of the Order for the Sacrament of the Lord's Supper.

First, we sketch a survey of the modern liturgical movement. For various reasons, the need to integrate the individual Christian into the corporate life of the Church was urgently felt at the turn of the twentieth century. In response to this need, many began to give increasing attention to the liturgy, since it is the liturgy that binds individuals together in the corporate act of worship. Second, we discuss the modern ecumenical movement. The formation of the World Conference on Faith and Order in the early twentieth century provided an unprecedented occasion for the churches to engage in interconfessional dialogue about the doctrines that have historically divided them. Since it is in the meaning and practice of the sacraments that the "deepest and most stubborn divisions among the churches" have emerged, it is no accident that Faith and Order was intensely concerned with the problem of the sacrament of the Lord's Supper.[2] Only in considering the impact of both these movements on the understanding of the Lord's Supper in the Reformed churches can we properly contextualize the modifications that the RCA made to the structure and content of its new order for the Lord's Supper. In the last part of the chapter, then, we will be prepared to chart the course of these modifications until they became incorporated in this new order adopted in the 1968 *Liturgy and Psalms*.

The Modern Liturgical Movement

In the foregoing chapter we focused on the changes in the approach to liturgy and worship introduced in the German and Dutch Reformed Churches in the mid-nineteenth century. The liturgical movements within the Reformed churches at that time had their counterpart in a project of liturgical restoration that the French Benedictine Prosper Guéranger (1805–1875) inaugurated in the Roman Catholic Church. Having felt called to a liturgical vocation in 1829, Guéranger refounded the Benedictine abbey at Solesmes, France in 1833 for the purpose of forming there a monastic community devoted to the celebration of the Mass and the Liturgy of the Hours and to the study of the Scriptures, the history of the liturgy, the lives of the saints and mystical and ascetical theology. Guéranger is credited as the first to enter the phrase "liturgical movement" into the historiography of the Roman Catholic Church, having used this phrase in his own day to designate the renewal of liturgical studies and the interest among both intellectuals and the faithful in reforming worship practices in the Catholic Church in France after generations of neglect.[3]

> Let us hope that the liturgical movement which is expanding and spreading will awaken also among the faithful the meaning of the Divine Office, that their attendance in church will become more intelligent, and that the time will come when, once more imbued with the spirit of the liturgy, they will feel the need to participate in the sacred chants.[4]

This *desideratum* of Guéranger received an official stamp of endorsement in 1903 when Pope Pius X issued his *motu proprio, Tra le sollecitudini*, on church music.[5] In this pronouncement Pius X advocated a return to the use of Gregorian chant in public worship as a means to encourage the active participation of all the faithful in the liturgy of the Church. Two years later Pius X reinforced this theme of the corporate character of the liturgy when he issued a decree calling for more frequent reception of Holy Communion.[6]

These papal pronouncements were certainly a harbinger of the changes that were to affect the thought and practice of the Roman Catholic Church in the sphere of worship. The point of departure for these changes has been associated with a Catholic Conference held at Malines in Belgium (*Le Congrès National des OEuvres catholiques de Malines*) in 1909. There the Belgian Benedictine Dom Lambert Beauduin (1873–1960) delivered a paper which historians identify as the origin of the modern liturgical movement.[7] Beauduin drew inspiration from an important theme in the *motu proprio* of Pius X, a theme destined to serve as the banner that the young Benedictine's paper helped raise for the liturgical movement: the true and indispensable source for the Christian spirit is the active participation in the holy mysteries and solemn prayer of the Church.[8] Beauduin asserted that the liturgy is the primary means of instructing the faithful in the holy mysteries of the Christian faith; it is from the liturgy that they must learn the language of the Church's prayers, which are necessary for the proper nourishment of their spiritual lives. Above all, the liturgy binds the lives of individual Christians by means of corporate prayer to the one visible Church, for which Jesus prayed in the Gospel of John (17:20–23).[9] But if the liturgy is to reclaim its central and integrating role of in the life of the Church, it must be rendered intelligible to all the faithful. Accordingly, Beauduin proposed to the conference the adoption of the following measures: (1) the translation of the Roman Missal, so that it might serve as the main devotional book among the faithful; (2) the promotion of the recitation of Compline in the home, and the encouragement of the attendance of the parochial mass and Vespers; (3) the restoration of Gregorian Chant, in keeping with the *motu proprio* of Pius X; and (4) the scheduling of annual retreats for parish choirs to centers of liturgical worship and life.[10]

These pragmatic proposals illustrate that pastoral concern for individual Christians in parish assemblies determined in large measure the aims of the modern liturgical movement during this early phase. Renewed interest in the liturgy was undoubtedly part of the pastoral response to the pressing need for genuine community in a modern world increasingly fragmented by the forces of urbanization and secularization.[11] In an amplified and longer version of the paper, *La Piété de l'Eglise, principes et faits*, published in 1914, Beauduin argued that liturgical renewal would generate a deeper sense of community amid these deplorable conditions, for the liturgy facilitates an inner understanding of the Church as the body of Christ. For Beauduin it was precisely through the Church's liturgy that Christ acts to unite organically the members of his body to himself and to one another: "By means of living the liturgy wholeheartedly Christians become more and more conscious of their supernatural fraternity, of their union in the mystical body of Christ."[12]

Restoring the *communio*-character to the liturgy and the sacraments would be a central concern in liturgical studies and reforms not only in the Roman Catholic Church but also in Protestant churches in the twentieth century. In the attempt on the part of the RCA to reclaim for the liturgy its rightful place in the thought and life of its congregations, we find precisely this concern emphasized. One member of its liturgical committee would insist that the "deepest meaning" of Christian personhood is expressed in the "communion and fellowship of Christians in their common worship of their God and Savior."[13] But at this early stage of the liturgical movement the insights that Beauduin and others sought to apply to the existential needs of the members of parish assemblies still required solid foundation in exegetical, historical, and theological research. The desire to provide for the growing liturgical movement an apologetic that conformed to the spirit of the liturgy as well as to Scripture and to the teachings of the church fathers distinguishes its next phase.[14] Among the most outstanding scholars here include the German Benedictine Dom Odo Casel (1886–1948), of the Abbey of Maria Laach, a leading center of liturgical scholarship; the Swedish Lutheran Bishop Yngve Brilioth (1891–1959); and the Anglican Benedictine Dom Gregory Dix (1901–1952). In the period between the two World Wars, these scholars published monumental studies that challenged conventional views of the history and meaning of Christian worship, and their ideas would alter dramatically the liturgical landscape of many churches — including that of the RCA — in the years that followed.

Odo Casel

Casel's seminal contribution to the liturgical movement was his "mystery theology" or "theology of the mysteries" (*Mysterientheologie*). By this term Casel intended to explain the very essence of the Christian faith. The content of the Christian message can be reduced neither to a set of dogmatic propositions nor to a moral code, but in essence is the mystery (*mysterion*) of God's saving plan (*oikonomia*), hidden in eternity, but revealed and realized progressively in time and in the world.[15] Its final revelation and first realization appeared in Jesus Christ. In this connection, Casel appealed to the Letters to the Ephesians and the Colossians, which refer to Jesus Christ as the "mystery of God's will"(Eph. 1:9), and the "mystery that has been kept hidden for ages and generations, but is now disclosed to the saints" (Col. 1:26).[16]

So then this mystery is no less than God's self-revelation in the incarnate Logos, the Son of God having become flesh. But at the heart of this mystery is the *pasch*, a term that designates the passing of the Son of God from this life, through his death on the cross, to his new life in the Spirit, through his resurrection and ascension into glory. The content of the mystery therefore comprehends the person of the incarnate Son of God and his saving actions for the Church. The Church is embraced in this mystery through these saving actions and is the form in which God's saving plan in Jesus Christ is further revealed and realized. According to the Letter to the Ephesians, the goal of this mystery is the unity of all human beings with God and with one another, when the "times will have reached their fulfillment—to bring all things in heaven and on earth together under one head, even Christ" (1:10).

The accomplishment of God's saving plan in the *pasch* of Jesus Christ is a unique and unrepeatable event that happened in the past. But it is Christ's will that his saving actions have a continuing presence in the Church to "give healing and life to the faithful."[17] In this connection, Casel applied the concept of mystery to Christian worship, which he saw as the ritual performance of the essence of the Christian message. In the Church's performance of its liturgical rites, especially the sacraments, Christ and his saving actions are objectively re-presented or re-actualized (*vergegenwärtigt*): "Christian liturgy is the ritual performance of the redemptive work of Christ in the Church and through it therefore, the presence of the divine salvific act under the veil of the symbol."[18] The redemptive work of Christ is made present in its ritual performance, so that those who participate in the liturgy are thereby made participants in the salvation accomplished through the passing of the Lord from death to life. This is attributable to the fact that Christ has entrusted the mystery of his *pasch* to the Church, which through its worship is drawn into this sacrifice of Christ as it is liturgically re-presented; for as Christ sacrificed for the Church, so the Church through its worship takes an active part in this sacrifice, and makes it its own. Thus there is a sense in which it is proper to say that in the liturgy "Bridegroom and Bride, head and members act as one." According to Casel, the liturgy is no less than the "fulfillment in ritual of what the Lord did for our salvation...We act out the mysteries as the body of Christ; as his body we do all that the head does."[19]

Casel's elaboration of the mystery of Christian worship (*Kultmysterium*) in this manner is determined in large measure by the place that he assigned to the Hellenistic mystery rites in God's progressive working out of his saving plan in history. Casel believed that the cultic form (*Kulteidon*) of the mystery rites adumbrated the fulfillment of God's saving plan in the *pasch* of Jesus Christ. For this reason he interpreted them as a providential preparation for what God was about to accomplish for humanity in Christ.[20] Out of the variety of these mystery rites, Casel believed an ideal type could be distilled. The lord (*kyrios*) of the mystery rite is a god who appears on earth to share in the struggle and misery of humanity, to suffer and to die. But then the god returns to life, thereby renewing the whole of nature and giving new life to his companions, those initiated into his cult. In the ritual reenactment of his myth, the companions of the dying and rising god are effectively united with his fate, and thereby acquire salvation (*soteria*). This salvation is realized in perfect communion with the god after death.[21]

In essence, then, the cult is a ritual memorial (*anamnesis*), a term used in this context to mean "a making present of some act of the god's upon which rests the existence and life of the community."[22] Casel saw in the form of the cult the longing of the *anima naturaliter christiana* for saving contact with God – a longing fulfilled in Christian revelation. But he did not mean to suggest that the mystery rites exercised a direct influence on Christian worship.[23] He did claim, on the other hand, that the common terminology implied an analogy between the two, if not in substance at least in mode of expression.[24] This he labored to show in adducing numerous texts from the New Testament and the church fathers in support of his theory.

The criticisms that Casel's antagonists leveled against his interpretation of the historical data, especially the links that he sought to forge between the Hellenistic mystery rites and the early Christian tradition, need not detain us here. It is enough to say that they do not diminish the enduring contributions that he made to a deepened understanding of the liturgy. The rationale for an objective and corporate, in contrast to a subjective and individualistic, conception of the liturgy sought by the pioneers of the liturgical movement is supplied here by a profound theology of worship grounded in a firm biblical and Christ-centered foundation. This theology proved to be enormously fruitful for continuing theological reflection on the meaning of the liturgy throughout the twentieth century, not only in Roman Catholic but also in Protestant circles. Casel's use of the category of *anamnesis* was significant for ecumenical dialogue about the doctrine of the sacrifice of the Mass, a painful subject of debate between the Roman Catholic and Protestant churches since the dawn of the Reformation in the sixteenth century.[25] As we have seen, the sacrificial dimension of the Eucharist in Casel's theory is bound up in the liturgical re-presentation of the unique and unrepeatable event of Jesus' *pasch*. In this interpretation the Anglican theologian, A.G. Hebert, a member of the committee on the "Ways of Worship" appointed by Faith and Order in 1939, claimed to find a promising basis for progress in dialogue about the controverted doctrine.[26] Presumably having Casel and his school at Maria Laach in mind, Hebert confidently reported in 1951 that the eucharistic sacrifice "is finding in our day a truly evangelical expression from the catholic side, when it is insisted that the sacrificial action is not any sort of re-immolation of Christ, nor a sacrifice additional to His one sacrifice, but a participation in it."[27]

Yngve Brilioth

Among the most influential early ecumenical studies on the meaning of the Eucharist that cannot be neglected in a survey of the modern liturgical movement is that of the Lutheran theologian Yngve Brilioth, *Nattvarden i Evangeliskt Gudstjänstliv*. First published in Swedish in 1926, it was translated in an abridged version in 1930 by A.G. Hebert as *Eucharistic Faith and Practice, Evangelical and Catholic*.[28] In this analysis of the tradition of the eucharistic celebration in the Western Church, Brilioth identified in the various liturgical forms and doctrinal statements four elements that he claimed were grounded in the institution narratives of the New Testament itself. These four elements are: thanksgiving (*eucharistia*), communion/fellowship, commemoration, and the eucharistic sacrifice. To these Brilioth added a fifth element, which he designated mystery—the element that suffuses and animates them all. Together these elements express the rich and manifold meaning of the Eucharist.[29]

The thanksgiving (*eucharistia*) is expressed primarily in the great prayer that the presider offers over the bread and wine of the Eucharist. In it God is praised not only for his gifts of creation, but also for the work of redemption in Christ and the fulfillment of the divine promises.[30] Communion/fellowship in the Eucharist has a double signification: It is communion with God in Christ at the same time as it is fellowship with those who belong to Christ. This fellowship extends to the whole Church on earth, and includes not only the living, but also those who have gone on to be with Christ.[31] Commemoration is the liturgical proclamation of the saving acts of God in history, which culminated in the passion and death of Christ. Closely related to the commemoration is the eucharistic sacrifice, because the climactic event of which this commemoration is made, which is represented and exhibited in the Eucharist, is precisely Christ's sacrifice on the cross. It is into Christ's sacrifice that the faithful are incorporated through communion; in the act of communion the faithful not only share in the benefits of Christ's atoning death, but also in his self-offering. Thus it is in the eucharistic sacrifice, according to Brilioth, that the four elements come together with one another.[32]

If it is in the eucharistic sacrifice that these elements are combined, it is the element of mystery that integrates them and ensures their proper balance. Mystery for Brilioth refers to the real presence of Jesus Christ in the eucharistic celebration. There are three modes of this presence as attested in the New Testament. In the Synoptic tradition, there is the "personal presence" of the Lord. Jesus Christ is the true celebrant at every Eucharist, presiding as Priest before God on behalf of the faithful, "at" rather than "on" the table.[33] In the Johannine tradition, there is the presence of the Lord in the sacraments. The Bread of Life uses the bread of the Eucharist as a "means of his presence" and "vehicle of his own self-communication."[34] The third is found in the Pauline tradition. Here the presence of Christ is in his mystical body, the Church, through which the faithful enter into the mystery of communion/fellowship.

These modes complement and complete each other. When in the history of the Church one or two were stressed to the relative neglect of the other(s), the four elements through which the meaning of the Eucharist is expressed disintegrated, and a period of liturgical decay inevitably followed. For example, in the late medieval period the exaggerated focus on the second of the three modes led to a "materialistic" interpretation of Christ's presence in the bread and wine. This incited reaction during the Reformation period. But in their concern to formulate an alternative definition of the real presence and to explain how the individual Christian appropriates the benefits of Christ's death through the reception of the sacrament, the Reformers only perpetuated this focus. In different ways, the Church during these two periods did not succeed in holding together the four elements, and so was unable to express adequately the meaning of the Eucharist.

In sum, the service that the historian Brilioth rendered to the churches in his own ecumenical context was to demonstrate that the meanings of the Eucharist are manifold, and that for historical reasons these received different accents in different periods and traditions.[35] No one church has ever possessed the total meaning of the Eucharist at any stage of its particular tradition. Each can learn from one another, and also help one another to deepen their appreciation of the greater tradition of Christendom as a whole. On the other hand, he also showed that certain elements must invariably be present in the eucharistic forms to ensure the expression of the manifold mean-

ing of the sacrament. These include praise, narrative recital, commemoration, self-offering, intercession, and doxology—elements that
most classic eucharistic prayers contain.[36] Brilioth's criticisms of the
liturgical forms and doctrines of the late medieval and Reformation
periods constituted an indirect charge to the Protestant churches in
his own day—especially those in the Lutheran and Reformed traditions—to recover the "objective expression of corporate faith and
worship in a service whose name means the Thanksgiving."[37] This
transparent allusion to "Eucharist" strongly suggests that only in reclaiming the eucharistic prayer in the proper sense would these
churches succeed in incorporating into their worship life the elements
necessary for the adequate expression of the manifold meaning of the
Eucharist.

Gregory Dix

Perhaps none of these historians did more to stimulate interest in the
potential inherent in the eucharistic rite of the early Church for liturgical renewal than Gregory Dix. Dix maintained that it was from the
late medieval and Reformation periods that the churches in the modern West inherited their ideas about the Eucharist. But in these ideas
the churches departed unfortunately from the conception of the eucharistic rite embodied in the liturgies of the early Church. In these
liturgies the intention of the rite can be seen to cohere more faithfully
with Jesus' command to his followers to "do this." Dix's understanding of the content of this command on the basis of the early liturgical
data won many adherents in Protestant worship committees. In fact,
there is evidence to suggest that it was precisely Dix's interpretation
of Jesus' command that informed the structure of the new eucharistic
liturgy in the RCA.

Dix's central thesis is implied in the title of his magisterial study,
The Shape of the Liturgy, which appeared in 1945.[38] In his analysis of
the great liturgical rites that have come down from the early Church,
Dix claimed to have discovered a single normal or standard structure
that underlies most of them. This structure or "shape" consists in four
essential actions, which in turn can be traced from the Last Supper
that Jesus shared with his disciples on the night before his crucifixion.
Dix observed that in these Last Supper accounts of the New Testa-

ment, Jesus is the subject of four verbs: he took; he blessed; he broke; and he gave. Since three of these verbs are repeated with respect to the cup, it is more accurate to see in the New Testament a "seven-action scheme" of the rite that Jesus then instituted. But in the liturgical tradition, these seven actions were condensed into four, which together constitute the "invariable nucleus of every eucharistic rite known to us throughout antiquity from the Euphrates to Gaul"[39] According to Dix,

> with absolute unanimity liturgical tradition reproduces these seven actions as four: (1) the offertory; bread and wine are "taken" and placed on the table together. (2) The prayer, the president gives thanks to God over bread and wine together. (3) The fraction; the bread is broken. (4) The bread and wine are distributed together.[40]

This theory of the "four-action shape" proved to be very influential among Protestant churches that initiated liturgical reforms in the second half of the twentieth century, including the RCA. In his essay on the new Order for the Sacrament of the Lord's Supper adopted by that denomination, Hageman explained that the liturgical committee modeled the order in which the events in this celebration were to unfold on the four actions Jesus performed during the Last Supper. After the service of the word, the celebration of the Supper was to proceed as follows:

a) The minister and elders gather around the Table and it is uncovered. This represents "He took."

b) There is a prayer of thanksgiving and blessing. This represents "He blessed."

c) This is followed by the recitation of the words of institution, accompanied by the breaking of the bread and the lifting of the cup. This represents "He brake."

d) The elements are then given to the elders and the people after the words of distribution. This represents "He gave."[41]

Hageman added provocatively that when the people assemble to "do this in remembrance of him," they should, on the basis of this scriptural mandate, follow Jesus' example not only in word but also *in action* (emphasis added).[42]

Hageman's assertion leads to a set of critical questions that we will need to explore in greater detail in the concluding chapter. Suffice it to say here that if in fact we have shown that the liturgical committee of the RCA endorsed the outline Dix proposed for the order of the eucharistic celebration, we find no evidence that they followed him in drawing out the implications of this "shape" for the meaning of the celebration. Hageman declared that the second principle that guided the composition of the new form was "responsiveness to the Reformed doctrine of the Supper as set forth in both the Belgic Confession and the Heidelberg Catechism."[43] Dix claimed, for his own part, that the shape itself performs the meaning of the action; the great eucharistic prayer, the second element in this shape, expresses the meaning integral to the action, however variable the content of this prayer in the liturgies that have come down from the early Church. In entering into this action, the people enter into the redeeming action of Christ himself, his death and resurrection made present and "operative by its effects" in the *anamnesis*.[44] There is heard here a clear echo of a theme that is at the heart of the *Mysterientheologie* propounded by Dom Odo Casel. For both Dix and Casel the Eucharist is an action in which Christ, incorporating the members of his own body into his *pasch*, transfers proleptically all who are in him into the Kingdom of his Father. More exactly, it is a corporate action of the whole body of Christ, head and members together, through which the redeemed, renewed and gathered into one, are presented to the Father in Christ as the one new humanity in him.[45]

If Dix is right, and it is in fact the case that liturgy itself articulates a theology as it is performed, then a critical issue that comes to bear directly on our thesis emerges. What is the precise relation between this theology and the theology of worship and sacraments enshrined in the Reformed confessions? Does the adoption of the "shape" that Dix outlined commit a church to a particular line of interpretation of the data of revelation? With perhaps very few exceptions, the Reformed churches until this stage in their history had not regarded their liturgies or forms for the Lord's Supper as a privileged norm for doctrine. Rather, as we have seen, these forms were more often seen as transcripts of theological propositions intentionally formulated for the purpose of catechetical instruction. For this reason, the meaning-intention of the Eucharist itself as a symbolic and ritual action had remained largely unaddressed in these churches. But the exegetical, historical, and theological studies engendered by the liturgical movement, as we have just reviewed them, were destined to play a critical role in the transformation of the Reformed understanding of the Lord's Supper. As we will see in the next part of this chapter, the ecumenical movement afforded a context in which the Reformed churches could interact with the ideas that the liturgical movement disseminated across the separated communions. As a result of this interaction, their conception of the place and meaning of the sacrament in the worship of their own congregations would undergo a substantive change.

The Modern Ecumenical Movement: The World Conference on Faith and Order

We have already indicated that the liturgical and ecumenical movements were intimately bound up with each other. This could hardly have been otherwise, since the principal concern of the liturgical movement was to recover the meaning of the Eucharist as the worship event *par excellence* through which Christians renew their unity with Christ and with one another. Indeed, insofar as it maintained that the ultimate goal of all sound liturgy is to unite Christians with the Church in all times and in all places, the liturgical movement was ecumenical in its very essence. One member of the RCA liturgical committee later perceived this clearly as he reflected on the impact that the liturgical movement had on his own denomination. "Some," he observed, "see in the liturgy not only a bridge over which men may join the ranks in the Body of Christ with Christians of every century, but also the means by which a divided Christendom may be healed of its many divisions."[46]

The intent of the ecumenical movement in the twentieth century was to provide a worldwide forum in which a divided Christendom could engage in interconfessional dialogue about the doctrines and practices that to this day continue to present obstacles to unity. Its ultimate goal remains to lead the churches through these dialogues to a visible manifestation of their unity willed by Jesus Christ. Between 1910 and 1948, the Faith and Order movement played an instrumental role in creating possibilities for the churches to progress toward this unity. One of the outstanding pioneers of this movement was Charles Henry Brent, who served in the Protestant Episcopal Church in the USA as bishop in the Philippines. Brent's frustrations as a missionary convinced him that the failure of the churches to deal effectively with the problems in the modern world, especially in "mission countries," was due to their inability to present a common witness. In October 1910, the day before the General Convention of his own denomination convened in Cincinatti, Ohio, Brent expressed to an audience largely composed of members of the convention his belief that the time had come for the churches from across the globe to assemble at a world conference to examine their differences.[47] His message met with overwhelming approval, and on 19 October the convention decided to adopt a resolution that a "Joint Commission" be appointed to summon a "World Conference" of "all Christian Communions throughout the world which confess our Lord Jesus Christ as God and Saviour." The movement adopted the working principle that "the beginnings of unity are to be found in the clear statement and full consideration of those things in which we differ, as well as of those things in which we are one."[48] Those "things" were comprehended by the terms "faith" and "order," which the commission later defined in its preparatory report:

> Of Faith, not of opinion, but of what is required or imposed as *de fide*, concerning God and Christ, concerning man and the future world; of Order, not of preferential practice, but of matters of discipline with regard to the Ministry, the Sacraments, Marriage, and Christian Life.[49]

In 1920 the Joint Commission held a preliminary meeting in Geneva for all the co-operating committees and commissions of the participating churches. After extensive preparations, the first World Conference on Faith and Order convened in Lausanne (Switzerland) in 1927. On this historic occasion, over four hundred representatives from the Orthodox, Anglican, Reformation, and free church traditions met to discuss their agreements in faith, as well as their disagreements that had divided them for centuries.[50] The Lausanne Conference marked the epochal moment in modern church history when

Christians worldwide began to collaborate on removing those barriers that had obstructed their path toward visible unity.

The sacrament of the Lord's Supper received attention not only at the first Faith and Order Conference in Lausanne, but also at the second held in Edinburgh in 1937. But at both the subject was treated only in the context of a general discussion about the sacraments (*sacramenta in genere*).[51] The drafters of the final reports were interested neither in resolving controversial issues nor in reconciling the conflicting interpretations of the individual sacraments. They were content merely to state the points on which there was a general consensus among the churches, and those on which there was a divergence of views. It was only after Edinburgh that Faith and Order sought to consider the implications of the liturgical principles and practices of the separated churches for ecumenical dialogue. In 1938 the "Continuation Committee" of the Edinburgh Conference discussed plans for the study of what it called the "liturgical question," but concluded that the time for the appointing of a special commission for this purpose had not yet come. Instead, it decided to appoint a theological commission to address the subject of "The Church." Before finishing its business, however, the Continuation Committee did entertain the suggestion that the problem of intercommunion should receive consideration, and agreed that this topic should be included in the discussion to be held at the next meeting.[52]

In August 1939 the Continuation Committee convened at Clarens for another meeting, where it decided to appoint two more international theological commissions. The committee instructed the first to the study the "ways of worship" characteristic of the various Christian traditions, and the second to deal with the problem of intercommunion. Both subjects were subordinated to the theme of the Church, to which the proceedings of the third World Conference on Faith and Order would be devoted. The cataclysm into which the war years plunged the world made communications between members and their respective commissions extremely difficult, and it was only in the summer of 1950 that the commissions managed to hold meetings long enough to prepare and approve their final reports. In the following year these reports, together with a selection of papers contributed by the members, were published and distributed to the delegates to the conference. These volumes were read and served as the basis for the discussions that were conducted over the course of the World Conference that opened on 15 August, 1952 in Lund.

Ways of Worship

The volume that the theological commission on Ways of Worship produced is especially germane to our present investigation for two reasons. First, it contains a report that not only surveys the historic worship traditions representing the member churches, but also registers the impact of the liturgical movement on them, suggesting the need to consider the consequences for ecumenical dialogue of the new liturgical forms and worship books that were already emerging as a result of this movement. Second, it contains significant papers submitted by theologians and liturgical historians representing the Reformed tradition.[53] An analysis of their papers reveals a remarkable change in orientation to the historic Reformed conception of the Lord's Supper, which these scholars subjected to criticism on the basis of the new insights they appropriated from the liturgical movement. For these reasons, we interrupt our narrative here to give a concise overview of the report, and then to highlight the most important themes that appear in select papers that Reformed members of the commission contributed to the volume.

According to the report, liturgical renewal was born from the rediscovery of the sacramental character of worship.[54] For Protestants, this meant that the preached word is no less sacramental than the sacraments, since the former also is a channel for the communication of God's grace, insofar as God uses human words for this purpose. In this respect, the value of the preached word is "not exhausted by its pedagogic worth, but involves a mystery, as do Baptism and Eucharist."[55] This recognition of the sacramentality of all worship in some cases led to a return to a more frequent celebration of the Lord's Supper.[56]

This new valuation of worship prompted many to reconsider the sources of their liturgical traditions. Worshippers in the churches of the Reformation studied the liturgical principles and forms that came out of the sixteenth century, while members of all churches, including Roman Catholic, were returning to the New Testament and the liturgies from the patristic age in order to regain the "purity and strength of worship as it was practiced in their classical periods."[57] There was a widespread consensus that the churches had to learn what the Holy Spirit "taught our fathers in the faith, first during the biblical period, and then in the period which followed."[58] This historical research and dialogue convinced many churches that the worship habits and practices of their own recent past were not entirely adequate. In Protestant churches, many determined that the privileging of the preached word at the expense of the table was unbiblical. On the basis of their study, they concluded that the assumption of a pure apostolic message that had degenerated into a sacramentalism rested on a misunderstanding, because Jesus distinctly enjoined his followers to break the bread and drink the wine.[59]

In this regard, the historical studies of Dom Gregory Dix and Dom Eligius Dekkers, OSB, stimulated discussion about a wide range of issues connected with the eucharistic prayer.[60] Among those in the report specifically singled out for mention include the function of the *epiclesis* and the content of the commemoration. Scholars were debating whether in the *epiclesis* the Holy Spirit is invoked upon the elements or the worshippers or on the entire sacramental act, including the elements, the worshippers and the action itself.[61] The attention given to the broader content of the classic eucharistic prayers led to the recognition that in the eucharistic celebration, the Church remembers not only Christ's death, but also his life, resurrection, ascension, and session in eternal glory.

Historical studies also revisited the problem of the sacrificial dimension of the Eucharist. Luther and Calvin rejected this dimension out of the conviction that the sacrifice of the Mass derogated from the sacrifice of the cross, which, having been offered once and for all, could never be repeated. But in light of recent research, scholars were asking whether the terms of this problem might be reconceived. In the report is recorded the enthusiastic reception granted to the *Mysterientheologie* of Odo Casel, whose notion that the sacrifice is re-presented rather than repeated in the eucharistic celebration was seen to have paved a way to "some understanding between the Roman Catholic and non-Roman Churches."[62] In addition, the idea that communion and offering can be seen as acts integral to each other implies that one cannot share in the sacrifice of Christ apart from participating in it through self-offering. According to the report, this idea tended toward the conclusion that in its self-offering, the Church is offering the body of Christ.[63] A milepost of the considerable distance that the separated churches had traversed since the eucharistic controversies of the sixteenth century is the following remarkable statement: "In the Eucharist the celebrant is the risen Lord, uniting the members of his earthly Body to himself in His offering of Himself to the Father."[64] This formulation unmistakably reveals the influence that Casel, Brilioth, and Dix exercised on the minds of those engaged in liturgical research during the time the commission met.

The report on the new developments in the conception of the Eucharist is concluded with reference to the attention given to the eschatological significance of this sacrament. In Luke's Gospel, Jesus depicts the Kingdom of God in the image of a heavenly banquet; the Last Supper that Jesus shared with his disciples was a "foretaste of the eternal life of the Kingdom of God."[65] This eschatological theme is accentuated in the Eastern liturgies. Nor is this theme ignored in the Reformed churches: the institution narrative that the sixteeth century Reformers drew from the First Letter to the Corinthians (11:23–26) to introduce their celebrations of the Supper contain the Apostle Paul's declaration: "For as often as ye eat this bread, and drink this cup, ye do shew the Lord's death till he come (v. 26)."[66] This expectation of the Lord's return in glory is also expressed in the "eucharistic Consecration Prayers" contained in the Church of Scotland's *Book of Common Order* and the English Congregational *Book of Public Worship*. Finally, renewed awareness of the eschatological dimension of the celebration is reflected in contemporary orders for the Lord's Supper. A petition from the *Didache* for the final ingathering of the Church and a *Maranatha* ("Come, Lord Jesus") concludes the prayer of intercession found in the Order for the Lord's Supper used in the Reformed Church of France.[67]

Reformed Contributions

It is significant that several members representing the Reformed tradition had already distinguished themselves as leading participants in the liturgical movement. Perhaps no one among them was more outstanding than the versatile scholar appointed by the Continuation Committee of Faith and Order as chair of the commission on Ways of Worship, Gerardus van der Leeuw (1890–1950). Internationally known for his research in the phenomenology of religion, van der Leeuw was professor of the history of religions at the University of Groningen, and later Minister of Education and Cultural Affairs of the Netherlands. His wide range of interests comprehended comparative religion, education, theology, religious art, music, and liturgical history. He was an assiduous student of recent developments in liturgical research, and maintained that the *Mysterientheologie* of Odo Casel was the most important theological contribution to the churches in the past 150 years.[68] Amid all his activities he still found time to serve as mentor of the *Liturgische Kring*, a group of pastors and laypersons in the Netherlands Reformed Church (*Nederlandse Hervormde Kerk*) dedicated to the renewal of the liturgical life of that communion. This group succeeded in adding to the 1563 Palatinate (1566 Dathenus) form for the Supper a number of eucharistic liturgies for use in Dutch Reformed congregations, and the *Dienstboek in Ontwerp* (Worship Book in Preparation) published in 1955 by the Netherlands Reformed Church bears the stamp of their labors.[69] Van der Leeuw helped the members of the Reformed churches in his own day see more clearly than their sixteenth century predecessors the rich liturgical heritage of the broader Eastern and Western ecclesial traditions. Perhaps his most enduring legacy will prove to be the foundation of *Studia Liturgica*, an international and ecumenical journal for liturgical research and renewal, which first appeared in 1962. Wiebe Vos, editor and founder, was a pupil and disciple of van der Leeuw, and from him "inherited a deep concern for an ecumenical approach to liturgical matters in the spirit of that great and gifted pioneer."[70]

Van der Leeuw drafted the report we just surveyed, and contributed one paper, which his death prevented him from revising and expanding. In this brief paper, he identified the challenge that the renewal in sacramental life posed to the Reformed churches in the twentieth century. That challenge was to overcome the separation of the sacrament from the word in typical Reformed worship. The Reformers themselves affirmed the unity of word and sacrament as the norm for worship on every Lord's Day, but sacramental practice in

Reformed churches very soon departed from the original intention of Calvin, who regarded lay participation in communion only a few times a year as a Roman Catholic abuse to be corrected. Against Calvin's wishes, however, infrequency of communion remained the rule in the congregations of Reformed churches into the twentieth century. Celebrated only on special occasions in a spirit of solemn reverence, the Lord's Supper was regarded as the "spiritual peak" in the life of the congregation.[71] For his part, however, van der Leeuw objected that "Holy Communion can never be the acme of worship, since it is itself worship, and every gathering of the members of Christ's body is essentially a gathering at the Table where He laid down the law of the New Covenant in his blood."[72] The growing recognition of the centrality of "Holy Communion," according to van der Leeuw, accounted for the recent demand for its increased celebration in the Reformed churches.

But van der Leeuw subjected not only the practice but also the form for the Reformed Supper to criticism. In the Reformed churches there had been an "almost exclusive relation between the Eucharist and the death of the Lord, with a total neglect of his resurrection." For this reason, the Lord's Supper resembled more a "funerary ceremony" than a "joyful feast."[73] Parenthetically, we may corroborate van der Leeuw's claim by adding that the drafters of the Palatinate form conceived the Lord's Supper as a celebration of a death, as the rubric at the head of the form implied: "On those days when Holy Communion is to be celebrated a sermon shall be delivered on the Lord's death and on His Supper."[74] But, according to van der Leeuw, the "resurrection is included in the sacrifice of the Lord," which helps explain why the Church of the apostolic era broke bread "with exultation," as is apparent in Acts 2:46. Here we see the ecumenical impulse to overcome the one-sided confessional stance by returning to the common heritage of the Church of the apostolic era.

In his paper, the Swiss Reformed liturgical historian Julius Schweizer echoed van der Leeuw's criticism of the classic Reformed forms for the Supper.[75] In these forms, public confession, the comfortable words, absolution, and the formularies for excommunication all precede communion. The cumulative result was an emphasis on sin and the need for forgiveness through the atoning death of Jesus, which introduced into the celebration a mood of somber repentance. But the New Testament reveals that the "eucharistic Supper of the Church stands between the Resurrection Supper of the Lord with his disciples and the eschatological Supper of the Lamb." Consequently, the Supper should be celebrated joyfully as a "meal with the Risen Lord and an anticipation of the messianic Supper of the returning Lord."[76] Schweizer appealed to the Reformed churches in his day, accordingly, to create new forms that guide the people to the table to receive the sacrament with the joy that is imparted by the presence of this resurrected Lord, who has promised to return to give his people a share in the eternal feast of his Kingdom.

Perhaps the most severe criticisms of classic Reformed sacramental theology and practice came from Richard Paquier (1905–1985). Paquier was the founder of *Eglise et Liturgie*, a group of Swiss Reformed pastors and laypersons intent on an "ecumenically-oriented renewal of the concept of the church and the reform of worship in line with an evangelical catholicity."[77] Paquier was drawn to the liturgical life of the Anglican world, and also profoundly versed in the liturgical traditions of the churches in both the East and the West. Paquier and his group were unwilling to deepen and extend the influence of the Calvinian liturgical tradition, but instead adopted an approach to liturgical reform shaped by their studies of the liturgies of the early Church. Paquier charged that the sixteenth century liturgies of Calvin were innovations; authentic liturgy developed from the apostolic times and found expression in the classic liturgies of the third and fourth centuries. The goal of the *Eglise et Liturgie* was to rehabilitate these liturgical sources, from which the Reformers departed in their protests against perceived abuses in the eucharistic theology and practice of the late middle ages.[78] In regard to new forms for the Lord's Supper, Paquier and his group succeeded already in 1931 in composing and distributing a "complete, ecumenically recognizable eucharistic prayer."[79] This prayer came out in several versions, and a final formulation was published in 1952.[80] *Eglise et Liturgie* played an instrumental role in assisting the Reformed Church of France (ERF) and the French Reformed churches of Switzerland in recovering the traditional structure of the eucharistic prayer, and the eucharistic liturgies that these churches created after the Second World War are profoundly indebted to its pioneering labors. We will see later that through the mediation of the ERF, the RCA also owed a debt to *Eglise et Liturgie* for its own new eucharistic liturgy.

Paquier's rejection of the Reformed liturgical tradition finds expression in the paper that he contributed to the volume. He believed that the sacramental life of the Reformed churches was vitiated by a flawed theological conception of the sacraments. The word of God in these churches is the "sole path from God to man." The sacraments do not have a value *sui generis*; rather they are accorded the status of a seal and a pledge of the grace that the word alone is sufficient to confer.[81] This conception, according to Paquier, led those in the Reformed tradition to interpret the sacraments only in terms of the word, as a *verbum visibile*, which God, in graciously condescending to frail human beings, instituted as a pedagogical aid, so that they might understand the promises addressed to them in Christ more adequately.[82] By reducing the sacraments to another form of the word, however, the Reformers were unable to prevent their churches from collapsing the one into the other. For the Reformers, in Paquier's judgment, "there [was] no difference between the Word and the sacraments, neither quantitative nor qualitative."[83]

Paquier objected that this "restricted idea of the sacraments" is simply not biblical. On the basis of relevant New Testament passages — Romans 6 for baptism, and John 6 for Eucharist — he sought to show that according to biblical teaching the sacraments "imply a unitive value, a grace of indwelling and, in a truly mystical sense, of assimiliation, which the Scriptures nowhere attribute to the Word as such."[84] He proceeded to cite two reasons for the neglect of this biblical teaching of the sacraments. The first concerns the christologies of Zwingli and Calvin, which Paquier denounced for their Nestorian tendencies. Too sharp a distinction between the human and divine natures in Christ tends also toward too sharp a distinction between the sign and signified in the sacraments. The second relates to the "liberal idealism" dominating the contemporary spiritual climate. The dualism of "spirit and bodily nature" that accompanies this liberal idealism expresses itself in the ecclesial realm in the reduction of the baptismal water and the eucharistic bread and wine to mere "symbols," understood in this context to mean "allegorical signs of a spiritual reality which is without a real and organic relation" to the *materia* of the sacraments. These two reasons help explain the "denial of any mystical and unitive element in faith, and the suspicion which this denial arouses regarding "sacramentalism" and "liturgism"" — accusations evidently brought against those in the Reformed churches intent on restoring to the sacraments what they regarded as their proper place and meaning in worship.[85]

Paquier approved the contemporary liturgical renewal in the French Reformed churches in Switzerland, in which he saw the embryonic stages of a movement to overcome the aversion to the sacramental dimension of the faith inherited from Zwingli and Calvin. One of the promising signs of change that he highlighted was the eucharistic liturgy of Lausanne, published in 1940. From this liturgy he cited in his essay the *epiclesis*, in which he discerned an attempt to forge a closer link between the elements and the fruit of the sacrament:

> We pray thee, O God, thyself to bless and to consecrate this bread and this cup: that through this perishable food thy Spirit may aid us to discern thy imperishable grace, and to find in this bread the body of our Lord Jesus Christ, and in this cup the blood of our Lord Jesus Christ.[86]

In spite of the positive changes reflected in this and other formulae, Paquier was nevertheless guarded in his optimism. He warned that only in drawing a proper theological distinction between word and sacrament could the Reformed churches establish a solid foundation on which to erect a liturgical practice that would ensure for the sacraments their proper place and meaning. Without this foundation, the sacraments and any new liturgies accompanying them would always appear as "invaders, or as needless postscripts, in the minds of Churches which wish to be fundamentally Churches of the Word."[87]

Swiss German Reformed pastor Arthur Graf also judged the exaggerated emphasis on the word to have diminished the sacramental dimension of faith in the Reformed churches. Graf argued that these churches inherited from the Reformers a distrust of mystery, of anything that is not transparent to reason.[88] This "rationalizing attitude" among the Reformers had at least three consequences on sacramental practice. First, what could not be based on the Bible was excluded from liturgical celebrations. Second, since celebrations were "public and accessible" to all, "everything [had to] be spoken aloud and audibly," and anything in them regarded as "mysterious" had to be removed. The people must understand the celebration, and for this reason the sacrament became above all a doctrine that must be "discerned and known."[89] In this connection, Graf noted that the phrase "explanation of the mystery" enters into the vocabulary of the Christian faith for the first time in the sixteenth century.[90] Finally, this intellectualization of the sacrament found expression in the "verbal and learned expositions inserted into the sacramental forms," which reduce the celebration to a catechism.[91] Graf's verdict was that as a result of the Reformation "reason" began to "carry so much weight that all mystery [became] on that account repressed."[92]

Graf added that the eclipse of the mystery of the Christian faith came to have more serious consequences on the Christian doctrine of God. Confidence in the authority of reason ultimately led to a "Universalist, Unitarian, understanding of God" in place of the "biblical, trinitarian belief in God." But where this "trinitarian belief fades" so too the "ground is taken away from beneath the sacraments."[93] The evidence to suggest that Reformed Christians in German Switzerland lived only according to the first article, that is, *Credo in unum Deum, patrem omnipotentem* [I believe in one God, the Father almighty] is found in their preference for the Jesus depicted in the "Lives of Jesus" to the "Christ present in the sacrament."[94] It is not the case in their worship that the "presence of the Lord in the Sacrament and in the congregation celebrating the Sacrament is taken for granted;" rather, the people adhere to an interpretation of the Lord's Supper as a mere "memorial" of the Lord's death.[95] But if the Swiss German churches clarified the concept of *anamnesis*, they would see that the "Church does not simply remember the death of the Lord: she 'represents' the sacrifice itself, letting herself enter into the suffering and death of Christ, into His obedience."[96]

In sum, the impact of the liturgical and ecumenical movements on the Reformed world prompted the liturgical historians and theologians representing this tradition to reflect on the place and meaning of the sacrament of the Lord's Supper in worship. The enormous amount of scholarship that these movements generated compelled them to test this tradition against the biblical and early liturgical sources that this scholarship brought to light. In the course of re-evaluating the history of Reformed sacramental theology and practice, they came to the realization that the separation of the sacrament from the word in worship was an undesirable development. This separation they attributed not only to a betrayal of the Reformers' original intentions, but also to the manner in which the Reformers conceived the sacrament. To the Reformers the sacrament was primarily a *verbum visibile* that served to confirm the promise of the forgiveness of sins through the atoning death of Jesus Christ — a message that the word alone was sufficient to convey. This "word-character" of the sacrament found expression in the forms for the Lord's Supper, which modern Reformed scholarship criticized for their ponderous, didactic tone. Consisting above all in exhortation and proclamation, the forms appear more concerned with moral and doctrinal rectitude than with the joy and spontaneity that accompany the celebration of the resurrected Lord, who has promised to return for his own.

The RCA was certainly sensitive to these currents moving through the churches outside the boundaries of its own denomination. In 1950 a young Howard Hageman, who was to become a distinguished leader in the RCA, published an article in *Theology Today* on the worldwide renewal of interest in liturgy and worship.[97] This article consists in an enthusiastic report of a personal encounter with the literature that emerged from the liturgical and ecumenical movements. It clearly reveals Hageman's own commitment to liturgical and sacramental renewal. Later in that same year the General Synod (GS) of his denomination would appoint him as one of four members to serve on its newly formed Committee on the Revision of The Liturgy. Guided by his liturgical scholarship and theological acumen, this committee attempted not only to restore a balance between word and sacrament in Lord's Day worship, but also to compose an order for the sacrament that adheres to the structure of the classic eucharistic prayers of the early Church. In the concluding part of this chapter, we will review selectively the stages that led up to this momentous event in the life of the RCA, singling out those decisions and strategies that account for the radical change from the classic Reformed form for the Lord's Supper to a eucharistic liturgy informed by the insights largely derived from the movements we have just described.

Liturgical Reform in the RCA:
On the Way toward the Communion Prayer

The Committee on the Revision of The Liturgy submitted their first report to the GS in 1951. The members expressed in this report their conviction that the successful outcome of any liturgical revision depended on the interest in the subject among the members of the congregations.[98] In order to avoid giving the impression that liturgical study and revision was merely a clerical pastime, the committee desired to inform the congregations as thoroughly as possible about the course of liturgical reform they intended to pursue. To this end, they sought and received the cooperation of the *Church Herald*, the official organ of the RCA, to print four articles to prepare the congregations to engage with them in reflecting on the place and need of liturgical revision.[99] These articles essentially had three aims: first, to assure the congregations that the project the committee was about to launch did not break from a tradition for which periodic revision of liturgy was the norm; second, to remind the congregations that the Constitution of the RCA mandates the use of prescribed liturgical forms; and third, to argue that the need existed. For a confessional church, standardized liturgical forms are necessary because they ensure the consistency of the theology enshrined in its doctrinal standards (Heidelberg Catechism, Belgic Confession, and The Canons of the Synod of Dort) with that expressed in its worship. Worship practices in many congregations were fragmented and incoherent, which resulted in ignorance of Reformed doctrine and confusion about the liturgical heritage of the Reformed traditions. Moreover, many of the forms still in use were unsatisfactory, which suggested the need for a revision comprehensive in scope.

Apropos the point about unsatisfactory forms, Hageman called attention to the "abridged" form for the Lord's Supper, which an earlier liturgical committee introduced into the 1906 *Liturgy and Psalms*. As we brought out in the concluding part of the second chapter, this form is a composite of formulae drawn from the Palatinate Supper form and from a eucharistic prayer that appeared in a selection of occasional prayers in an earlier revision of *Liturgy and Psalms* (1873). The order in which this eucharistic prayer unfolds is interrupted by the interpolation of an exhortation to self-examination and an exposition on the meaning of the sacrament—sections borrowed from the Palatinate form. It then resumes with its own formula for the prayer of self-offering, which is assigned the status of an alternate to the prayer for worthy reception from the Palatinate form. The abridged form concludes with the Apostles' Creed, the Reformed *Sursum corda*, distribution of the elements, and the post-communion psalm and prayer of thanksgiving—consistent here with the order of the Palatinate form.[100]

Hageman complained that the dismembered eucharistic prayer reveals an "utter disregard of the liturgical tradition and of common sense," and no doubt had in mind to reunite the parts of this prayer that had been severed by the Palatinate material inserted into it by the committee responsible for the 1906 revision.[101] It is not surprising, therefore, to find that his committee proposed as early as 1952 to address his complaint. Appended to the report on their progress to the GS of that year is a series of revised orders for Sunday and occasional services. Among these include (1) a complete "Order for the Preparatory Service for the Sacrament of the Lord's Supper;" and (2) a complete "Order of Worship to be used when the Sacrament is to be celebrated," in which a rearrangement of the parts of the form for the Supper is recommended.[102] The proposal of these two orders provides a solution to the problem of the dismembered eucharistic prayer, as we intend to explain briefly here.

We can clarify the significance of the proposed order for the preparatory service when we recall the strict relation between church discipline and the Lord's Supper in the sixteenth century Reformed churches. According to Reformed doctrine, as we saw in the first chapter, the sacrament serves to attest and confirm the union of the members of the body of Christ with their head and with one another. For this reason, persons living in unrepented sin were excluded from the table, because their participation would violate the integrity of the holy community and profane the body and blood of Christ. In order to avoid this danger, ministers exhorted the people and, when necessary, excommunicated the unrepentant and the hypocrite. The public occasion for the exercise of this ministerial duty was the preparatory service. In this connection, we will remember that the people in the Reformed churches of the Palatinate assembled for this service on the

Saturday afternoon before the Sunday on which the Supper was to be celebrated. In it they reaffirmed their commitment to Christ by examining themselves and assenting to a series of doctrinal propositions as they responded to the form the minister read aloud from the pulpit.

Their recognition of the purpose of this institution seems to have suggested to the members of the committee what to do with the exhortation to self-examination in the abridged form: they simply removed it from its place and incorporated it into the proposed preparatory service for the Lord's Supper. In this new order it stands between the sermon and the prayer of confession—obviously more suited here to the purpose of preparing the people to approach the Lord's table with a purified heart and conscience. The committee intended that this order be used either on the Sunday or a weekday before the celebration of the Lord's Supper, a practice which they correctly regarded to be consistent with that of the first Reformed churches.

The provision for a complete order of worship for use when the sacrament is celebrated accomplished two purposes. First, it intimated the committee's intention to reclaim an order of word and sacrament for use on every Lord's Day. Second, it enabled them to transpose the exposition on the meaning of the sacrament from the abridged form to a place between the sermon and the institution narrative. In this place, it accords with the Reformed insistence that the Supper cannot be celebrated properly unless the people are prepared to approach it intelligently. The restored prayer (now designated the Prayer of Consecration) follows the institution narrative. It is essentially the Eucharistic Prayer that appeared in the Revised Liturgy of 1873, which became the denomination's official service book in 1882.

The committee requested the GS to authorize its revised 1952 "Liturgical Orders and Forms" for three years of provisional use and to urge the study of them by the consistories and Classes of the RCA.[103] In 1955 the GS voted to approve and authorize final drafts and referred the now completed "Revised Liturgy" to the Classes for final adoption. The Revised Liturgy of 1955 failed, however, to gain from the Classes the two-thirds majority vote necessary for a proposed amendment to the Constitution of the Church. Consequently, the GS was forced to recommit the drafts prepared in 1955 to the committee, together with the reactions and comments issued by the Classes of the RCA. We must add here, however, that the adoption failed not because the RCA opposed the agenda of the committee. The reports from the Classes in fact indicated that the congregations for the most part were favorably disposed to the work that the committee members had already accomplished. But many felt that more work was necessary before the revision would be acceptable. It became clear that the denomination desired a liturgy that met contemporary needs and that was expressed in "simple and forthright language."[104]

It is entirely possible that the demand for forms in simple and forthright language helped seal the eventual fate of the 1873 Eucharistic Prayer, but at least at this stage the committee proceeded to move slowly. This prayer (now designated the "Communion Prayer") appears unmolested in the form for "The Sacrament of the Lord's Supper" contained in the revised 1958 "Orders and Forms of Worship." These in turn now constituted the "Provisional Liturgy" that the committee recommended to the GS in 1958 for continued study and evaluation over an additional five year period.[105] In the 1958 form for the Supper, the exposition on the meaning of the sacrament from the Palatinate source appears under the heading "The Instruction," and precedes the institution narrative, as we should expect.[106] But it is interesting to see that there is added an alternate provided for use at the discretion of the minister. This new composition is largely dependent on the Palatinate source, recounting in similar language the suffering and death that Jesus Christ had to undergo to obtain for sinners a place in God's covenant of grace and reconciliation. There follows a brief account of the meaning of communicating in the Supper, which draws inspiration from the Palatinate source in theme if not in content. But in the third paragraph there appears something new:

> But in this Supper of remembrance and communion we must also lift up our hearts in hope. For we do this, as He commanded, till He come. As we eat this bread and drink this cup, we do so as a pledge and foretaste of that feast of love of which we shall partake when His kingdom has fully come. Under the veil of earthly things we now have communion with Him. But with unveiled face we shall behold Him, rejoicing in His glory, made like unto Him in His glory. Even so, come, Lord Jesus.[107]

We have already seen that renewed attention was given to the eschatological dimension of the Supper under the impetus of the ecumenical movement. We have also witnessed the concern among the Reformed members of the commission on Ways of Worship to recover for their churches the spirit of joy and anticipation proper to the celebration of the Supper. In this respect, it is especially interesting to observe that the insertion of this new paragraph coincides with the publication in English of Oscar Cullman's influential essay "The Meaning of the Lord's Supper in Primitive Christianity."[108] The Reformed ecumenist argued in this essay that in their eucharistic celebrations the first believers experienced the presence of Christ in a threefold relation with Easter, the community meal, and the parousia. Cullman appealed to the churches in his own day to restore to the Aramaic expression *Maranatha* the liturgical significance that it originally had in these celebrations, so that the term might again express the "double desire [of the faithful] of seeing Christ descend into [their midst as they gather in his name] and of discovering for themselves, in that coming, an anticipation of his final Messianic return."[109] It is not possible to demonstrate that Cullman's essay lies directly behind the new paragraph, but certainly this paragraph furnishes tangible evidence that the committee members had been drawing on contemporary biblical scholarship as they addressed themselves to the meaning of the Lord's Supper in contemporary Reformed Christianity.

Apart from these changes in the form proposed for the sacrament of the Lord's Supper, the revised orders and forms contained in the 1958 Provisional Liturgy were substantially the same as those the classes voted down in 1956. This fact simply indicates the desire of the committee for greater input from the congregations before it proceeded to introduce further revisions. To this end, the committee made a second recommendation to the GS to instruct each Particular Synod (PS) to appoint a committee for liturgical study. The formation of additional committees would broaden the base of the involvement among the congregations by providing clearinghouses for responses to the proposed revisions. The original committee added the further suggestion that the GS appoint members from among them to serve on these PS committees, so as to facilitate studies and conversations between the two groups. This would enable members of the original committee to learn better the mind of the congregations regarding their work. The GS adopted this recommendation, and thereby opened the way for wider participation in the ongoing process.[110]

This strategy seems to have succeeded. At the GS of 1959, the committee reported the need for a fourth printing of the Provisional Liturgy authorized the preceding year.[111] Many workshops were subsequently held, and members of the congregations were engaging critically with the orders and forms contained in the Provisional Liturgy. For their part, the members of the two committees were involved in helping the participants in the workshops both to understand the basic principles of liturgy and to apply them to the study of these orders and forms. In 1960 the original committee pledged to the GS that the results of the deliberations of the workshops would be consulted and seriously considered in the preparation of the final draft of the Provisional Liturgy, which they intended to present to the GS at the conclusion of the five year trial period (1963).[112]

The New Communion Prayer

The intervening years proved decisive in the evolution of the Order for the Sacrament of the Lord's Supper. The committee continued to stay current on the liturgical reforms that by now were making advances in Reformed churches almost everywhere. In 1960 the committee listened to an audio tape of a Communion service celebrated in a congregation of the Reformed Church in the Netherlands.[113] In the following year the committee reported to the GS that they had been conducting a correspondence with liturgy committees from the United Presbyterian Church, USA and the Presbyterian Church, US, the Christian Reformed Church, the Presbyterian Church in Canada, and the *Nederlandse Hervormde Kerk.*[114] In this same year Hageman also shared with the committee a translation of several liturgical forms from the Reformed Church of France (ERF).[115] The outcome of this concentrated activity was an Order for the Sacrament of the Lord's Supper that is a significant departure from the one contained in the 1958 Provisional Liturgy. The former appears in a further revision of the Provisional Liturgy, which the committee presented to the GS in 1963 for permission for an additional year of study.

In considering the general structure of this new order, we note in the first place that its drafters did not conceive the Lord's Supper to be an occasional office independent from the order of worship used when the sacrament is not celebrated. A rubric directs that the normal order of worship is to be used through the offering, after which the minister recites the "Instruction" to prepare the people for the service of the sacrament. During the singing of a hymn, the minister and the consistory (elders and deacons) assume their places around the Lord's table.[116] The minister then addresses to God on behalf of the people a prayer that appears for the first time in the 1963 Provisional Liturgy. An analysis reveals that it is in large part a translation of several formulae from the eucharistic liturgy of the ERF, which is found in the *Liturgie de l'Eglise réformée de France*, first published in 1950 before it appeared in a definitive edition in 1963.[117] An arrangement of the material from both liturgies in parallel columns will provide a clear picture of what the RCA borrowed from the ERF for its prayer. The italicized texts in the RCA prayer indicate other sources than the ERF.

Table 2: ERF and RCA Eucharistic Liturgies

1. Elevons nos coeurs vers le Seigneur!	Let us lift up our hearts unto the Lord!
2. Il est vraiment digne et juste, il est équitable et salutaire de te rendre graces en tout temps et en tout lieu, Dieu tout-puissant, Père éternel et saint, par Jesus-Christ notre Seigneur, car tu as créé les cieux et toute leur armée, la terre et ses magnificences; [tu nous as donné l'etre et la vie et tu nous conserves par ta providence.] Tu as manifesté la plénitude de ton amour en envoyant dans le monde ta Parole éternelle et ton image visible, en ton Fils bien-aimé, qui s'est abaissé jusqu'à nous pur nous élever jusqu'à toi.	Holy and right it is and our joyful duty to give thanks unto thee at all times and in all places, O Lord, Holy Father, Almighty and Everlasting God. Thou didst create the heaven with all its hosts and the earth with all its plenty. Thou hast given us life and being and dost preserve us by thy providence. But thou hast shown us the fulness of thy love in sending into the world thy eternal word, even Jesus Christ our Lord, *who became man for us men and for our salvation.*

Continued on next page

Table 2—*Continued*

Pour le don précieux de ce puissant Sauveur, médiateur charitable qui nous a réconciliés avec toi, pain vivant donné pour la nourriture du monde, nous te louons et nous te bénissons, o Seigneur Dieu! C'est pourquoi, avec les cieux et toutes les puissances des cieux, avec l'Eglise entière, en une commune allégresse, nous adorons ton infinie majesté et nous chantons à ta gloire, te célébrant et disant:	For the precious gift of this mighty Savior who has reconciled us to thee we praise and bless thee, O God. Therefore, with thy whole Church on earth and with all the company of heaven we adore thy majesty and bless thy glory.
Saint, saint, saint est l'Eternel! [Toute la terre est remplie de sa gloire. Hosanna au plus haut des cieux! Béni soit celui qui vient au nom du Seigneur!]	Holy, Holy, Holy, Lord God of Hosts, Heaven and earth are full of thy glory. Hosanna in the Highest! Blessed is he that cometh in the name of the Lord. Hosanna in the highest!

Institution

Prions Dieu:

1. Père saint et juste, en commémorant ici le sacrifice unique et parfait, offert une fois pour toutes sur la croix par notre Seigneur Jésus-Christ, dans la joie de sa résurrection et l'attente de sa venue, nous nous offrons nous-memes à toi en sacrifice vivant et saint	Holy and righteous Father, as we commemorate in this Supper that perfect sacrifice once offered on the cross by our Lord Jesus Chirst for the sin of the whole world, in the joy of his resurrection and in expectation of his coming again, we offer unto thee ourselves as holy and living sacrifices.
Toi qui connais les coeurs, purifie-nous et renouvelle en nous ton pardon et ta grace. Faisnous vivre de la vie du Ressuscitè: qu'il demeure en nous et nous en lui!	

Continued on next page

Table 2—*Continued*

Envoie sur nous ton Saint-Esprit, pour qu'en recevant ce pain et cette coupe il nous soit donné de communier au corps et au sang de notre Seigneur Jésus Christ. Car c'est par lui que tu crées, que tu sanctifies, que tu vivifies, que tu bénis et que tu nous donnes tous les biens

Send thy Holy Spirit upon us, we beseech thee, that the bread which we break may be to us the communion in the body of Christ and the cup which we bless the communion of his blood.

Grant that being joined together in him we may attain to the unity of the faith and grow up in all things into him who is the Head, even Christ our Lord.

Comme les épis jadis épars dans les campagnes et comme les grappes autrefois dispersées sur les collines sont maintenant réunis sur cette table dans ce pain et dans ce vin, qu'ainsi, Seigneur, toute ton Eglise soit bientot rassemblée des extrémités de la terre dans tu Royaume.

And as this grain has been gathered from many fields into one loaf and these grapes from many hills into one cup, grant, O Lord, that thy whole Church may soon be gathered from the ends of the earth into thy kingdom.

Viens, Seigneur Jésus! Amen.[118]

Even so, come, Lord Jesus. And now as our Savior Christ has taught us, we are bold to say OUR FATHER...

The Communion[119] [Institution Narrative]

In essence, this prayer is the "Communion Prayer" that the RCA adopted for inclusion in its new *Liturgy and Psalms*, published in 1968. Let us point out that with the exception of only one relative clause ("who became man for us men and for our salvation"), the committee completely abandoned the Eucharistic Prayer of 1873 in favor of a translation of the eucharistic liturgy of the ERF. The prefaces in this French liturgy are variable; the committee opted for the second, to which it joined a translation of the first *anamnesis/epiclesis* sections from the two provided as variants to be chosen at the discretion of the minister. It is noteworthy, however, that the committee did not include in its translation the second section interposed between the *anamnesis* and the *epiclesis* in the French Reformed liturgy. We also find that the committee decided to replace the doxology that concludes the *epiclesis* (third section) with a prayer for the unity and maturity of the liturgical community. Drawn from the language of the Letter to the Ephesians (4:13), this prayer comes from the eucharistic liturgy of the Church of South India, published in 1954.[120] Both the ERF and the RCA prayers borrow a text from the *Didache* (9.4) to conclude their petition for the unity of the Church.

But the most conspicuous deviation from the eucharistic liturgy of the ERF is the position of the institution narrative. In the French prototype, the institution narrative immediately precedes the *anamnesis/epiclesis* sections. This connection reveals more clearly how the anamnesis functions liturgically as a response to Jesus' command that the meal be celebrated in memory of him: the community commemorates Jesus by acknowledging his sacrificial death, and his resurrection and return in glory in the act of its own self-offering. But for reasons that none of its members spelled out anywhere, the committee decided to sever this connection, and place the institution narrative at the end of their prayer. This position creates problems for the internal coherence of the prayer, as well as raise critical issues for the interpretation of its theological meaning. We will return to address these issues in the final chapter.

The distribution of the bread and wine immediately follows the proclamation of the institution narrative, and is accompanied by words drawn from the First Letter to the Corinthians (10:16). The post-communion thanksgiving consists in a responsive reading from Psalm 103, which continues a traditional practice in the Reformed celebration of the Lord's Supper. The intercessions conclude the service. In his essay on the new Order for the Sacrament of the Lord's Supper, Hageman later explained that their position at the end of the service is meant to impress on the people that it is from the Lord's table that they receive strength for their witness in the world: "Having begun our witness to them [sc. those in need] by lifting them up before the throne of grace, we go out into the world to continue our witness as a priestly people."[121]

On the recommendation of the committee, the GS granted the congregations an additional year to study this most recent revision as it was found in the 1963 version of the Provisional Liturgy. Meanwhile, the members of the committee continued to entertain the suggestions from the congregations on this liturgy, and to make progress on the Treasury of Prayers, the Lectionary, and Psalter, which they intended to include in a new *Liturgy and Psalms* when the GS authorized its publication. In 1964, the GS adopted the motion to provide yet another year of study of the orders for baptism and the Lord's Supper in the Provisional Liturgy, and to permit suggestions for the revisions of these orders to be sent to the chairman of the committee until 1 January, 1965. The GS hoped that at last a final vote on the liturgy might be taken when it met later in that year. At this meeting the final series of revisions for the orders and forms were presented to the GS and sent to the Classes for final adoption. Having obtained this time the necessary majority vote from the classes, the GS in 1966 officially ratified these orders and forms, directing at the same time that the older ones of the 1906 revision be published with them. The intention here seems to have been to afford sufficient latitude to congregations with varying liturgical sensibilities and preferences. In the following year, the GS authorized the inclusion of new translations of the RCA's doctrinal standards in the service book. By 1968, the new *Liturgy and Psalms* was ready to be presented to the GS.[122] And so after eighteen years of exacting liturgical study and experimentation, the committee succeeded in providing their denomination with a service book that it hoped would serve widely to improve the worship of God. The new Order for the Sacrament of the Lord's Supper was perhaps the most promising sign that this hope would be realized.

Conclusion: The Aims of the Committee

It is possible to make summary observations about the significant changes that the Committee on the Revision of The Liturgy introduced to its church's order for the celebration of the Lord's Supper. We may do this from two angles of approach. In the first place, we have sought to demonstrate that these changes cannot be understood apart from an appreciation of the spirit of liturgical and sacramental renewal that inspired churches worldwide during the first sixty years of the twentieth century. We have suggested that Howard Hageman, principal architect of the new order for the Lord's Supper, and the committee on which he served, were animated by this spirit to lead the RCA toward a conception of the eucharistic celebration that departed from one that the denomination had fully known before this committee began to launch its liturgical reforms in 1951. But in the second place, we must also bear in mind that the committee introduced these liturgical reforms not only on the basis of the liturgical scholarship they embraced from the movements influencing almost all the churches in their time, but also on the basis of what they regarded as sound Reformed theology, classically defined in the works of John Calvin and in their own doctrinal standards. The subsequent attempt to integrate contemporary liturgical scholarship and classic Reformed theology into the new Order for the Sacrament of the Lord's Supper has resulted in tensions of which the committee did not seem to be entirely aware. We will indicate these tensions in the final chapter, but for now we need only to respect the committee's aims, and to attempt to interpret what we regard those aims to have been.

It seems certainly to be the case that the committee obeyed the call of the Reformed scholars appointed to serve on the commission on Ways of Worship. Deeply influenced by the liturgical and sacramental renewal movements, those scholars called for a new form for the Supper that would be devotional rather than didactic, joyful rather than somber, and oriented to Jesus' resurrection as well as to his death. They were of the firm conviction that the Lord's Supper is a joyful celebration of praise and thanks. In contrast to what the classic forms for the Reformed Lord's Supper (e.g. Palatinate) envisage, this celebration should be a corporate action, not a sermonizing discourse given by the minister. This helps explain why the celebration in the order the RCA adopted opens with an invitation to the members of the community to lift up their hearts. The community responds with the *sanctus* and the *benedictus* — liturgical formulae that no doubt serve to express awe, wonder, and joy, and thereby to maintain the community in the jubilant mood. The motivation for this joyful celebration is the Christ event. But this is not restricted to a memorial of the "perfect sacrifice that Christ offered once and for all on the cross for

the sin of the whole world." "The joy of his resurrection and the expectation of his coming again" impress on the people that the Supper
is not a "funerary ceremony" but a Supper of intimate communion
with the resurrected Christ who was crucified. Moreover, this Supper
anticipates the final fulfillment of this communion on the day of redemption, depicted in the New Testament image of the eschatological
Supper of the Lamb. This is why the community is eagerly to look
forward to Jesus' *parousia*, when his Church will be gathered from the
ends of the earth into the kingdom (cf. *Didache*). Thus the doxological
note on the joy of the resurrected and triumphant Christ is sustained
from beginning to end.

But if the drafters intended the new order to reflect and embody
the *desiderata* of the Reformed participants in the ecumenical movement, they also intended it to respond to the demands of the classic
Reformed conception of the Lord's Supper. In support of this claim,
we need only consider the decision of the committee to retain the didactic section, the "Instruction," which appears in the 1968 *Liturgy
and Psalms* under the heading "Meaning of the Sacrament."[123] According to traditional Reformed sacramental practice, a doctrinal statement of the meaning of the action always precedes that action itself.
We have already seen that in 1958 the committee reformulated this
doctrinal statement by adding a paragraph that confesses what the
Reformed tradition believes about the eschatological dimension of the
Supper. By 1963 Hageman revised the statement, so that it might
more adequately express the Reformed doctrine of the Lord's Supper
in toto. The Supper in the Reformed churches is a "feast of remembrance, of communion, and of hope." By this time the committee concluded that while the Palatinate form succeeded in conveying the
faith that the Supper is the "remembrance of the atoning death of Jesus Christ," it did not spell out clearly enough that it is also communion with the present Lord. To correct this deficiency, Hageman added
to the statement another paragraph to define the Reformed doctrine
of real presence:

> We have come to have communion with this same Christ who has promised
> to be with us always, even to the end of the world. In the breaking of the
> bread he makes himself known to us as the true heavenly Bread that

strengthens us to life eternal. In the cup of blessing he comes to us as the Vine in whom we must abide if we are to bear fruit.[124]

There is an undisguised appeal here to the Melanchthonian-Calvinist conception that the presence of the Lord at the Lord's Supper is located in the use or action of the distribution. But it is noteworthy that there is nothing in this paragraph to suggest that Hageman drew on the language of the new Communion Prayer itself in formulating this doctrinal statement. The statements on the eschatological hope and on the work of the Holy Spirit in uniting all in one body also appear to have been drafted independently of the Communion Prayer. From these observations, we may with good reason suppose that the "exposition on the meaning of the sacrament" remains the privileged place in which the RCA expresses its eucharistic faith. But even if this accords with traditional sacramental thought and practice in the Reformed churches, it reveals little recognition that the eucharistic celebration itself articulates and expresses a theology as it is performed. To explain how it does this constitutes the task of the remaining two chapters. Therefore, in the next chapter we aim to clarify the structure and dynamic of the eucharistic prayer at its origins, so as to provide a basis on which to evaluate the Communion Prayer in the concluding chapter (chapter 5).

PART TWO

Liturgical and Theological Evaluation

Chapter Four

The Lord's Supper in the Early Church:
A Return to the Sources

In his *Pulpit and Table* Howard Hageman articulates a series of programmatic theses to be used as criteria for judging any composition of Reformed liturgy. Germane to our present concern is his thesis that the biblical factor must be primary.[1] The refusal of the Reformed churches to enshrine a confession as a binding norm for the Church universal has indirectly expressed their commitment to be the Church reformed and always reforming on the basis of the word of God alone (*ecclesia reformata semper reformanda secundum verbum Dei*). The Church must always be returning to the Scriptures as the standard against which to measure its own doctrine and practice.

With respect to the liturgy of the Lord's Supper, due regard for the biblical factor motivated Hageman and the committee to espouse the central thesis that Gregory Dix advanced in his *The Shape of the Liturgy*, as we saw in the preceding chapter. Dix informed the committee that in the institution narratives of the New Testament there is a taking, a blessing, a breaking, a sharing of the bread, on the one hand; and a taking, blessing and sharing of a cup, on the other. To this we may add the words of Jesus over the bread and the cup. On the basis of the early liturgical data, Dix argued that the series of events that transpired in the Last Supper constitute the model from which the various actions of the early eucharistic celebrations were drawn. Accordingly, "taking" corresponds to the presentation of the gifts; "blessing" relates to the eucharistic prayer; "breaking" is represented by the fraction rite; and "sharing" is continued by the distribution of the gifts. Dix's observations convinced Hageman that a Reformed liturgy of the Lord's Supper is faithful to the New Testament witnesses to the extent to which it conforms to this fourfold "shape."

Dix played an instrumental role in helping the RCA to reclaim what was then affirmed as the basic structure of the eucharistic celebration. But he left to the succeeding generation of liturgical historians to investigate the more limited problem of how the eucharistic prayer itself was born. This problem will form the subject of our investigation in this chapter. At first glance, the New Testament witnesses do not appear to be the proper place from which to set out. The institution narratives are silent about what Jesus said when he "blessed" the bread or "gave thanks" over the cup at the Last Supper. For this reason no one has ever claimed to reproduce the exact words Jesus used on this occasion. Nevertheless, scholars have inferred from the accounts and from historical research into Jewish meal rituals significant clues about the blessings possibly used by Jesus and the post-resurrection community that continued to meet in obedience to his mandate at the Supper: "Do this in memory of me." If the hypotheses that these scholars have constructed are correct, then it is imperative to investigate the institution narratives in their historical and literary contexts in an attempt to determine the order of the shared cup(s), and broken bread, and contemporary forms of blessings that Jesus might have said over them. This must serve as the starting point in the search for the origins of the Christian eucharistic prayer.[2]

This is what we propose to do here. We begin with a general overview of the problems that these narratives have posed for research. This will prepare us to give more focused attention to the elements in the Jewish meal ritual that underlie what is recorded in these narratives. In this context, we will give special consideration to the blessings pronounced over the cup at the end of the meal. For it is this series of blessings, which we know as the *Birkat ha-mazon*, that many liturgical historians have determined to be the antecedent of the eucharistic prayer. In the second part of this chapter, we will extend our consideration of the *Birkat ha-mazon* by addressing ourselves to the earliest recorded formulary of a Jewish Christian meal ritual. This is contained in a document called the *Didache*, the earliest of a literary genre conventionally known as "church order." Many scholars affirm that the prayer formulae that accompany the celebration of the Christian meal described in chapters 9 and 10 of the *Didache* represent a Christian transformation of the Jewish meal ritual into a nascent eucharistic celebration. In the concluding part, we will bring the results of our investigation into these sources to bear on the question of the structure and dynamic of early Christian eucharistic praying. Our ultimate goal in this chapter is to provide a fundamental basis on which to evaluate the Communion Prayer and any future compositions of a Reformed eucharistic liturgy.

The Institution Narratives:
The Problem of Historical Reconstruction

There are four texts that give us an account of the Last Supper Jesus shared with his disciples on the night of his betrayal: Mark 14:22–25; Matthew 26:26–29; Luke 22:14–20; and 1 Corinthians 11:23–26. To be sure, there are several more biblical sources at our disposal for learning about the eucharistic thought and practice of the early Christian communities. Among them we may mention the story of the two disciples on the way to Emmaus, who encounter Jesus in the "breaking of the bread" (Luke 24:13–35); at least four more references by Luke in the Acts of the Apostles (2:42–47; 4:32–35; 5:12–16; 20:7–8); the commentary that the Apostle Paul gives on the cup and the bread rite in the First Letter to the Corinthians (10:16–17); and the Bread of Life discourse in the Gospel of John (6:25–58). But it is in the first four texts to which we referred that the institution narratives are found. As we have already seen, these texts report an episode in which Jesus gathers his disciples to share with them a last meal before he suffers and dies. In two of the texts, Jesus is reported to have commanded his disciples to repeat this Supper in memory of him (Luke 22:19; 1 Cor. 11:24–25). Hence, the Christian churches from their very origin have kept this command and celebrated this Supper, which has come to be known as the Lord's Supper or the Eucharist.

Most critics do not dispute the assumption that in these four accounts we have an historical foundation for the origins of the eucharistic celebration in the early Christian liturgical communities. But some are less confident in supposing that the "Upper Room is the origin for the Lord's Supper in Christianity, at least in a single direct-line cause."[3] These critics claim that it is impossible to reconstruct in precise detail the words and actions of Jesus at the Last Supper; for the accounts contain significant differences that perhaps reveal more about the liturgical practices and theological interpretations drawn from those practices than about the founding event itself. They argue that access to this event and to early Christian celebrations of the death and resurrection of Christ is mediated through the different interpretations of the New Testament accounts. Thus, these should not be seen to provide transcriptions of the events that occurred on the night preceding Jesus' death, but rather to reflect rites and practices already in habitual use.[4]

This problem concerning the historical foundation for the Lord's Supper in early Christianity is complicated by the fact that difficulties emerge from the accounts about the occasion of the meal itself. The synoptic Gospels maintain that the Last Supper was a Passover feast (Mark 14:12–16 and par.). The Gospel of John, however, evidently contradicts these accounts when it indicates that Jesus shared a final meal with his disciples before the festival of the Passover (13:1–2). According to John's chronology, Jesus is crucified at the same time that the lambs were slaughtered in the temple. John's purpose in relating the immolation of the lambs to Jesus' sacrifice on the cross is no doubt theologically motivated: the offering of Christ, the Lamb of God, fulfilled the offering prescribed under the Mosaic law (cf. 1 Cor. 5:7). But the fact remains that his dating of the final meal of Jesus with his disciples is incongruent with that of the synoptics.

Those for whom the theological significance of the Last Supper depends on its historical coincidence with the Passover feast have tried to resolve these chronological difficulties. The New Testament exegete Joachim Jeremias argued rigorously that the Last Supper was a Passover meal. He sought to demonstrate that the report contained in the Fourth Gospel about this event is not uniform, and so cannot be regarded as decisive for its dating.[5] Others have tried to harmonize the synoptic and Johannine accounts by proving that there were two different calendars followed.[6] More recently, the Italian liturgical historian Cesare Giraudo revived interest in the thesis of Jeremias by bringing out the "figurative dynamic" at work in the Passover rite in the manner in which it was celebrated at the time of Jesus. To these scholars the historical coincidence of the Last Supper with the Passover feast is indispensable because the paschal *seder* provides the framework within which to interpret the meaning of Jesus' words and actions. According to Jeremias, Jesus is the "eschatological Passover sacrifice," of which the former is the prototype. For Giraudo, the Passover rite is a "prophetical sign" that makes the participants in the feast present to the event of salvation, God's gracious action that delivered his people from their oppressors and constituted them in a covenant relationship. As prophetical sign, the Passover reveals the dynamic of the Last Supper, for through the ritual commemoration of this Supper, Christians are made present to the founding events of their salvation, the death and resurrection of Jesus Christ.[7]

Despite the welter of historical and textual evidence that these two scholars amassed, many critics remain skeptical about the possibility of establishing the claim that the Last Supper was indeed a Passover feast. Yet there seems to be a general consensus today that even if it is not possible to be certain that the Last Supper was a Passover, it is nevertheless important to recognize that the former is situated in a Passover setting. We should point out, however, that the observations that liturgical historians make concerning the institution narratives generally do not depend on the outcome of these debates. They observe that since every Jewish meal is a religious meal, in virtue of the blessings pronounced at the beginning and at the end of the meal, it is not necessary to prove that the Last Supper was a Passover feast.[8] On the basis of their observations, then, we need only presuppose that neither Jesus at the Last Supper nor the post-resurrection community at its common meals invented new rites for the purpose of sharing a religious meal. Rather they adopted and adapted rites already in use in the Jewish environment of which they were part. To the extent to which we can depend on the fragmentary historical evidence about Jewish meal customs in the first century C.E., it is sufficient for our purposes to direct our attention to the meal ritual generally as it is embedded in the four accounts.

The Last Supper and the Jewish Meal Ritual

That the accounts are couched in the framework of a meal ritual is revealed by the stylized material that they share in common (see the italicized words in the following table). They nonetheless diverge from one another characteristically in the ordering of this material and in the formulating of its details, as will also become apparent below:[9]

Table 3: Institution Narratives

1 Cor. 11:23–25	Luke 22:17–20	Mark 14:22–24	Matt. 26:26–29
	and he received a cup and when he had given thanks he said		
the Lord Jesus	and	*and as they were eating*	*and as they were eating*
on the night he was delivered up			
took bread	*taking bread*	*taking bread*	Jesus *taking bread*
and *having given thanks broke* (it)	*having given thanks broke* (it) and *gave* (it) *to them*	*having said the blessing broke* (it) and *gave* (it) *to them*	and *having said the blessing broke* (it) and *giving* (it) to the disciples
and *said*	*saying*	and *said*	*said*
in the same way also the *cup* after supper	and the *cup in the same way* after supper	*and* taking the cup	*and* taking the cup
		having given thanks he gave it to them and they drank of it	and *having given thanks he gave it to them*
saying	*saying*	and he *said* to them	*saying*

In this division of the four accounts, we assume that the Pauline/Lucan tradition and the Markan tradition are independent from one another, and do not derive from a common Greek source. The phrase "after supper" in the former indicates a separation of the actions connected with the bread and the cup, and thereby reflects more accurately the course of the Jewish meal ritual as it has been re-constructed. Liturgical historians have considered it significant that in Luke's account a preliminary action over the first cup and the words said over it precedes the two main actions connected with the bread and the cup. This first cup is attested in the First Letter to the Corinthians (10:16–17), but critics are divided about whether this reflects the order of the celebration in that community. In the Lucan account, the following statement about the coming kingdom of God accompanies the first action that Jesus performed after he and his disciples reclined at the table:

> And he had received a cup, and when he had given thanks, he said, Take this, and divide it among yourselves: for I say unto you, I will not drink from henceforth of the fruit of the vine, until the kingdom of God shall come (Luke 22:17–18).

If this saying is to be regarded as a distinct blessing connected to a first cup, then an interesting feature emerges when this account is compared with its parallels. In all of them a cup and the words that accompany it appear at the end of the meal. In Luke, however, a cup not only follows but also precedes the meal.

This cup-bread-cup order featured in the Lucan narrative has suggested to liturgical historians parallels with the course that Jewish meal rituals might have followed in Palestine in the first century C.E.[10] Before the meal commences, the table is prepared and the table candles are lit for the solemn occasion. Then the master of the house stands, lifts a cup of wine in his right hand, directs his gaze at the cup and says:

> You are blessed, Lord our God, King of the universe, you who created the fruit of the vine.

This blessing of the first cup before the meal proper began is known as the *Kiddush*.[11] It is a blessing prounounced at the beginning of the Sabbath or a special feast day for the purpose of consecrating it to God. To this short *berakah* (blessing) the presider adds a longer *berakah*, which praises God in a more elaborate manner for the gift of the Sabbath and the various meanings attaching to it. Afterward, the guests received wine into their own cups from the cup that the master blessed, and drank after him.

The rite of the bread proceeds as follows. The master of the house places his hand on the bread and while raising it says:

> You are blessed, Lord our God, King of the Universe, you who have brought bread forth from the earth.

After this short *berakah*, the master of the house breaks the bread with his hands, eats some himself, and distributes enough for each guest at the table. This action marked the indispensable beginning of the meal proper. The principal aim of the blessing is to praise and thank God for the abundant goodness that he has shown to his creatures.[12] At the same time, it is to acknowledge God as the giver of the goods of this earth, and thereby to express and realize the intention to receive them from him precisely as gifts. Thus, it is through the act of blessing that the master of the house receives these goods stamped with the value of divine gifts. In this perspective, the blessing of God is not without an element of reciprocity. Since the giver is always present in the gift, the blessing returns, as it were, as the very presence of God in the form of the bounty of his good creation.

The guests at the table make the presider's intention their own by responding with an "Amen." The act of "breaking" that continues the rite involves a parting with the goods received from God in order to share them with others. In this way, according to the New Testament exegete Xavier Léon-Dufour, "the sharing of the pieces effectively established a table fellowship; those at table henceforth formed a single body, and God the giver was considered to be present [among them]."[13] Léon-Dufour adds that this Jewish conception underlies what Paul tells the Corinthians about the Eucharist: "As there is one loaf, so we, although we are many, are one single body, because we all share in the one loaf" (1 Cor. 10:17).[14]

Parenthetically, we may remark that Jesus not only performed the rite of the bread, but also added the words that identified the bread with his body. Here we must distinguish at least three senses in which these words re-interpret the complex of actions composing the rite. In the first place, the words endow a rite through which God reveals himself to the table fellowship as the generous giver of the

earth's goods and the sustainer of its common life with a new signification: God is manifested through Jesus' very act of "blessing" the
bread as the one who gives Jesus himself to the disciples. In a very
real sense, therefore, the Last Supper becomes the completion of what
the disciples anticipated symbolically in every religious meal: "the
perfected reception of human life from the abundance of divine
life."[15] Second, the words re-interpret the act of "breaking." Some critics see in this action a prophetic gesture; Jesus' gesture is a parable in
act, which dramatizes an event that demands a response from his disciples. Just as the prophet Jeremiah broke the potter's vessel (Jer.
19:10) or as Ezekiel cut his hair, burned some of it, scattered some of it
to the wind, and bound the rest in the skirts of his robe (Ezek. 5:1–4),
so Jesus gestures to the disciples to see the word of the Lord that he is
prophesying in the bread that he breaks.[16] The Supper, therefore, is
an "announcement in the form of an action, a gestural-verbal proph-
esy of [Jesus'] imminent death on the cross."[17] Finally, the words
"given for you" attested in the Pauline/Lucan tradition invite reflection on the meaning of the "sharing." Here recourse to the interpretation of the concept of sacrifice that ritual theory provides is
instructive. The meal Jesus shares with his disciples is eaten in view
of his impending death on the cross and receives its meaning from it.
According to the Pauline/Lucan tradition, as we have already noted,
Jesus intends that his disciples repeat the meal after his death, until he
eats it with them anew in the kingdom of God. But the death of Jesus
initiates a process that threatens to end in the disintegration of the table fellowship. In this respect, his death is an "act of deconstitution,"
which is symbolized in the "breaking" of the bread. At the same time,
however, this very death is the "deconstituting" act of the disintegrating forces that his sacrifice is meant to overcome. The act of "sharing"
the bread, then, is a "mending process" that signals that "life enhanc-
ing processes" will continue as a result of this sacrifice. Paradoxically,
then, the table fellowship regains its life and integrity through an
event that at first threatens to annihilate it.[18]

Some critics might object that the order in which we outlined the
Kiddush rite here presupposes the veracity of the historical claim that
the Last Supper was in fact a Passover feast, since it is clear that none
of the accounts presents Jesus as holding the Last Supper on the Sab-

bath. But even if these scholars do not accept this claim, we must keep in mind that Luke and the other two evangelists intend to present it as a Passover, so that evidence of elements that properly belong to a putative Pasch *seder* should not surprise us. In any event, we have no good reason to suppose that blessings in one form or another were absent from a solemn meal in Jesus' time, whether a Passover or not.

We cannot determine exactly the chronological origin of the blessing formulae we cited above, but they must date at the very least to the second century C.E. The texts are preserved in the tractate *Berakhot* of the Jewish *Mishna*, a codification of Jewish law consisting of sayings that bear the names of rabbinic authorities who lived in the late first and second centuries. This document is supposed to have received its final recension about 200 C.E.[19] Consequently, there is sufficient reason to suppose that the formulae were known and used in the time of Jesus. Some scholars find this supposition confirmed in the words of Jesus about the "fruit of the vine" (Luke 22:18); in this eschatological saying they hear a clear echo of a blessing formula similar to the one that we have given above.[20]

The *Birkat ha-mazon*

After the meal, the master of the house took a cup of wine in his two hands, and when he was about to pronounce the blessing, shifted the cup to his right hand, and lifted it up in his palm. This longer blessing is actually a series of blessings, which we know as the *Birkat ha-mazon*, the prayer of thanksgiving after meals. The *Mishna*, however, tells us that before the presider began to say these blessings, he appointed an honored guest from the table to invite the others to join their praise with the presider's by means of an invitational formula. The text is recorded in the *Mishna*:

> [Leader]: Let us bless our God.
> [Guests]: Blessed is the Lord our God, the God of Israel, God of the Hosts, who sits upon the cherubim, for the food we have eaten.[21]

Unfortunately, neither the *Mishna* nor any other ancient authority gives us a text of the *Birkat ha-mazon* that we can reliably locate in first century C.E. Palestine. The *Mishna* does instruct, however, that this grace after meals contain three *berakoth*.[22] Some liturgical historians see in this instruction support for their position that the texts of the *Birkat ha-mazon* preserved in two Jewish *siddurim* (prayer books) that date from the ninth and tenth centuries C.E. bear testimony to a tradition of considerable antiquity, since they find in them three *berakoth*. These late texts also include a fourth *berakah*, but the formula is supposed to have been added in the second century C.E.[23] Although the earliest extant text is preserved in the first of these two *siddurim*, that of R. Amram, the ninth century Gaon (president) of the Babylonian academy at Sura, it is considered to represent a later stage in the tradition. For this reason, liturgical historians interested in creating a text that comes close to a putative early Palestinian version turn to the shorter text found in the *siddur* of R. Saadia, Gaon from the following century.[24] On the basis of this text and the fragmentary textual evidence from earlier centuries, the Jewish Scholar Louis Finkelstein proposed as a model for the first century form of the *Birkat ha-mazon* the following text:[25]

> Blessed are you, Lord our God, King of the Universe, because you nourish the whole world in goodness, kindness, and mercy. Blessed are you, Lord, who nourishes the world.

> We thank you, Lord our God, because you have given to us a desirable land as our inheritance, so that we may eat from its fruit and be satisfied from its goodness. Blessed are you, Lord our God, for the land and for the food.

> Have mercy, Lord our God, on your people Israel, on your city Jerusalem, and on Zion, the habitation of your glory and your altar and your sanctuary. Blessed are you, Lord, who build Jerusalem.[26]

We direct our attention in the first place to the *chatimah* ("seal" = eulogy), with which the second strophe concludes: "Blessed are you, Lord our God, *for the land and for the food.*" The italicized phrase indicates that the prayer of thanksgiving after meals is based on Deuteronomy 8:10: "You will eat and be satisfied and will bless the Lord your God for the good land he has given you." This is the text that governs the logic of the Jewish table blessings, and generates the composition of the *Birkat ha-mazon*, as it were, from within. In the bread and the cup, the earth's bounty is present as God's generous gift that nourishes and sustains everything that lives. But these immediately bring to mind the land that was to provide the wheat and wine to the Hebrews when they came to end of their journey through the wilderness.[27] Having liberated the people from their Egyptian oppressors and at last settled them in this land, God demonstrates his gracious intention to establish Israel in an abundant life when he enters into covenant with them, a covenant that he seals with the gift of the Torah. That is why, probably at an early stage in its development, this second strophe was expanded to include the mention of the gifts of covenant and Torah for which God is thankfully remembered, as a *baraita* in the Babylonian Talmud shows:

> R. Eliezer says: "One who does not say the words "A goodly, pleasant, and broad land" (in describing the Holy Land) in the second benediction...has not fulfilled his duty. Nahum Ha-Zaken says: "One must also mention (in the second benediction) thanks for the Covenant." R. Jose says: "One must also include the Torah."[28]

It is the thanksgiving for the gifts expressed in the second strophe that has prompted liturgical historians to regard it as a commemorative recital of the saving interventions of God in Israel's history. In this connection, it is worth noting that a rubric in the later *siddurim* indicates that the second strophe can be expanded by embolisms (insertions of material) as appropriate to the particular feast that is celebrated. At the feast of Hanukah, for example, the master of the house gives thanks for the saving interventions of God in the time of the Maccabean revolt, when God delivered into the hands of the priest Matthias and his sons the "impious kingdom of the Greeks, which made the people of Israel forget [God's] laws and turn away from his statutes."[29] To the student of Christian liturgy interested in the background of the early eucharistic prayers, the memorial character of this strophe is among the most suggestive features of the *Birkat ha-mazon.*

In the confidence arising from the memorial recital of God's saving interventions in the past, the prayer moves to a petition that God act in the present to bring to fulfillment his blessings on his chosen people in the future. The central accent in the third strophe, accordingly, is on the hope for redemption and the longing for its ultimate realization. For this reason, liturgical historians see intimated in the *chatimah*, "Blessed are you, Lord, who builds Jerusalem," an eschatological orientation of this hope. This orientation emerges clearly in the more developed text found in the *siddur* of Amram Gaon. The supplication here is protracted to include a prayer for the advent of messianic age:

> And may Elijah and the Messiah, the Son of David come in our lifetime, and let the kingdom of the house of David [your anointed] soon return to its place, and reign over us, [since] you alone [are], and save us for your name's sake, and bring us up and make us joyful in it and comfort us in Zion your city. Blessed are you, O Lord, who builds Jerusalem (emphasis added).[30]

The embolism introduced into the third strophe of the *Birkat ha-mazon* designated for the Passover rite contains a similar prayer:

> Our God, and God of our Fathers, may there arise, and come, and come unto, be seen accepted, heard, recollected and remembered, the remembrance of us and the recollection of us, and the remembrance of us, and the remembrance of our fathers, and the remembrance of the Messiah, son of David, your servant...and the remembrance of Jerusalem your holy city, and the remembrance of all your people, the house of Israel. May their remembrance come before you, for rescue, goodness.[31]

The wording of this embolism provides an important key to Jeremias' interpretation of the meaning of the command that Jesus gives to his disciples: "do this in remembrance of me." In the context of the Passover feast, on which this petition exercised a strong influence, the command can only mean, "This do, that God may remember me." According to Jeremias, "God remembers the Messiah in that he causes the kingdom to break in by the parousia."[32] Recited in the context of a meal ritual, the words in both texts no doubt point to the prophetic promises of the messianic banquet, a classic image of the kingdom of God (Isa. 25:6; Amos 9:13; cf. Matt. 8:11; Luke 13:29). Whether or not Jesus' thanksgiving over the "cup of blessing" included any of the themes that these later texts contain, it is at least worthwhile to speculate how these themes would have formed a bridge to Jesus' announcement of the new banquet that he will share with his disciples in the coming kingdom of God (Mark 14:25 and par.). In any event, the prayer in chapter 10 of the *Didache* will appear to transpose this supplication for the building of Jerusalem into a petition for the perfecting of the Church until the *parousia*, as we will see below.

Jesus and the *Birkat Ha-Mazon*

In the foregoing analysis of the *Birkat ha-mazon*, we have drawn on texts that are admittedly very late. But some confirmation for the hypothesis that the general structure and themes of the *Birkat ha-mazon* were already known before the time of Jesus is found in the Book of the Jubilees 22.6–9, dated from the second century B.C.E. In this passage the patriarch Abraham blesses the God "who created heaven and earth and who made all the fat things of the earth and gave them to mankind…;" gives thanks to God for the blessings of a long life; and asks God to show mercy to him and his posterity, "so that they might become your chosen people and a heritage…"[33] It has been suggested that the concern of the author to avoid anachronism prevents him from placing in the mouth of Abraham the content found in the later forms.[34] But the fact that the same blessing-thanksgiving-supplication order is attested here suggests at least a structural continuity between the *Birkat ha-mazon* that is attributed to Abraham and those later forms.

For the reasons that we have given here, then, many liturgical historians have become convinced that the devout Jew in Palestine in the first century C.E. would have been familiar with the threefold prayer of thanksgiving after meals. It is another matter, of course, to claim that Jesus himself recited the *Birkat ha-mazon* in the manner in which we have presented it. Liturgical formulae were not codified in the first century, and many historians today maintain that the presider at a liturgical setting would have exercised considerable freedom in composing the blessings in whatever way he wished. On the other hand, even if it is the case that the blessings were spontaneously improvised, they no doubt eventually came to inherit through their oral transmission a certain form or structure.[35] Our observation of the prayer of Abraham gives evidence that the thanksgiving after meals acquired constant elements through its historical development even as it remained flexible enough to accommodate variable content. Therefore, if we really can assume that the general structure and themes of the *Birkat ha-mazon* were already present in general outline by the first century C.E., then there is no good reason to exclude the possibility that Jesus used some form of it in his thanksgiving after meals.

Moreover, since the *Birkat ha-mazon* was no prescribed text, but a flexible set of norms that could adapt itself according to the circumstances, it is possible to imagine it as a suitable vehicle through which Jesus might have expressed the new meaning that his life and mission had in the economy of God's saving acts. We have already seen how the second blessing not only included mention of those acts that the Jew regarded as saving interventions in the history of God's chosen people, but also admitted embolisms for commemorating particular saving acts. If Jesus had said the *Birkat ha-mazon* over the last cup, he might have given thanks in this context for all that God was about to accomplish through his sacrificial death.[36] Could it be that what he might have said about the relation of this death to the covenant that is recalled in the second blessing prepared the disciples for the words that he said over the last cup?

> Then he took a cup, and after giving thanks he gave it to them, and all of them drank from it. He said to them, "This is my blood of the covenant, which is poured out for many" (Mark 14:23–24).

And in connection with this cup it is reported in the First Letter to the Corinthians:

> In the same way, he took the cup also, after supper, saying: "This cup is the new covenant in my blood. Do this, as often as you drink it, in remembrance of me" (11:25).

To be sure, such a reconstruction rests almost entirely on formal considerations and so remains speculative and unrooted in any secure knowledge gained from solid textual evidence. But if the preceding analysis of Jesus' actions as they are attested in the institution narratives is correct, then it is reasonably clear that Jesus announced the new covenant in his blood within the framework of a Jewish meal ritual, at least according to the reports as we have them. From this we can infer that when Jesus commanded his disciples to "do this," they most likely understood "this" to refer to the actions, i.e. the *berakoth*, that belong to the meal ritual as they had known and performed it as Jews. But when Jesus added to the command the phrase "in memory of me," the disciples were constrained to adapt the meal ritual to express the new meaning that Jesus introduced into it.[37] Subsequently, the motive for their thanksgiving would no longer be the gift of the land and God's covenant with Israel as the chosen people, but the culmination of God's saving acts in Jesus Christ. For "if Christ is the true bread that has come down from heaven and if he is the true vine, then it is no longer for the land and for the vine of David that thanks must be given."[38] It is these considerations that will help us account for both the structure and the thematic contents of the prayers that accompany the depiction of the early Christian meal ritual in the *Didache*, to which we now turn.

Didache

The *Didache* or "The Teachings of the Twelve Apostles" is an early "church order" that scholars have dated somewhere between the late first and early second centuries C.E. There is no consensus on the place of origin of the *Didache*, but almost all scholars agree that the content of the document bears a strong Jewish stamp. For this reason they see reflected in it the religious beliefs and values of first century Jews who accepted the message about Jesus Christ. The *Didache* has generated an enormous amount of research since 1883, when Philotheos Bryennios, the Greek metropolitan of Nicomedia, published the text which he discovered in an eleventh century manuscript housed in the library of the patriarch of Jerusalem at Constantinople ten years earlier. Scholars continue to regard it as an invaluable source of knowledge about the teaching, rites, and the ecclesiastical disciplines of a Jewish Christian community in the first or early second century C.E.

The *Didache* contains sixteen chapters, which can be divided into four parts. The first contains the treatise on the "Two Ways," a series of moral and catechetical instructions that distinguish godly conduct that leads to life from sinful conduct that leads to death (chs. 1–6). The second addresses the practices and rites to be observed in the community: baptism, fasting, daily prayer and the prayers said at the community meals (chs. 7–10). The third part gives instructions concerning the obligations proper to the life of the church: the reception of itinerant ministers, hospitality, material support for prophets, the order of Sunday worship, and the election of bishops and deacons (chs. 11–15). The last part contains final admonitions in expectation of the parousia (ch. 16).

We restrict our attention to the prayers to be said at community meals as they are given in chapters 9 and 10. For the convenience of the following analysis we provide the text here.

Table 4: *Didache* 9 and 10

Chapter 9	Chapter 10
1. Concerning the Eucharist give thanks thus:	1. After you have eaten your fill, give thanks thus:
2. First concerning the cup: We give thanks to you, our Father, for the holy vine of David, your servant, which you have made known to us through Jesus your servant. To you be glory forever. [Amen].	2. We give thanks to you, holy Father, for your holy Name which you have made to tabernacle in our hearts and for the knowledge, faith and immortality which you have made known to us through Jesus, your servant. To you be glory for ever and ever. [Amen.]
3. And concerning the broken (bread): We give thanks to you, our Father, for the life and knowledge which you have made known to us through Jesus your servant. To you be glory for ever. [Amen.]	3. You, almighty Lord, have created all things for the sake of your Name; you have given food and drink to the sons of men for their enjoyment so that they might give you thanks; but to us you have given the spiritual food and drink for eternal life through Jesus your servant.
4. Just as this broken (bread) was scattered upon the mountains and gathered together has become one, so let your church be gathered into your kingdom from the ends of the earth because yours is the glory and the power for ever. [Amen.]	4. For all these things we give you thanks because you are mighty. To you be glory for ever.
5. Let know one eat or drink from your eucharist except those baptized in the name	5. Remember, Lord, your church, to deliver it from evil and to perfect it in your love. And gather it, sanctified, from the four winds

Continued on next page

Table 4—*Continued*

of the Lord; for indeed concerning this the Lord has-
said: "Do not give what is
holy to the dogs."

into your kingdom which
you have prepared for it
because yours is the power
and the glory for ever.
Amen.

6. Let grace come and let this
    world pass away. Amen.
    Hosanna to the God of
    David. If anyone is holy let
    him come; if anyone is not,
    let him repent. Maranatha.
    Amen.

7. Permit the prophets to give
    thanks as much as they
    wish.[39]

Fellowship Meal or Eucharist?

The character of the meal that these prayers frame has posed problems for interpreters from the time the texts first came to light. The
texts designate the meal as a Eucharist (9.1, cf. 9.2, 9.3; 10.2, 4), and
there is ample evidence to suggest that the meal ritual does in fact refer to a celebration of the Eucharist or Lord's Supper, as we will soon
see. But interpreters have raised several objections that radically call
into question the acceptance of this *prima facie* attribution. First, the
cup-bread order in the rite indicated in 9.2–4 does not correspond to
the canonical form of the celebration of the Eucharist, in which the
blessing over the bread precedes that over the cup. Second, the thematic contents of the prayers do not appear to draw inspiration from
those associated with the Last Supper traditions; in this regard, we
find no direct reference to the body and blood, the covenant, or the
death and resurrection of Jesus. And third, the texts do not include
the words of institution. This last objection is perhaps the most serious, and we will have to return to it later. But it is enough to say here
that for these reasons, it is problematic to affirm that the meal ritual
described in chapters 9 and 10 is one that intends to respond to the
command given by Jesus at the Last Supper, "do this in memory of
me."

Because the data about the meal ritual found in these chapters do
not square easily with the institution narratives of the New Testa-

ment, interpreters have proposed various hypotheses about the character of the meal featured in them. An early response to the problems as we have presented them was to see in the rite a description of an agape or fellowship meal, and not a Eucharist in the strict sense.[40] Another reference to the Eucharist later in the *Didache* evidently confirms the supposition that chapters 9 and 10 do not envisage the community's Eucharist; in chapter 14 the *Didache* instructs the members of the community to assemble on the Lord's Day in order to "break bread" and to offer the Eucharist, and to prepare for this celebration through confession and reconciliation, so as to avoid the profanation of the sacrifice. This text has suggested to J.P. Audet the hypothesis that the expression "breaking of the bread" refers to a "minor Eucharist" (chs. 9 and 10), which must be distinguished from the "major Eucharist" (ch. 14). 10.6 provides the transitional formula that links the two rites together. We are to read this formula, accordingly, as an invitation to come forward to participate in the Eucharist proper, for the command "let him come" would be senseless if it did not precede the sacramental celebration.[41]

Many interpreters have adopted a variation of this hypothesis, according to which 9.1–10.5 depicts a fellowship meal that precedes the Eucharist announced in 10.6.[42] But it is evident that the validity of this hypothesis about two independent rituals stands or falls with the function assigned to the invitational formula in 10.6. To be sure, the liturgical acclamations (e.g. "Hosanna to the God of David" "*Maranatha*") followed by the "amen" manifestly seem to conclude the ritual introduced in 9.1. In this perspective, it seems very plausible to regard the lines in 10.6 as a liturgical dialogue between the celebrant and the community; moreover, they can be seen as serving not only to conclude one ritual, but also to prepare the community for the one that is about to begin:

> Celebrant: Let grace come and let this world pass.
> Community: Hosanna to the God of David
> Celebrant: If one is holy let him come, if not let him be converted. *Maranatha*.
> Community: Amen.[43]

The celebrant prays for the passing away of this world and for the coming of Jesus, since "grace" is probably a christological title. By responding with a line from a royal messianic psalm, with which it heralds the expected Jesus, the community makes this intention their own. The *"maranatha"* that concludes the invitation probably has a twofold signification: not only is it a petition for the *parousia* ("Lord, come!"), but also a confession of the "sacramental" advent of the Lord in the Eucharist that is about to begin ("The Lord has come!").[44] With the response of the "amen" the community affirms that it is prepared to greet the approaching Lord in the celebration that is about to take place.

Despite the cogency of this reading, recent scholarship has shown that the meaning and function of 10.6 cannot be established with absolute certainty. There are two considerations in particular that complicate this liturgical interpretation of the passage.[45] In the first place, if the phrase "if one is holy let him come" were meant as an invitation to the participants to "come forward," it is more likely that the compound Greek verb *proserchesthō* would have been used instead of *erchesthō*. The simple verb signifies an invitation "to come" without indicating a specific place. Second, it is significant that 9.5 closely parallels 10.6. If we read the later in light of the earlier passage, we may assume that those who are called "holy" in 10.6 are the same as the "baptized" in 9.5, and that the invitation "let him repent" implies "let him be baptized." In addition, the warning issued by the Lord, "do not give what is holy to the dogs" (cf. Matthew 7:6) may have its counterpart in the *"maranatha,"* which in this case has the force of a prohibition, a solemn warning that reinforces the demand for repentance by calling on the presence of God as witness.[46] On the basis of these parallels, recent interpreters see the content in 10.6 as a "recapitulation and further development" of what is found in 9.5.[47] Moreover, noting that 9.5 does not form a part of the prayer, but rather is a general admonition to the community to guard the eucharistic celebration against profanation, some suggest that 10.6 may have also functioned in this way. If this reading is correct, then the invitational formula is not a part of the liturgy recited by the celebrant (and community), but rather a rubrical instruction that perhaps a final editor added for the purpose of reminding his community about the requirements (sc. repentance and baptism) for admission to the eucharistic celebration.

This alternative reading of 10.6 has the advantage of freeing the interpreter to attend seriously to the data in chapters 9 and 10 that favor the hypothesis that the meal ritual envisages the eucharistic celebration. First, the introduction to the prayers in 9.1, *Peri de tes eucharistias* ("concerning the Eucharist"), bears a verbal parallel to the introduction to the section on baptism in 7.1, *Peri de tou baptismatos* ("concerning baptism"). This parallel indicates that we have in both passages a definite rule for the conduct of church ceremonial.[48] Second, the term "Eucharist" in 9.5 designates not only the prayers of thanksgiving (9.2–4; 10.2–5), but also that over which they are said, namely, the eucharistic food and drink (cf. 10.3b). The object of the thanksgiving in 10.3b is the spiritual food and drink that have been consecrated by the meal prayers and consumed by the community in the context of a meal that has already happened (cf. 10.1). On this reading, then, there is no need to postulate a second eucharistic celebration. Nor does the objection that the mention of the Eucharist recurs in chapter 14 refute this claim. The phrases "breaking of the bread" and the "Eucharist" found in chapter 14 do not necessarily have to refer to two independent rites; rather the phrases can be seen to constitute a *hendiadys*, which signifies the single meal ritual of "breaking the bread with thanksgiving" described in chapters 9 and 10.[49] The term "Eucharist" in these two chapters, therefore, refers to the "meal ritual that is certainly the Eucharist," and "every claim which presses for a non-eucharistic interpretation in *Didache* 9–10 stands in patent contradiction to everything these prayers want to say."[50]

For the preceding reasons, then, we prefer to see the rites in chapters 9 and 10 as a complex unity that embraces the elements we have already identified as belonging to the Jewish meal ritual. The entire sequence of events in these two chapters unfolds a pattern that we have already traced in our analysis of this meal ritual. Accordingly, we find in them two short blessings over the cup and the broken bread respectively before the meal (ch. 9), and a longer threefold blessing that comes after the meal (ch. 10). Two phenomena, therefore, can be seen to converge in the texts before us. On the one hand, there is the Jewish meal ritual, which embraces the *Kiddush* rite, and the *Birkat ha-mazon*, the thanksgiving after the meal; on the other hand, there is an early Christian eucharistic celebration. We can see that neither one excludes the other; we also see, however, that the traditional Jewish table blessings have undergone significant structural and thematic modifications as they have been made to assimilate the christological content that the *Didache* prayers introduce into them. We intend to bring this out more clearly as we turn now to examine the structure and themes of these prayers. Since we are primarily interested in investigating the role that the *Birkat ha-mazon* played in the formation of the eucharistic prayer, we will focus our attention for the most part on the material found in chapter 10.

Didache 10 and the Structure of the *Birkat ha-mazon*

Ever since Louis Finkelstein sought to establish parallels between the thanksgiving after the meal in *Didache* 10 and the ancient Jewish *Birkat ha-mazon*, which he attempted to reconstruct with the help of the former, a general consensus among scholars emerged very early that the blessing formulae in chapter 10 represent a reworking of the threefold series of blessings that concludes the Jewish meal ritual. Liturgical historians today, however, are reluctant to press the structural parallels too closely, since they maintain that the prayer formulae in Jewish liturgy of the first few centuries were fluid and not bound by rules, which were in any case established only during the later Tannaitic and Amoraic traditions.[51] We have already seen that the oldest Jewish sources that contain a complete text of the *Birkat ha-mazon* date only as early as the ninth century C.E. Thus, they can hardly serve as bases for the reconstruction of a first century version.[52] On the other hand, we have argued that postulating an ancient version of the thanksgiving after meals is not entirely misconceived, since the prayer that appears in the Book of the Jubilees 22.6–9 suggests that the general structure and themes of the *Birkat ha-mazon* were already known by the time that the prayers in the *Didache* were composed. We consider it legitimate, therefore, to adopt Finkelstein's proposed text, if not with the aim of deciding the original wording of the ancient *Birkat ha-mazon*, at least for the heuristic purpose of seeing how the blessing formulae in *Didache* 10 might have both presupposed and reconfigured their putative Jewish counterparts, whatever content they may have had.

The first indication that the prayers in chapter 10 correspond to the custom of the *Birkat ha-mazon* is found already in 10.1. The verbal noun phrase *meta de to emplesthenai* ("after you have eaten your fill") appears to refer to the prescription in Deuteronomy 8:10 (LXX): "And you shall eat and be filled (*kai phage kai emplesthese*) and shall bless the Lord your God for the good land which he has given to you." As we have already seen, this text determines the composition of the Jewish liturgy after the meal and provides the basis on which the "prayer becomes obedience to a Word contained in the Law."[53] We will return to this point later when we develop its implications in an attempt to address the problem of the absence of the words of institution from the *Didache* prayers. For now let us recall that in its most basic form the *Birkat ha-mazon* reveals a tripartite structure. This consists of a blessing for food; a thanksgiving for the gift of land; and a supplication for mercy on the people of Israel, the city of Jerusalem, and the temple. The rubric (10.1) suggests that the *Didache* community grounded its liturgy after the meal in the injunction contained in Deuteronomy 8:10, but a comparison between the *Didache* prayers (10.2–5) and the reconstructed Jewish table blessings reveals that the composer did not adhere strictly to the order according to which this tripartite structure unfolds.

That the prayers in chapter 10 begin with a thanksgiving (*eucharistoumen*) for the saving intervention of the Father through Jesus (10.2), and then proceed to the themes of creation and food and drink (10.3a), has suggested to liturgical historians that the *Didache* has inverted the order of the first two strophes in the *Birkat ha-mazon*. The thanksgiving for God's saving intervention in behalf of his people occupies the first place; only then is God acknowledged as creator and as the nourisher of human beings. Structurally, the supplication for the Church (10.5) is relatively unproblematic, since it corresponds with the prayer for Jerusalem, the temple, and its restoration as found in the third strophe of its Jewish counterpart. Thus, at first glance it seems that tripartite structure has been retained, even if its elements have been rearranged. A closer analysis, however, reveals a more complicated picture than the assumption of a simple inversion of the first two strophes suggests.

Basic to this analysis is a determination of the extent of the thanksgiving formula with which the prayers after the meal opens. It is significant to find that the summarizing thanksgiving formula in 10.4a, *Pro panton eucharistoumen* ("For all these things we give you thanks") has a clear parallel in the second strophe of the *Birkat ha-mazon* as it is recorded in the *siddurim* of the ninth and tenth centuries.[54] Finkelstein omitted the formula from his reconstruction because he considered it to be a later addition. To be sure, it is easy to see that the simple text he proposed would not have required a summarizing formula. A Rabbinic rule (third century C.E.) stipulating that there must be a return to the theme of thanksgiving before the *chatimah* presupposes that the body of the prayer was becoming so complex as to stray from the thanksgiving mode.[55] But recent scholarship has challenged Finkelstein on this point, and on the basis of parallel phrases in liturgical prayers of considerable antiquity, concluded that the formula could have derived from contemporary Jewish usage.[56] Consequently, if 10.2 and 10.4a encompass the first thanksgiving in the *Didache* prayer, then the acknowledgment of God as creator in 10.3a cannot be seen to constitute a discrete unit that corresponds to the first strophe in the *Birkat ha-mazon*. Rather, it gives the appearance of an interpolation that in this instance disturbs the thematic integrity of the one thanksgiving articulated by doxologies at the middle and at the end.[57] If this in fact is the case, then it is probably more meaningful to speak of the assimilation of the first Jewish blessing into the second than to speak of the inversion of the first two strophes. The alteration, in effect, has reduced the threefold blessing-thanksgiving-supplication pattern to a twofold thanksgiving-supplication pattern. We may say that in a broad sense Christian eucharistic prayers will subsequently conform to this basic pattern, consisting of a thanksgiving for the saving acts of God through Jesus Christ (*anamnesis*) and a petition for eschatological fulfillment on the basis of these acts (*epiclesis*).

Themes in the Prayers of *Didache* 10

Already in the *Didache* community this means that it is now no longer the gift of the land that constitutes the object of thanksgiving, but the new gift that God has bestowed through Jesus his *pais* (servant/child). In the prayers in chapter 10 that gift is first described as the "holy name which you have made to tabernacle in our hearts" (10.2a). The term "name" appears as a christological title in the New Testament, as well as in early Jewish Christian literature (Acts 2:21; Rom. 10:12; John 17:6; 1 Clem. 60:4; Polyc. Phil. 10:1–3).[58] It designates the ineffable essence of God, which is revealed only through the Son. It is appropriate to attribute this title to the Son, because he is the one closest to God, and thereby able to disclose and communicate God's life, which is hidden in itself. The verb "tabernacle," predicated of the "name," supports this christological interpretation of the term, insofar as it is used to indicate the incarnate existence of the Logos in John 1:14.[59] From these considerations it is reasonable to infer that the gift for which the cultic community gives thanks is no less than the very presence of Jesus himself, who once descended and now has come to dwell in the hearts of the members of the community.

But this interpretation has been contested on the basis of what immediately follows. In 10.3a we read: "You, almighty Lord, have created all things for the sake of your name." If "name" is identified with God's *pais*, then we have to conclude that God created all things for the sake of Jesus. But this is a theme that does not accord with what the prayers say about God's *pais*, namely, that he is the means of revelation and of the divine gifts (10.2b, 3b; cf. 9.2,3). For this reason, liturgical historian Enrico Mazza has preferred to dissociate the two terms (name and *pais*), having appealed instead to the temple theology in the Old Testament to explicate the meaning of the term "name."[60] In Deuteronomy 12:11 the temple is the place where God has caused his name to dwell, so that it may be invoked. According to Mazza, in later Jewish theology the name is regarded as a "sort of hypostasis entirely like but not perfectly identical with God."[61] That is to say, the name is conceived as God's intermediary through which God interacts with his people. The temple is the site of this interaction, the place where God's servants can call on God's name in prayer (cf. 1 Kings 8:27-30).

According to *Didache* 10.2, it is no longer the temple, but the hearts of the community's members that serve as the place of the divine presence, mediated by the name that now dwells there, and "in this place a liturgy consisting of prayer is celebrated."[62] Thus, the message of 10.2 is that God the Father, through Jesus, has created a "new place of worship and a new liturgy." In so doing, God has revealed the "deepest nature of Israel and the temple," acting through Jesus to reveal knowledge, faith, and immortality to those Jews who have accepted the message about him.[63]

This is certainly a cogent reading, but it is nevertheless difficult to avoid seeing in the thanksgiving in 10.2 an explicit image of eucharistic indwelling. In this regard, it has been suggested that the themes of knowledge, faith, and immortality introduced in a meal context derive from the the wisdom theology of the late Old Testament period.[64] The attributes and activities of personified Wisdom in Proverbs, Sirach, and Wisdom of Solomon described in hymnic form offer illuminating parallels with those of God's *pais* in the *Didache*. Thus Wisdom is identified with the Torah (Sir. 24:23) or personifed as revealer (Wisd. of Sol. 7–9). Wisdom descends to find a dwelling place in Israel (Sir. 24:8), to set up a tabernacle in Jacob (Sir. 24:11). Wisdom has even the power to grant immortality and provide an eternal memorial to those who find her (Wisd. of Sol. 8:13). Moreover, Wisdom is described as food and drink (Sir. 24:21); she is the source of true nourishment as the tree of life (Prov. 3:18). Wisdom gives the bread of understanding to eat and the water of wisdom to drink (Sir. 15:3). Wisdom hosts a feast, to which she invites the simple to eat the bread and drink the wine that provide life, knowledge and wisdom (Prov. 9:1–6).[65]

This list of texts strongly suggests that the christology of the prayer's composer was influenced by the Jewish writers of the Wisdom school. Against this background, then, the thanksgiving formula in 10.2 appears to affirm that the function of wisdom is realized in God's *pais* and is disclosed and communicated by him especially in a meal context. That the thanksgiving is linked with the acknowledgment that God has given "spiritual food and drink and eternal life through Jesus your *pais*" (10.3b) lends support to this interpretation. It is therefore legitimate to suppose that the eucharistic indwelling envisaged in 10.2 is mediated by the eucharistic food and drink. This is not far from the conception of the Fourth Gospel, which refers to the "bread which has come down from heaven" (6:58), and identifies this with the Jesus who gives eternal life to those who eat his flesh and drink his blood. Granted, it cannot be said that the *Didache* explicitly identifies the flesh and blood of Jesus with the "spiritual food and drink" that has been consecrated and consumed by the community. But it nevertheless seems that the eucharistic gift—the presence of God's *pais* and the gifts revealed and imparted through him in the context of the meal—constitute the primary object of its thanksgiving.

We have already indicated that the acknowledgment of God as creator and provider of food and drink in 10.3a appears to interrupt the christological train of thought we have observed in 10.2 and 10.3b. But the presence of this text does not seem anomalous when we remember that the prayers are to be recited after the completion of a meal that satiates (cf. 10.1). It is here especially that we may call to mind the relationship between the Jewish thanksgiving after meals and the Christian eucharistic celebration as we have it in the *Didache*. Liturgical historians have seen in 10.3a evidence of the community's intention to celebrate its meal ritual according to the mandate in Deuteronomy 8:10. By forging a link between these two texts, Mazza has elaborated an answer to the problem concerning the absence of the words of institution from the *Didache* prayers.[66] It will be helpful to summarize his position here in order to facilitate a grasp of the dynamic at work in both the Jewish meal ritual and the eucharistic celebration featured in the *Didache*.

According to Mazza, the words of institution serve as the theological locus that "grounds and makes sense" of the actions in which the community engages during its religious meal celebration.[67] When the devout Jew asks why Israel is enjoined to recite the prayer at the end of the religious meal, the answer is that the obligation comes from Deuteronomy 8:10. This function is rendered more explicit in later texts of the *Birkat ha-mazon*, in which this verse itself is introduced into the second strophe.[68] But the insertion of the entire text is not necessary to bring out the connection between the community's present action and the divine command that established and instituted it. Even an indirect reference indicating clearly that this action is done in obedience to the command issued in Deuteronomy 8:10 is sufficient. Since, in Mazza's interpretation, 10.3a provides this indirect reference, it is legitimate to conclude that this text serves as the words of institution in the prayers of Didache 10.[69]

But this reading evidently leaves open the question how the Christian eucharistic celebration depicted in the *Didache* conforms to what Jesus instituted on the night of his betrayal. According to Mazza, this is not a problem with regard to this early Jewish Christian celebration. Because of the "particular relationship between Christianity and Judaism in the *Didache*," there would have been no need to "explain or formulate this conformity by making direct reference to [Jesus'] institution."[70] The structure of the celebration itself, consisting of the elements proper to the Jewish meal ritual, already indicates its conformity with the Lord's Supper.[71] In this perspective, the community enacts its obedience to Jesus' command to "do this in memory of me" precisely by celebrating a meal ritual similar to what Jesus and his disciples would have known and celebrated as Jews.[72] But so as to render this meal ritual suitable as a vehicle to carry the memory of Jesus, it modified the typical Jewish table blessings to convey the soteriological themes of the nascent Christian faith. Thus, "the Christian celebration continues to flow from the rite and logic of the Jewish ritual supper" even as it undergoes a transformation to bear new revealed content.[73]

But this transformation means that the liturgy of the Christian meal can no longer be reduced to the Jewish meal ritual prescribed by Deuteronomy 8:10. Mazza has argued that the text of 10.3b reflects the community's consciousness of the difference of its own celebration from that of the Jews. By placing this text in parallel with what immediately precedes it in 10.3a, Mazza has drawn attention to the emerging contrasts:

—The recipients change from "children of men" to "us."
—The verb changes from "you have given" (*edokas*) to "graciously bestowed" (*echariso*).
—The gift changes from "food and drink" to "spiritual food and drink."
—The outcome changes from "for their enjoyment so that they may thank you" to "eternal life."[74]

From an analysis of what gives the strong impression of deliberately formulated contrasts, Mazza has concluded that the *Didache* community self-consciously defined its identity in contrast to that of the Jewish community even as it articulated its own faith in the framework of the Jewish meal ritual. In this respect, he notes the absence of any reference to the "promised land" in the *Didache* prayers. In the horizon of the Jewish understanding, God gives food from the abundance of the land; for the Christian, God gives "spiritual food" through Jesus, the *pais* of God. The promised inheritance is and will be Christ; in him, a new relation among peoples is rendered eschatologically possible by the power of God to bring the Church from the four winds of the earth into the kingdom of God.

To this end, the final section of the prayer in *Didache* 10 consists in a petition for the sanctification of the Church and its gathering into the kingdom of God. As we have already noted, this petition appears to bear formal and thematic parallels with the third strophe of the *Birkat ha-mazon*, which consists in a supplication for the temple, Jerusalem, and its restoration. But a closer analysis reveals that the *Didache* prayers after the meal depart here from their putative Jewish models to draw on phraseology and formulae employed in other Jewish liturgical prayers. The theme "to gather from the four winds" in 10.5 (cf. 9.4b) is reminiscent of the tenth blessing of the *Shemoneh Esreh berakhot* (the eighteen benedictions), the obligatory statutory prayers also known as the *Amidah* or as simply *Tefilla* (prayer).[75] The text according to *siddur* of Rav Amram reads:

> Sound the great trumpet for our freedom, and lift up the ensign to gather together our captives, and announce our freedom for gathering us together into one from the four corners of the earth. You are blessed, Lord, who gathers the exiles of the people of Israel.[76]

The same theme is also found in the *Ahablah Rabbah*, the second of the blessings before the *Shema*:

> ...And bring us to peace from the four corners of the earth and let us enter our land as a free people.[77]

Of course, it is impossible to trace the texts of these formulae to the time of the composition of the *Didache*. But liturgical historians point to Sirach 36, in which one can find a series of petitionary prayers that parallel some of those in the *Amidah*, as a possible source for the idea of "gathering" expressed in *Didache* 10.5.[78] In Sirach 36:10–13, there is a series of petitions to God to gather together all the tribes of Jacob (v.10); to show mercy on the people of Israel, whom God calls his first-born (v.11); to have compassion on Jerusalem (v.12); and to fill the temple once again with the divine glory (v.13). It is noteworthy that this text also reflects the themes of the third strophe of the *Birkat ha-mazon*. In any case, we can say that the petition for the gathering of the scattered was a typical theme in Jewish liturgical prayer generally, regardless of the context, because it is intrinsic to the theme of the covenant, which is the object *par excellence* of thanksgiving and the very ground of possibility for the prayer of the devout Jew.

If the petition in Jewish liturgical prayer, then, expresses the hope for the gathering of the Diaspora and the restoration of Israel, that in *Didache* 10.5 expresses the hope for the gathering of the Church and its entering into the kingdom of God. The prayers after the meal conclude with a final doxology.

Conclusion: Structure and Dynamic
of Early Christian Eucharistic Praying

One of the principles that guided the composition of the Order for the Sacrament of the Lord's Supper adopted by the RCA for inclusion in its 1968 *Liturgy and Psalms* was "faithfulness to the New Testament understanding of the meaning of the Supper."[79] We have already indicated that Howard Hageman, the chief architect of this order, learned from Gregory Dix that the institution narrative is not only a typical part of eucharistic prayers, but also constitutes a model from which the various ritual actions composing the eucharistic celebration have been drawn. From this Hageman and his committee concluded that faithfulness to the New Testament required, among other things, that after the minister and the elders assemble around the Lord's table, a prayer of thanksgiving must be said.

We have sought in this chapter to return to the New Testament and to the period of Christian origins to investigate the prayers of blessing and thanksgiving that the earliest Christian communities said over their meals dedicated to the celebration of the saving acts that God accomplished through Jesus Christ. In this investigation we were guided by the research that liturgical historians have done on the Jewish table blessings, especially the *Birkat ha-mazon*. Through an analysis of the stylized material that the New Testament accounts of the Last Supper share and of the structure of the early Christian eucharistic celebration depicted in chapters 9 and 10 of the *Didache*, we have sought to demonstrate that the prayers of blessing and thanksgiving were couched in the framework of the Jewish meal ritual, of which the *Birkat ha-mazon* forms the most significant component. For this reason, we devoted much of our attention to the *Birkat ha-mazon*, in the hope that gaining an understanding of the Jewish thanksgiving after meals would yield insight into the structure and dynamic of early Christian eucharistic praying.

In this concluding section, then, it remains for us to clarify this structure and dynamic on the basis of our foregoing study of the early Jewish and Christian meal rituals. It is possible to do this from three angles of approach. First, we wish to consider the relationship between the blessings and the consumption of the food and drink. Then, turning to the structure of these blessings themselves, we will examine the relationship between thanksgiving and petition. To clarify this bipartite structure in the form in which we recognize it in eucharistic praying today, we will need to introduce a brief excursus on the oldest surviving eucharistic prayer text as it is contained in the *Apostolic Tradition*, a church order conventionally attributed to the schismatic (and later reconciled) Roman presbyter Hippolytus (c.170–235).[80] Our consideration of this eucharistic prayer will prompt us, finally, to ask about the words of institution and their place and function in early Jewish and Christian liturgical prayer. Our goal in this section, as we have already stated, is to provide some basis on which to evaluate critically the Communion Prayer in the chapter to follow.

We have pointed out repeatedly that according to Jewish faith the *Birkat ha-mazon* is an act of obedience to the command recorded in Deuteronomy 8:10: "You will eat and be satisfied and will bless the Lord your God for the good land he has given you." Through the acts of blessing, the liturgical community acknowledges the food and drink that they have consumed as gifts from God. But these gifts are the produce of the land that God gave to the people as a pledge of the covenant that he concluded with them, through which he elected them as his own holy people. That is why in the meal ritual the liturgical community also thankfully recalls this covenant and why its eating of the produce of this land constitutes in itself an ongoing symbolic acceptance of the covenant and reception of its identity as God's holy people. Thus, it is through its faith expressed joyfully in the table blessings and in its eating and drinking that the liturgical community effectively renews its participation in the blessings of the covenant relationship.

We have tried to show that the rites that Jesus probably performed at the Last Supper with his disciples, at least as they are adumbrated in the institution narratives, represent a similar phenomenon. However, the common relationship to God that this liturgical community enjoys is no longer mediated through the land, the covenant, and the Torah, but is reconstituted through the person of Jesus himself. In this connection, we have speculated that in the threefold series of blessings over the cup at the end of the meal, Jesus might have seized the occasion afforded by the second strophe to direct the disciples' attention to the relation of his own saving death to the covenant. In any case, the texts tell us that the cup that he shares with them is the cup of his "blood of the covenant" (Mark/Matt.) or is the "new covenant in [his] blood" (Luke/Paul). For the disciples, then, participation in the dispensation of this new covenant, for which God probably was acknowledged in the thanksgiving after the meal, is similarly received through the faith expressed in the table blessings and in the drinking of this cup (and in the eating of the bread).

In the eucharistic celebration depicted in the *Didache*, there is no evidence that the meal elements are ordered to the covenant, the body and blood, or the saving death and resurrection of Jesus Christ. But we have seen that Jesus, God's *pais*, is nevertheless confessed as the bearer of a new relationship with the Father, and it is this new revelation and the gifts that accompany it that constitute the objects of the thanksgivings that we studied in *Didache* 10. In this chapter we also saw that these eucharistic gifts are appropriated by the liturgical community through the "spiritual food and drink" that God graciously bestows through Jesus, his *pais*. This signification of the meal elements marks them as distinct from those that are consecrated and consumed in the context of the typical Jewish meal ritual. The contrasts between this meal ritual and that in the *Didache* are deliberately formulated in 10.3a and 3b, which reflect the new realization of the Christian consciousness: Jesus and not the land is the true source of nourishment for the Christian community.

The relationship between God and the liturgical community that is celebrated and renewed in these meal rituals is established and sealed in the past. God has intervened decisively in history to bring into existence a people that will praise him by proclaiming the *mirabilia Dei*. But this covenant has still to be fulfilled. While Israel patiently awaits its fulfillment, she calls to mind the major episodes in her life that demonstrate God's ongoing commitment to provide for her, to deliver her from her enemies, and to restore her. We have seen that the second strophe in the *Birkat ha-mazon* is expanded on special feasts to include embolisms that commemorate these episodes. In bringing them to mind and expressing them in the *berakoth*, the liturgical community not only experiences their saving presence anew, but also finds in them the assurance that God will act on its behalf in the future in a manner consistent with how he has already acted. From this assurance that God has acted in saving ways in her past, Israel can move from thanksgiving to petition for the consummation of those acts. We have seen that this petition finds concrete expression in the third strophe of the *Birkat ha-mazon*, in which the devout Jew boldly prays for the restoration of Jerusalem and the Temple, the place where God's glory dwells.[81]

In the New Testament and in the *Didache* the object of the eschatological hope of the liturgical community is no longer this restoration, but the kingdom of God. We have seen in the *Didache* the transition from thanksgiving (10.2–4) to petition (10.5) and have suggested that it reveals the same dynamic as operative in the Jewish *Birkat ha-mazon*. The past grace (self-communication of the Father through Jesus, his *pais*) grounds the present petition for future blessings, which can be regarded as the telos of the saving acts of the Father through Jesus (sanctification of the church and its gathering into the kingdom of God). We have claimed that this basic anamnetic-epicletic structure revealed in the *Didache* prayers constitutes the nucleus of later eucharistic prayers, which began to attain by the third century more or less the form in which we recognize it today. It is to a consideration of the eucharistic prayer proper that we turn here.

Excursus: The Eucharistic Prayer in the *Apostolic Tradition*

Space does not permit us to trace the complex historical development of the later eucharistic prayers.[82] But it may be helpful to review briefly the earliest surviving text of a eucharistic prayer to clarify how thankful memory and confident petition express the dynamic of the covenant relationship, founded and renewed by God in Jesus Christ, and continually celebrated and actualized in the liturgy of the community. We refer here to the eucharistic prayer in the document known as the *Apostolic Tradition*.

> The Lord be with you.
> And with your spirit.
> Lift up your hearts.
> We have them with the Lord.
> Let us give thanks to the Lord.
> It is right and just.

> We give you thanks, God, through your beloved child Jesus Christ, whom you sent to us in these last times as savior and redeemer and messenger of your will. He is your inseparable Word, through whom you made all things, and with whom you were well pleased. You sent him from heaven into the womb of the Virgin. And, having been conceived in the womb, he became incarnate and was shown to be your Son, born of the Holy Spirit and the Virgin.

> Fulfilling your will and gaining for you a holy people, he stretched out his hands when he suffered, so that by his suffering he might free those who have believed in you. And when he was betrayed to voluntary suffering, so that he might destroy death, break the chains of the devil, tread down hell, illuminate the just, fix the limit, and manifest the resurrection, he took bread, gave thanks to you, and said:

> Take, eat, this is my body that is broken for you. In the same way also the cup, saying: this is my blood, which is poured out for you. Whenever you do this, you do it to commemorate me.

Therefore, remembering his death and resurrection, we offer to you the bread and the cup, giving thanks to you, because you have held us worthy to stand before you and to minister to you. And we ask you to send your Holy Spirit on the offering of the holy Church. Gathering them into one, grant to all who participate in the holy things the filling of the Holy Spirit, to confirm their faith in the truth, so that we may praise and glorify you through your child Jesus Christ, through whom be glory and honor to you, to the Father and Son with the Holy Spirit in your holy Church both now and in the age to come. Amen.[83]

In regard to its literary structure, the text of this prayer differs dramatically from those that we have considered. In contrast to a simple thanksgiving for the saving intervention of the Father through Jesus, as we have seen in *Didache* 10, here the "thanksgiving becomes a narrative and has for its subject the history of salvation with all its stages,"[84] ranging from eternity to the incarnation and culminating in the death of Christ, his descent into the world of the dead, and his resurrection. This elaboration on the redemptive acts of Jesus Christ no doubt reflects the community's profession of faith, to which the extended thanksgiving gives privileged expression.[85] Moreover, instead of a petition to God for the perfecting of the Church, as in the *Didache*, there appears here an *epiclesis* for the Holy Spirit, which can be divided into two parts:

1. And we ask you to send your Holy Spirit on the offering (*oblationem*) of the holy Church.
2. Gathering them into one, grant to all who participate in the holy things (*sanctis*) the filling of the Holy Spirit, to confirm [their] faith in the truth.[86]

The final purpose of this twofold petition is expressed in the bridge to the concluding doxology: "that we may praise and glorify you through your child (*puerum*) Jesus Christ." The doxology in turn develops this formula by specifying the object of this praise in trinitarian language:

through whom [be] glory and honor to you, to the Father and Son with the Holy Spirit in your holy Church both now and in the age to come. Amen.[87]

From the opening narrative to the concluding doxology the eucharistic prayer of Hippolytus maintains a continuous flow from thanksgiving to petition. But two important observations are in order here. In the first place, the more complex literary structure of the prayer reflects and clarifies a greater theological awareness of the liturgical community's covenant partner, as well as of the basis and goal of the covenant relationship. The prayer shows that through its eucharistic celebration the community understands itself as entering into the presence of the triune God. On behalf of this community, the presider addresses the prayer to God, through the Son, in the faith inspired by the Holy Spirit. In the unfolding of its content, the prayer reveals that it is patterned on the trinitarian activity of God in the history of salvation: the Father is the source and therefore the end of all creation and salvation; the Son is the "savior and redeemer and messenger of the [Father's] will"; and the Holy Spirit is the power whereby God unites the members with one another, and strengthens them in the common faith they profess. In recognition of the particular role each of the three divine Persons plays in the history of salvation, the community prays for communion in the Holy Spirit with the body and blood of Jesus Christ (*sanctis*), through which the community is confirmed in its faith and enabled to praise and glorify God. As we have seen, the doxology elaborates on the object of this praise by rendering "glory and honor" to the "Father and the Son with the Holy Spirit...both now and in the ages to come." Thus it is in these explicit trinitarian terms that the *epiclesis* and concluding doxology give content to the eschatological hope of the saving acts of God through Jesus Christ. That hope is nothing less than to be drawn into the unending fullness of the very life of the triune God.

But it is not only the extensive narrative development of the trinitarian activity of God in salvation that makes the literary structure of Hippolytus' eucharistic prayer more complex. Following a rather protracted catalogue of the events that constitute the Easter mystery, there appears at the end of the anamnetic section the institution narrative, to which an *anamnesis*/offering formula is closely connected:[88]

> ...taking bread, and offering thanks to you, he said: take, eat, this is my
> body that is broken for you. In the same way also the cup, saying: this is my

blood, which is poured out for you. Whenever you do this, you do it to commemorate me.

Remembering therefore his death and resurrection, we offer to you the bread and the cup, giving thanks to you that you have held us worthy to stand before you and to minister to you.

Before its appearance in this eucharistic prayer, there is no textual evidence that any reference to the institution narrative formed a part of the eucharistic celebration. It is understandable, then, that the interpolation of these formulae in Hippolytus' prayer has prompted liturgical historians to account for their presence in this and in the more developed prayers that emerged in the course of the fourth and fifth centuries.

Reflection on the place and function of the words of institution in Jewish liturgical prayer has suggested to these historians clues to understanding the role of the institution narrative in the later Christian eucharistic prayers. Louis Ligier was among the first to attempt an answer to the question why the institution narrative became incorporated into the eucharistic prayer, which seems otherwise complete without it.[89] He did not, however, begin with Deuteronomy 8:10, the words of institution of the *Birkat ha-mazon*, as the starting point in his investigation. Rather, he contended that the introduction of the institution narrative into the eucharistic prayer paralleled the Jewish practice of introducing into the second or third strophe of the *Birkat ha-mazon* on special feast days an embolism that mentions God's particular action in founding the feast and in calling for its observance. We have already seen that on the feast of Hanukah the master of the house recites the saving acts of God in the time of the Maccabean revolt. In this way, the function of the embolism is to introduce a specific motive for the celebration, linked to the special feast day. Similarly, the insertion of the institution narrative, including its memorial command, into the anamnetic or epicletic sections of the eucharistic prayer, functions as the motive for the prayer offered in commemoration of Jesus Christ. In this perspective, "the narrative is not recited for its own sake, as if it alone should constitute the action of the Church; rather it serves to prepare and authorize the action of the Church."[90] As a memorial recital of the greatest of God's saving acts, the institution narrative instructs the liturgical community that its celebration is to be done as a memorial of Jesus Christ, which it carries out in obedience to his command. It is legitimate to explain in these terms the role the institution narrative plays in the eucharistic prayer of Hippolytus.

Cesare Giraudo has extended the discussion about the function of the institution narrative through the important thesis he advanced on the genesis of the literary structure of the eucharistic prayer.[91] In his study Giraudo has traced the literary origins of the eucharistic prayer from the Old Testament *todah* rather than from the *Birkat ha-mazon*. With the former Hebrew term Giraudo designated a literary genre that he identified in a number of Old Testament prayer formulae relating to the formation or restoration of the covenant relationship between God and Israel. These prayer formulae typically consist in two related parts: (1) a commemorative recital of God's fidelity to the covenant and a corresponding confession of Israel's failure to live in accord with her covenant obligations; and (2) a petition for God's continuing fidelity to the covenant expressed in answer to a specific request. Inserted into either of the two parts is an embolism in the form of a scripture passage relevant to this request. To cite one example, in a prayer for the exiles in Nehemiah 1:5–11, we find an acknowledgment of the God "who keeps covenant and steadfast love with those who love him and keep his commandmants" (v. 5); and a confession of the sins of the people of Israel, who have not "kept the commandments, statutes, and ordinances" that God gave to his servant Moses (vs. 6-7). Following this we find in the form of a citation from Deuteronomy 30:1–5 an appeal to God to remember the promise that he gave to Moses (vs. 8–9). From this embolism the prayer moves to a petition to God to grant the request in a manner consistent with what he has promised (vs.10–11).

Giraudo has drawn attention to the function of the embolism in the Old Testament *todah* to suggest that it illuminates the function of the institution narrative in the eucharistic prayer. With the aim of grounding the appeal to God to act on behalf of the exiles, namely, to return them to their land, Nehemiah inserts into the prayer a biblical text that is appropriate to the request. Nehemiah can be confident that God will respond to the request, because the text serves as a "prophetic oracle" that announces in advance that God will certainly grant it on the basis of his fidelity to the covenant promises.[92] According to Giraudo, just as Nehemiah inserts into his prayer a prophetic oracle according to which God has promised to repatriate the exiles, so also the Christian liturgical community inserts into its prayer the institution narrative according to which Jesus proleptically gives himself under the signs of bread and wine in view of reuniting the scattered children of God.[93] This community can enjoy the same confidence that its subsequent *epiclesis* will be heard, because it is likewise grounding its request on God's fidelity to the covenant promises sealed by the sacrificial death of Jesus Christ.

In the last analysis, then, if the preceding hypotheses about the function of the words of institution are correct, then we may see in the institution narrative the structural and thematic link between the anamnetic and epicletic sections of the developed eucharistic prayer. For the former section, it serves as the basis and warrant for the joyful acknowledgment of the saving acts that God has accomplished through Jesus Christ. For the latter section, it provides a firm foundation for the liturgical community's confidence that God will bring to fulfillment the covenant relationship, which is the final goal of Christian eucharistic praying. In our concluding chapter we will need to keep the foregoing observations before us as we examine more closely the Communion Prayer itself, its structure and dynamic, in order to attend to what it is revealing about its own Church's communion with the triune God.

The Lord's Supper in Light of Liturgical Theological Principles: A Critical Interpretation

At the very outset of this investigation we claimed that the decision of the RCA to substitute its Communion Prayer for its traditional form for the Lord's Supper entailed a change in the shape of its celebration of the Supper. In the first three chapters we saw in the history of this ecclesial communion the processes by which it gradually came to abandon the Palatinate form for the Holy Supper in favor of the Order for the Sacrament of the Lord's Supper, which it adopted for inclusion in its 1968 *Liturgy and Psalms*. Our aim has not been merely to traverse this evolutionary path, but also to become aware of the "why" of the various changes. We found that the liturgical and ecumenical movements in the twentieth century were a watershed in this history. Under the impact of these movements, Reformed theologians and pastors worldwide began both to subject to criticism the liturgical forms that their tradition inherited from the sixteenth century Reformation and to reconceive the nature and meaning of the celebration of the Supper. For these tasks they received generous help from the wealth of biblical, liturgical, and historical research that emanated from these movements. In the fourth chapter we drew from some of this research in our own attempt to discern the structure and dynamic of early eucharistic praying to the extent to which we were able to determine it at the origins of the Christian tradition. We maintained the hypothesis that the Christian eucharistic celebration derived its origins from the Jewish liturgical heritage (*Birkat ha-mazon*). This heritage passed over into the Jewish Chrisitan churches, and provided the framework within which the early Christian liturgical community expressed the *anamnesis* of the *mirabilia Dei* and the *epiclesis* for the fulfillment of the new covenant relationship that God has established in Jesus Christ. With respect to this framework, we then examined the eucharistic prayer in the *Apos-*

tolic Tradition of Hippolytus. We did this in an attempt to clarify the principles, the essential elements and their relations, that constitute the Christian eucharistic prayer in the form in which we know it today. Without pretending to provide a set of inflexible critieria, we declared our intent to bring these to bear on a critical evaluation of the Communion Prayer.

We have now arrived at the juncture at which we are prepared to realize this intent. In this chapter we aim to demonstrate that the decision of the RCA to adopt the Communion Prayer involved not only a change in the shape of celebration of its Lord's Supper, but also a change in the expression of its meaning. The methodological presupposition that will guide us in this demonstration is the traditional adage in liturgical studies: *lex orandi, lex credendi.*[1] That is to say, the manner in which an ecclesial community prays is precisely the manner in which it believes. To examine the meaning of the Communion Prayer, then, means to uncover what the community that offers it is seeking and what transformations it must undergo to obtain what it seeks through it. This is the place from which we must set out. In the course of this analysis we will encounter the important question how the grace of the covenant is received through the sacrament of the Lord's Supper. To this question we will see that the traditional Palatinate form and the Communion Prayer give two different answers. We continue the analysis of the Communion Prayer by addressing the problem introduced by the position of the institution narrative after the prayer itself. The drafters of the prayer provided no explanation why they decided to place the narrative in this position. We will advance the hypothesis that its position is meant to continue a sacramental practice that is consistent with the teaching about the Lord's Supper formulated in the theology of John Calvin and in the Heidelberg Catechism. We will argue, however, that in this position the institution narrative does not harmonize with what our analysis will have shown concerning its function in eucharistic praying. This observation will furnish us with the occasion to urge future committees to reconsider the place of the narrative in the composition of future eucharistic prayers.

The Meaning of the Communion Prayer

In the foregoing chapter we found that early eucharistic praying consists in a bipartite anamnetic-epicletic structure. Following the lead of several liturgical historians, we argued that this structure can be located in the second and third pericopes of the *Birkat ha-mazon*, which in turn probably formed the template for the organization of the content of the prayers in *Didache* 10. We suggested that this structure emerges even more clearly in the eucharistic prayer in the *Apostolic Tradition* of Hippolytus, the earliest surviving text of a eucharistic prayer. An analysis of the content common to this way of praying has shown that it is composed generally of (1) thankful recognition of the fidelity of God in initiating and maintaining the covenant; and (2) confident petition to God to restore and build up the covenant people on the basis of his ongoing fidelity to the covenant relationship.

In view of this basic anamnetic-epicletic structure, liturgical theologian Edward J. Kilmartin has proposed that the eucharistic prayer articulates a theology of covenant modeled on that of the old covenant that God has established with the people of Israel.[2] But in the developed eucharistic prayers, as we saw in the prayer of Hippolytus, this theology is patterned after the trinitarian activity of God in establishing the new covenant in Jesus' blood. God enters into relationship with the new people of God from the Father, through the Son and in the Holy Spirit. For this reason, the Christian petition for the fulfillment of the covenant relationship (the goal of the eucharistic prayer) is ordered to a twofold communion in the Holy Spirit with Christ (and through him with the Father), on the one hand, and with the ecclesial body of Christ in the unity of this same Spirit, on the other. We have already indicated this twofold communion as the goal toward which the eucharistic prayer of Hippolytus is directed. It remains for us to determine whether or in what manner the community that offers the Communion Prayer is seeking the same goal. To facilitate the analysis that follows, we reproduce the text of this prayer here.

Let us lift up our hearts unto the Lord!

Holy and right it is and our joyful duty to give thanks to thee at all times and in all places, O Lord, holy Father, almighty and everlasting God. Thou didst create the heaven with all its hosts and the earth with all its plenty.

Thou hast given us life and being and dost preserve us by thy providence. But thou hast shown us the fullness of thy love in sending into the world thy eternal Word, even Jesus Christ our Lord, who became man for us men and for our salvation. For the precious gift of this mighty Savior who has reconciled us to thee we praise and bless thee, O God. Therefore with thy whole Church on earth and with all the company of heaven we worship and adore thy glorious name.

Holy, holy, holy, Lord God of Hosts. Heaven and earth are full of thy glory. Hosanna in the highest! Blessed is he that cometh in the name of the Lord. Hosanna in the highest.

Holy and righteous Father, as we commemorate in this Supper that perfect sacrifice once offered on the cross by our Lord Jesus Christ for the sin of the whole world, in the joy of his resurrection and in expectation of his coming again, we offer to thee ourselves as holy and living sacrifices. Send thy Holy Spirit upon us, we pray thee, that the bread which we break may be to us the communion of the body of Christ and the cup which we bless the communion of his blood. Grant that being joined together in him we may attain to the unity of the faith and grow up in all things into him who is the Head, even Christ our Lord.

And as this grain has been gathered from many fields into one loaf and these grapes from many hills into one cup, grant, O Lord, that thy whole Church may soon be gathered from the ends of the earth into thy kingdom. Even so, come, Lord Jesus.

And now, as our Savior Christ has taught us, we are bold to say:

Our Father, who art in heaven, hallowed be thy name. Thy kingdom come. Thy will be done on earth as it is heaven. Give us this day our daily bread. And forgive us our debts, as we forgive our debtors. And lead us not into temptation, but deliver us from evil; for thine is the kingdom, and the power, and the glory, forever. Amen.

The Lord Jesus, the same night in which he was betrayed, took bread; and when he had given thanks, he broke it and gave it to them, saying, "Take, eat; this is my body which is broken for you: this do in remembrance of me." After the same manner also, he took the cup, when they had supped, saying, "This cup is the new testament in my blood: this do ye, as oft as ye shall drink of it, in remembrance of me."

The bread which we break is the communion of the body of Christ.

The cup of blessing which we bless is the communion of the blood of Christ.[3]

It is clear that in the Communion Prayer the community speaks to God both in thankful memory and in petition that God strengthen it in the covenant relationship. In the opening thanksgiving (preface), the community expresses its recognition of the Father's goodness and love through giving thanks for the gifts of creation and life, which the Father preserves by his providence. But it renders praise to the Father especially for "sending into the world [his] eternal Word." In contrast to the prayer of Hippolytus, the Communion Prayer does not subsequently proceed to elaborate on the saving acts that God accomplished through Jesus Christ; it is content to sum these up by reciting the principle of the whole economy of salvation: "for us men and for our salvation." Closer analysis of this christological section of the preface, however, reveals the awareness that the mission of the Word has two dimensions: one relative to human beings (Jesus Christ the Lord is the experiential manifestation of the "fullness of the [Father's] love for human beings"); the other relative to God (Jesus Christ the Lord, "who became man for us men and our for salvation," is the agent of the implied acts by which he has "reconciled" the community to God). We will need to consider whether this awareness reflects the community's perception that its Eucharist is "both a receiving of Christ as the Father's gift to us and a sharing in his offering to the Father of our nature, indeed of us."[4] For now let us observe that in the confidence that arises from the recognition that this "mighty Savior" has reconciled the worshippers to God, the community can dare to claim that its worship has communion with the "whole Church on earth and with all the company of heaven who cry, "Holy, Holy, Holy!"[5]

The memorial proclamation of the saving intervention of God through Jesus Christ naturally leads to joyful petition for fulfillment of the covenant relationship established in Jesus. Before the *epiclesis*, however, there appears an *anamnesis*-offering formula: commemorating the "perfect sacrifice once offered on the cross by our Lord Jesus Christ for the sin of the whole world," the worshippers express their desire to offer themselves to the Father as "holy and living sacrifices." We have witnessed a similar phenomenon in the prayer of Hippolytus. But in this ancient prayer there are outstanding elements in the *anamnesis*-offering formula, including the immediate context in which the formula stands, that set it apart from that in the Communion Prayer. In the first place, the formula in the prayer of Hippolytus is closely linked with the preceding institution narrative, to which is added the memorial command. This makes the transition to the *anamnesis* more seamless, because it appears as a response of obedience to Jesus' command that the meal be celebrated in memory of him. By forging this link, the community ensures the continuity of its Eucharist with the Last Supper, which serves to ground and authorize its celebration. In the second place, the *anamnesis* leads into the offering—but it is not of the worshippers expressly, but of the bread and the cup. In offering the bread and the cup (with thanksgiving), the community signifies paradoxically its grateful reception of Jesus Christ's sacrificial act as it is symbolically represented in the eucharistic gifts of his body and blood, which are designated as such by the institution narrative. By extension, then, insofar as the worshippers acknowledge that they live and serve only in strict dependence on Christ, it is also possible to see in the ritual offering of the bread and cup a symbolic gesture of the offering of the worshippers themselves. In other words, the worshippers accept the grace of God in Jesus Christ—the gift of their own new lives in him—precisely through the offering of themselves in faith to the Father.

The sense of the *anamnesis*-offering formula in the Communion Prayer is not as clear, not least because it is severed from the institution narrative. The relationship between the institution narrative and the Communion Prayer is a problem to which we will need to return later; for now let us point out that in the absense of the institution narrative from this section, the prepositional phrase at the beginning of the *anamnesis* ("as we commemorate *in this Supper*" [italics added]) has no immediate referent. Consequently, it is not at all clear how to render the tense of the verb. If it refers to an action that is already in process ("as we have been commemorating"), then the interpreter can only assume that the object of the *anamnesis* (sacrifice of the cross) is included among the *mirabilia Dei* already recounted in the preceding thanksgiving, even though it is not explicitly mentioned there. If not, the interpreter must conclude that it refers to an action anticipated later in the celebration ("as we are about to commemorate"), when the institution narrative will have been said, in which case the offering here appears misplaced. Of course, this ambiguity could have been avoided if the drafters of the Communion Prayer had decided to retain the order of the celebration as they found it in the eucharistic liturgy of the ERF, which they otherwise carefully followed (see chapter 3). There the order "institution narrative-*anamnesis*-offering" makes more explicit that the community's self-offering, renewed at each celebration of the Lord's Supper, is somehow closely associated with Christ's own sacrifice, commemorated and sacramentally represented both in the institution narrative and in the *anamnesis*.[6]

The sense of the *anamnesis*-offering in the Communion Prayer is further complicated by the construction of its offering formula. To verify its acknowledgment of the perfect sacrifice once offered by Christ for sin, as we have already seen, the community pledges itself as a holy and living sacrifice. The prepositional clause ("in the joy of his resurrection and in the expectation of his coming again") that precedes this vow of intent, however, raises the question whether the intention of the community really is to associate its own self-offering with the sacrifice of Christ. It is conceivable that this clause refers to no more than the subjective state of mind in which the community offers itself. It is joyful and expectant because in faith it regards itself as the beneficiary of Christ's sacrificial act; it expresses this faith by offering itself as the only response appropriate to his offering of himself for it. Thus the offering is its own action. The formula then means no more than this: confident in the reality of Christ's resurrection and assured that he will come again in glory, the community is encouraged and motivated to live for him.

A case can certainly be made for this reading, especially against the background of the radical rejection of the sacrificial character of the Mass by the sixteenth century Reformers. But let us suggest that there are at least three reasons to contest this reading. First, if the self-offering is made in response to the love of Christ for the community, then we should expect to see Christ, and not the Father, as the object to whom the formula is addressed. Second, it is inconsistent with the insights of classic Reformed liturgy and theology to assume that the faithful are capable of offering themselves or anything at all apart from the power of the Holy Spirit. In this regard, it is instructive to refer to Diebold Schwarz' adaptation and vernacular translation of the Latin Mass in Strassbourg in 1524, the earliest attempt to compose a Reformed Mass. In place of the offertory exhortation, the *Orate Fratres*, Schwarz provided a clever reformulation that underlines the relationship between the Holy Spirit and the Christians' self-offering:

> Dear brothers and sisters, pray God the Father through our Lord Jesus Christ that he send us the Holy Spirit, the Comforter, that he may make our bodies a living sacrifice, holy, acceptable unto God, which is our reasonable service. May this happen to all.[7]

Third, it is plausible to infer that the language in the prepositional phrase designates as much an objective basis for the action of the worshippers as it does an attitude of mind in them. Indeed it is hard to conceive how the worshippers could offer themselves in the joy of his resurrection if it did not somehow really involve them in it and thereby serve as the ground for their action. In this perspective, the meaning of the *anamnesis*-offering formula could be clarified if the references to Christ's resurrection and return in glory were removed from the offering and placed in the *anamnesis*. We propose, accordingly, the following reworking of the formula:

> Holy and righteous Father, as we commemorate the perfect sacrifice of our Lord Jesus Christ, which he offered on the cross once and for all for the sin of the whole world, his resurrection from the dead, and his coming again in glory, we offer to thee ourselves as holy and living sacrifices.

This reworked formula not only avoids detracting from the unique, sufficient, and unrepeatable sacrifice of the cross, but it also has the advantage of placing the death of Christ in the totality of his saving acts. In their *anamnesis*, their efficacy becomes present somehow in an objective mode, not merely in their subjective recalling by the worshippers. Because and as these saving acts become anamnetically present, this is also the place for the community to participate in them, to let them happen to them, to be caught up into them. For this reason the prayer of offering follows the *anamnesis*: the worshippers appropriate the gift of their new lives in Christ precisely under the mode of their self-offering to the Father.

The prayer of offering serves as a bridge to the invocation of the Holy Spirit to transform the worshippers so that their desire to participate in the divine blessings presented to them in the *anamnesis* of the *pasch* of Jesus Christ may be actualized. In view of the *epiclesis* that immediately follows, then, we may say that the Spirit not only mediates the worshippers to Christ, so that in and with him they may be presented as holy and living sacrifices to the Father, but also Christ to the worshippers, so that they may enjoy communion with him and with one another already now and in the kingdom of the Father yet to come.[8] To this end, the community asks the Father to send the Holy Spirit upon it in the expectation that the confirmation and completion of the covenant relationship will be signified and sealed in sacramental communion. An analysis of the epicletic section in the Communion Prayer, accordingly, reveals the desire of the community (1) to obtain communion in the body and blood of the Lord under the mode of the actions of breaking the bread and blessing the cup; (2) to become what it has received (That is, anticipating the reception of the sacramental body of Christ, it seeks to become the ecclesial body of Christ.); and (3) to participate in the kingdom fully realized when the Lord Jesus comes again and the "whole Church [is] gathered from the ends of the earth into [this] kingdom." In these words adapted from *Didache* 9.4, we see an expansion of the *epiclesis* into an eschatological perspective: the community seeks to be transformed into the ecclesial body of Christ, "grow[ing] up in all things into him who is the Head, even Christ our Lord," in the hope of what has not yet been achieved. In other words, the community expects to experience in sacramental communion with Christ and with members of his body the anticipation of the joy of the Kingdom. For this reason, it is not surprising that the Communion Prayer concludes with the corporate recitation of the Lord's Prayer. In this prayer that Jesus taught to his followers, the community above all is "asking the Father to manifest with power that of which in the Eucharist he gives a foretaste."[9]

Critical Evaluation

The foregoing literary-theological analysis of the Communion Prayer provides conclusive support to our thesis that the celebration of the Lord's Supper in the RCA has undergone a decisive change in the expression of its meaning. We can now make our case: in this prayer communion with Christ (and in and with him reconciliation with the Father) is mediated by the Holy Spirit through the faith of the community expressed in an effective memorial proclamation of the *pasch* of Jesus Christ. In other words, the worshippers open themselves to the Father's descending movement (*katabasis*) toward them through Jesus Christ, a movement recreating and renewing the covenant people, precisely through their own ascending movement (*anabasis*) toward God in prayer and petition. To enlarge on this even further, we may say that through the prayer there is a "binding" and "actualization" of the covenant relationship in which the self-offering of the Father through Christ in the Holy Spirit finds the faith response in the self-offering of the community in the Holy Spirit through Christ to the Father.[10] In this perspective, the celebration determined by the Communion Prayer conveys a dialogical understanding of the Eucharist, in which the divine *katabasis* in word and sacrament renders possible the human *anabasis* in praise, thanksgiving, and petition. The simultaneity of these two movements in this prayer of the Eucharist results in the divine communication of life and the introduction of the worshippers into the plenitude of this new life.[11]

It is not necessary to re-examine extensively the structure and dynamic of the Palatinate form for the Holy Supper to see how far this performance of the meaning of the Eucharist departs from the meaning attributed to the celebration of the Lord's Supper by the sixteenth century Reformers. We have already seen in this form that the celebration commences with the audible recitation of the institution narrative, continues with instruction on the moral disposition necessary for the fruitful reception of communion, provides an explanation of the meaning and benefits of Christ's sacrifice, then proceeds to the prayer, the distribution, and the post-communion thanksgiving. It is important to stress that participation in these benefits (forgiveness of sins, communion in the Holy Spirit with the resurrected and glorified Christ) is not mediated by the accomplishment of the eucharistic action by the liturgical community (*actio ecclesiae*). Rather faith is awakened, confirmed, and nourished in the worshippers through the word and the Spirit by the proclamation of Christ's sacrifice, a proclamation that is signed and sealed in the elements of bread and wine. According to the classic Reformed theology of the Lord's Supper, as we have already seen, the sacrament functions as a sign and seal of what has been proclaimed in the word. And it does this precisely as another form of the word (*verbum visibile*). That is to say, the elements, whose meaning is interpreted by the form that accompanies the celebration, renders the Supper a visible manifestation of an event of proclamation. Consequently, the Supper is no more or no less than an extension of the proclamation. The testimony about God verbalized in the form and portrayed in the bread and wine is accepted through the obedient assent of the worshippers to the content of the form and confirmed for them in both the breaking of the bread and the eating and drinking of the bread and wine.

The Mediation of the Grace of the Covenant

If the preceding interpretation of the liturgical function of these two orders for the Lord's Supper in the RCA is correct, then we are obliged to conclude that the question how the grace of the covenant is mediated receives two different answers. Grace in the Palatinate form is conceived as an act that emanates from God's sovereign will; it consists in his merciful condescencion in granting favor and forgiveness through the Spirit to undeserving human beings on the basis of the satisfaction that Christ made for their sins in his life of perfect obedience and his death on the cross. The sufficient ground of their salvation, accordingly, is a twofold imputation of the righteousness that Christ gained for them: on the one hand, the sins of human beings are imputed to Christ, who bears them in his anguish in the Garden of Gethsemane and in his dereliction on the cross; on the other hand, Christ's perfect obedience is imputed to human beings, as if they themselves fulfilled perfectly the demands of the law. This is the faith embodied and proclaimed in the form, as we have already seen, a faith to which the worshippers are invited to assent. The self-examination, which in the form precedes the explication of this faith, is a test to determine whether or not they are sincere in this assent. Thus the blessings that Christ died to purchase can be received on fulfillment of the conditions of repentance, faith, and obedience, by which the worshippers are granted access to the table of the Lord. It is not necessary to elaborate any further on this form to see here a reception-oriented understanding of grace. In contrast to this understanding, our analysis of the Communion Prayer has revealed that the grace of the new covenant is mediated through the liturgical action of giving thanks to God for his saving intervention in Jesus Christ. Put otherwise, God is conceived as acting to unite worshippers through Christ in the power of the Holy Spirit with himself and with one another precisely through their own prayer of thanksgiving and petition offered to the Father in faith.

It is important to bear in mind that we are saying no more here than what we have already demonstrated with regard to eucharistic praying in the preceding chapter. Let us recall that in Jewish liturgical prayer, it is through the table blessings (*Birkat ha-mazon*) that the presider expresses and realizes the intention of the community to receive the meal its members have enjoyed precisely as divine gift. Since the produce comes from the land that God gave to the people of Israel as a pledge of the covenant into which he entered with them, the table blessings appropriately include thanksgiving for the covenant (and the law by which this covenant relationship is lived out). From this observation we concluded that the offering of the table blessings for the meal can be seen to constitute the community's symbolic reception of God's gift of the covenant (and the law) together with its own identity as God's elect people. In other words, it is the recognition of the meal as bearing these significations that confers on it the status of divine gift. Of course, we cannot say that the faith itself expressed through the blessings makes of the meal a mediation of the grace of the covenant. We recognize the theological danger of suggesting that the saving encounter between God and human beings is dependent on human action, or that the saving acts of God somehow lie dormant until they are conjured up by the liturgical activity of the community. To be sure, God is not bound by the sacraments (*Deus non alligatur sacramentis*). Moreover, it is our conviction that the grace of God is reducible neither to a privileged scheme of representation nor to any academic explanation. But through the approach to the path of understanding the dynamic of eucharistic praying we have adopted in this investigation, we are led to maintain that insofar as the language of faith reveals the grace of the covenant by thankfully expressing it, this language at the same time makes that grace effective for those whom it inserts into a shared symbolic order to which the liturgical celebration itself belongs. In this perspective, liturgical rites are neither the celebration of an already-there grace nor the instrumental means for the production of this grace; they are linguistic mediations that allow the "real" to become meaningful and therefore effective for the liturgical community.[12]

Excursus: Jewish Rite of the First Fruits (Deuteronomy 26:1–11)

By the path opened up by this approach we can extend the insights we have gained thus far even further. An analysis of the Jewish rite of the first fruits offering recorded in Deuteronomy 26:1–11 will reinforce what we have already established, as well as further illustrate the dynamic of eucharistic praying that we have argued is discernible also in the Communion Prayer. Let us indicate at the outset the historical context in which the rite is to be performed. Israel has already come into the promised land, and is now concerned whether the God who demonstrated his power by bringing the people out of Egypt and giving them a land to possess is also able to make its fields fertile, so that the people may prosper in it. This is the concern to which this text responds by showing that it is the very "God of the Exodus, the God who has made Israel 'come into' the land… who also will make it possible for Israel to make food 'come forth' from the soil that God is giving them."[13]

   The rite instructs each Israelite to take some of the first fruit of the ground after harvest, place it in a basket, and present it before the priest at the temple (vs. 2). The presentation of the offering to the priest is accompanied by a declaration that interprets the ritual gesture: "Today I declare to the Lord your God that I have come into the land that the Lord swore to our ancestors to give us" (vs. 3). The Israelite repeats this declaration at the conclusion of the series of verbal-gestural acts that compose the rite: when he prostrates himself before the Lord at the altar with the offering, he is to say: "So now I bring the first of the fruit of the ground that you, O Lord, have given me" (vs. 10). Here too we may discern the same dynamic as we have been describing: it is through the offering of the first fruits that the Israelite (and all Israel as represented in the collective "I" of the first person singular) receives the land that God promised to give Israel to possess. The formal recognition of the fruits of the first harvest as a symbol of the fertile land with which God has blessed the people confers on it the status of a gift to be received from God.

But it remains to ask how this liturgical rite can be regarded as a "real" event of the mediation of God's grace. In other words, how is it possible that the Israelite can assert that it is "today" that "I have come into the land that God swore to our ancestors to give us" (vs. 3)? After all, the Israelite is temporally separated from the acts by which God rescued the people of Israel from Egypt and established them in the land he promised to give them to possess. A clue to the answer to this question can be found in the narrative that the two declarations frame. When the priest receives from the Israelite the basket and sets it before the altar of the Lord, the Israelite is to respond:

> A wandering Aramean was my ancestor; he went down into Egypt and lived there as an alien, few in number, and there he became a great nation, mighty and populous. When the Egyptians treated us harshly and afflicted us by imposing hard labor on us, we cried to the Lord, the God of our ancestors; the Lord heard our voice and saw our affliction, our toil, and our oppression. The Lord brought us out of Egypt with a mighty hand and an outstretched arm, with a terrifying display of power, and with signs and wonders; and he brought us into this place and gave us this land, a land flowing with milk and honey (vs. 5–9).

We can recognize in this narrative the dramatic story of Israel's origins. At the same time, however, we may see that in the context of the rite the events of the past relate to the Israelite as founding present.[14] According to liturgical theologian Louis-Marie Chauvet, it is in this context that "the epic deed of the Exodus is simultaneously event and advent."[15] It is legitimate to interpret the liturgical appropriation of the story of Israel's origins in these terms on the basis of two semantic observations. In the first place, the story is framed by declarations in the first person in the present tense, "Today I declare...", and "Now I bring..." These performative statements convey the formal recognition of the present reception of the land: it is not to our "ancestors," but to "us, who are all of us here alive today" (Deut. 5:3)—that the Lord has given the land.[16] In the second place, the narrator situates himself (and all Israel "alive today") in those past saving events by the use of the pronoun "we." By this linguistic change of register the narrator effectively transforms the story from only a mere report of historical events to a memorial confession of faith.[17] The verbal-gestural oblation of the first fruits that surround this memorial confession acts out what the memorial (*anamnesis*) grounds and authorizes. In light of the preceding analysis, then, we may conclude that this "liturgical process renders each Israelite contemporary with the divine history of the past, since the Lord gives fertility today just as he gave the land. To come into the sanctuary with the first fruits is to identify with the entrance of the people into the land of Canaan."[18]

When we return to a consideration of the eucharistic prayer of Hippolytus, it becomes clear that we are involved in a similar liturgical process. We have already shown that the dynamic of this prayer obeys the same internal logic as we have revealed to be evident in Jewish liturgical prayer. But in view of what we have just demonstrated with regard to the Jewish rite of the first fruits, we are now in a position to specify further how we understand the role of the institution narrative in this prayer. Let us acknowledge in the first place that this narrative is a story of the "institution" of the Christian Church. In the context of the eucharistic celebration we may regard it to function analogously to the story of Israel's origins in the Jewish rite of the first fruits. If this reading is permissible, then we may say that it does not function only as a report of a past event—in this case the Last Supper that Jesus and his disciples shared two thousand years ago. It functions also as founding present. This is evident in the fact that this narrative, although related as past event in the third person, is framed by a prayer of "you" and "we" addressed to God in the present tense. In this regard, let us note especially the transition from the words of Jesus in the institution narrative "Whenever you [the disciples] do this, you do it to commemorate me" to the words of the presider in the *anamnesis* of the eucharistic prayer "Remembering…we [the liturgical community in the present] offer." By substituting here the "we" for the "you," the prayer situates the community in the place of the disciples, thereby enabling it to hear the memorial command as if it were addressed to it. It is as if the community is avowing, "it is not to the disciples that Christ is addressing his command, but to us, all of us who are assembled here today."[19] The verbal-gestural oblation of the bread and the cup carry out what the institution narrative grounds and authorizes: the community signifies its reception of the bread and the cup as the sacramental body and blood of its Lord precisely through offering them in memorial thanksgiving. In this connection, the words of Louis Ligier will bear repeating: "The narrative is not recited for its own sake, as if it alone should constitute the action of the church; rather it serves to prepare and authorize the action of the church."[20]

The Problem of the Institution Narrative

Ligier's observation returns us to a problem that we have already identified in this and in earlier chapters. In the Order for the Sacrament of the Lord's Supper, the institution narrative is located after the Communion Prayer. At first glance, this position suggests that it is in fact recited for its own sake. That the committee was deliberate in placing the narrative in this position is seen when the Communion Prayer is compared with the eucharistic liturgy found in the *Liturgie de l'Eglise réformée de France*, from which the committee borrowed extensively. We have already emphasized that in the French eucharistic prayer the narrative is embedded in the context of the prayer itself, appearing before the *anamnesis/epiclesis* sections. Furthermore, we have argued that in this position it reveals more clearly that the *anamnesis* functions liturgically as a response to Jesus' command that the meal be celebrated in memory of him. Thus the French prayer appears to accord to the institution narrative a function that is similar to what we have attempted to demonstrate in the prayer of Hippolytus. To our knowledge, none on the committee explained the decision to depart here from the order in which the French prayer unfolds, which the committee otherwise carefully followed. Consequently, the interpreter can only advance hypotheses about the reasons. For our part, we suggest that a clue to the riddle may be the unexpressed *desideratum* of the committee to accommodate the structure of the order to the classic Reformed sacramental practice of "breaking the bread" (*fractio panis*). To clarify what we mean here, let us set this practice in its historical context.

In the first chapter we referred to the practice of "breaking the bread" when we surveyed the changes that the churches in the territory of the Palatinate were undergoing at the time of the Reformation.

The practice emerged as a distinguishing mark of these churches in the wake of the theological disputes between Lutheran and Reformed camps over the proper interpretation of the "real presence" of the Lord in the Supper. Tilman Hesshus, the Gnesio-Lutheran and fanatically anti-Calvinist superintendent of the churches, argued for an interpretation according to which the body and blood of the Lord are corporeally present in the elements of bread and wine. Against him the leaders of the Reformed camp insisted on a conception according to which the presence of the Lord is located in the action or use of the sacrament. The elector Frederic III eventually championed the Reformed conception, and ordered the churches in his territory to introduce the fraction rite, in which the minister was to break the bread ceremonially before the eyes of the worshippers before distributing the elements to them during communion. This practice was understood to express ritually the Reformed conception of the mode in which Christ is present in the celebration of the Lord's Supper. To affirm the modality of Christ's presence in the action of the "breaking" averted the danger of *verdiglichung*, of making of this presence a "thing"—a charge to which the Gnesio-Lutherans were open.[21] According to the Reformed camp, Christ cannot be enclosed in bread or otherwise corporeally present. To maintain this is to reduce the communion between Christ and the worshipper to a "physical" relationship, a *Bauchgemeinschaft* [communion of the belly] with Christ.[22] It is appropriate to refer to the "substantial presence" of the body of Christ only in the fraction and the distribution of the bread to the worshippers, who are nourished on Christ's body and blood through the instrumentality of the Holy Spirit. Apart from this action the bread is only bread.

How this conception is expressed through the rite of "breaking the bread" is explained in the seventy-fifth question and answer of the Heidelberg Catechism, which contains the theological presupposition for the practice:

> Question 75: How are you reminded and assured in the holy Supper that you participate in the one sacrifice on the cross and in all his benefits?
>
> In this way: Christ has commanded me and all believers to eat of this broken bread, and to drink of this cup in remembrance of him. He has thereby

promised that his body was offered and broken on the cross for me, and his
blood was shed for me, as surely as I see with my eyes that the bread of the
Lord is broken for me, and that the cup is shared...(emphasis added).[23]

We have already remarked that this statement reflects the conviction
of John Calvin, who maintained that Christ instituted the Supper so
that the faithful can see in the form of the action and the use of the
elements the very promises of the word displayed before the eyes. For
Calvin the sacrifice of Christ is shown in the Supper as if to set the
spectacle of the cross before the eyes of the faithful.

It is no accident that at the same time the Heidelberg Catechism
was published in 1563, there appeared a pamphlet that came to be
known as *Das Büchlein vom Brotbrechen* [The Little Book on Bread-
Breaking], written by Thomas Erastus, the rector of the University of
Heidelberg and relentless opponent of Hesshus.[24] Frederic III regarded the tract significant enough to include it with the letters that
he sent to the electors of Baden, Zweibrücken, and Württemberg in
May 1563 for the purpose of introducing the Catechism. This suggests
that if he had not actually commissioned Erastus to provide an apol-
ogy to the Lutheran princes for this practice in the churches of the Palatinate, at the very least he accepted the *Büchlein* as an official
explanation.[25] Erastus outlined three reasons on which the practice of
"breaking the bread" was based. In the first place, Jesus himself had
instituted it at the Last Supper; there is an obligation to imitate Jesus'
example in this regard in order to express proper obedience to his
command, "do this in memory of me." Second, this command appears to be implied in the phrase "breaking of bread", which is used
in Acts 2 and 20 to designate the apostolic Church's Eucharist. And
finally, the people need a visual action to instruct them concerning
two truths that the Supper sets forth: (1) the bread broken and the cup
poured out are images of the suffering of the death of the Lord on the
cross; and (2) the breaking of the one bread teaches and reminds the
worshippers "through their eyes" that they are all members of the one
body of Christ, since they all receive from the one loaf of bread.[26]

In our estimation it is the theological consideration suggested by
this third reason that probably determined the decision of the committee to place the institution narrative after the Communion Prayer.
At the moment in the eucharistic liturgy where the presider recites

the institution narrative, he or she at the same time is to dramatize the actions of Jesus as they are recounted in the text, at the places in the narrative that the rubrical instructions designate:

> The Lord Jesus, the same night in which he was betrayed, took bread [here he shall take the bread in his hand]; and when he had given thanks, he broke it [here the minister shall break the bread] and gave it to them...After the same manner also he took the cup [here the minister shall take the cup in his hand]...[27]

When the committee decided to link the *fractio panis* with the recitation of the institution narrative in this way, it could not do otherwise than to place the narrative outside the Communion Prayer itself. The interpreter will realize this necessity when he or she discovers that worshippers in the congregations of the RCA pray with their heads bowed and their eyes closed; therefore, to include the *fractio panis* within a prayer of the Eucharist would defeat its purpose. It is important for the worshippers to see as well as to hear the promises of their redemption through the sacrifice of Christ for them, a sacrifice that is both proclaimed and portrayed in the Lord's Supper.

The decision to place the institution narrative after the Communion Prayer is in our opinion the signal case in which the attempt to integrate contemporary liturgical scholarship and classic Reformed sacramental theology has created tensions of which the committee did not seem to be aware. This decision clearly is not congruent with the conclusions that recent liturgical research has drawn concerning the institution narrative, as we have already brought out. According to the analysis of the eucharistic prayer of Hippolytus, as we have been developing it here, the institution narrative is not an independent formula to be enlisted in the service of expressing a confessional identity-marker, but an embolism that receives its meaning on the basis of its position relative to the other elements that constitute the prayer. We have already described its functions in both this prayer and the ERF prayer. If we have done this correctly, it will have already become apparent that the institution narrative, *anamnesis*, and self-offering belong together as a complex unit. The absence of the narrative from this complex in the Communion Prayer does not frustrate the dynamic movement of this prayer as we have carefully traced it in the first section of this chapter. But in its position after the Communion Prayer it certainly does not cohere with this movement.

If the isolation of the institution narrative from this prayer of the Eucharist in fact has its origins in the polemic waged against the Gnesio-Lutherans over the proper conception of the "real presence," then it is necessary to revisit the question about its position. Future committees will critically appreciate that sacramental concepts and practices forged in the fire of confessional controversies ought not to be abstracted from their historical contexts. While developed in their own contexts to defend the faith against distortion or misinterpretation, these concepts and practices certainly need to be re-evaluated in the current ecumenical context to determine whether they still function in this role for the faith today. We do not approach the problems today with the same concerns, the same patterns of understanding and interpretation, that the Reformers imposed on the texts and traditions in their day. Even John Nevin over a century and half ago observed that the Reformers revealed no awareness of the early liturgies. To this we may add that neither did they give evidence of a knowledge of the origin, development, and shape of the early eucharistic prayers, which only later liturgical scholarship has reconstructed. Familiarizing themselves with this scholarship, future committees will perhaps conclude that a theology of the Eucharist derived from the *lex orandi* suggests, *inter alia*, that the institution narrative ought to be restored to the complex, which consists in narrative-*anamnesis*-self-offering.

Conclusion

T his investigation has encompassed over four hundred years. We have engaged in the exercise of historical retrieval and interpretation to determine the elements of the order of the Lord's Supper as it has been celebrated in the RCA from its origins in the Palatinate Reformation. Only in narrating this history from the very beginning has it proved possible to demonstrate convincingly that the tradition of this celebration has undergone a real transformation.

We began in the German territory of the Rhine Palatinate at the time of the Reformation. We learned through an investigation of the political and ecclesial vicissitudes of this territory about the instrumental role that elector Frederic III (r. 1559–1576) played in the origin of this tradition. In order to promote and consolidate the ecclesiastical reforms in his territory, he commissioned early in 1562 a group of theologians to produce a church order. Central to the Church Order of the Palatinate is the Heidelberg Catechism. Intended to serve as a norm for life, doctrine, and worship in the Reformed churches of the territory, this catechism understandably influenced the composition of the form for the Holy Supper. This form bears the impress of the Heidelberg Catechism in structure, theological content, and even wording. For the drafters of the form, the celebration of the Lord's Supper provided the occasion *par excellence* to expound precisely in the terms of the catechism the saving death of Christ and the manner in which it must be appropriated. The pedagogical purposes for which the drafters enlisted the celebration emerged in the course of our analysis of the structure and content of the form. The heavy emphasis on penitential preparation, the careful elaboration of doctrine (christology, soteriology, and sacramentology), and the extensive post-communion thanksgiving reflect the *desideratum* of the drafters to recapitulate the threefold scheme of the catechism in their form. To live and die in the comfort of the Christian faith, according to the Heidelberg Catechism, worshippers must know their own sin and misery, how they have been freed from this sin and misery, and the gratitude they owe to God for this redemption.

The Reformed Churches in the Netherlands and in America sought to adhere to the Christian faith articulated in the Heidelberg Cathechism and the form for the Holy Supper. Petrus Dathenus, pastor of a small congregation of Dutch refugees in the Palatinate territory, prepared a translation of the form into Dutch already in 1566. In 1618-1619 the national Synod of Dordrecht (Dort) authorized this form, and directed that it be added to the public documents of the Reformed Church in the Netherlands. The form, contained now in the Netherlands Liturgy, accompanied the Dutch colonists who began to immigrate to the new world only ten years after the Synod of Dort concluded its sessions. In 1788 the General Synod of the Dutch Reformed Church in North America appointed a committee to translate and revise the entire Church Order of Dort, as well as the doctrinal standards and the Netherlands Liturgy. Although this committee introduced changes to the Church Order of Dort to adapt it to new conditions in the now independent United States of America, it did not alter the form for the Supper. Until the liturgical reforms implemented in the twentieth century, it continued its official life in the renamed RCA as the principal form for the celebration of the Lord's Supper.

But already in the mid-nineteenth century there were developments that presaged these later liturgical reforms. In an attempt to establish itself more firmly in a rapidly changing American frontier, the Dutch Reformed Church in North America (DRC) sought to enter into an alliance with the emergent German Reformed Church in the United States (GRC). These two ecclesial bodies traced their origins from the Reformation in the Palatinate, formally adhered to the Heidelberg Catechism as a confessional standard, and acknowledged the Palatinate liturgy as the source of their common worship tradition. Because of these strong affinities, it was only natural that they began to devise plans for merger in the early nineteenth century. These plans failed to materialize, however, due to the rise of the Mercersburg theology in the GRC in the 1840s. The crisis precipitated by the

Mercersburg theologians, the most outstanding among whom were John Nevin and Philip Schaff, concerned foundational issues in the worship life of the Reformed churches on the American frontier. Nevin especially decried the churches' adoption of revivalistic techniques, which not only eroded the order of worship, but also reflected a distorted conception of the nature of the Church. Nevin and his supporters soon found a platform on which to promote the themes of the Mercersburg theology. In 1847 the GRC commissioned them to prepare a new liturgy. Against their detractors the Mercersburg theologians insisted that they had no intention of undermining the substance of the Reformed faith; they only refused to defend and consolidate the liturgical traditions that originated in the sixteenth century Reformation. Instead they appropriated patristic sources to establish a liturgical order of worship on the foundation of an "evangelical catholicity," which relativized the Reformation. They argued that they were not thereby abolishing their confessional heritage, but preserving its true essence. Indeed John Nevin was convinced that his rehabilitation of John Calvin's doctrine of the mystical union (*unio mystica*), according to which union of the faithful with the risen and glorified Christ is mediated by the symbols of bread and wine in the power of the Holy Spirit, necessitated the liturgical reforms they were advocating. The omission of the sacrament of the Lord's Supper from regular worship distorted the reception of the distinctive features of the tradition that originated in Calvin. To the chagrin of Nevin and his supporters, the liturgical reforms experienced very limited success in the congregations of the GRC. But the liturgies that they published exercised a wide influence beyond the boundaries of their small denomination. Even the DRC (later RCA), which had severed its ties with the GRC in the 1840s, was prepared already in the early 1870s to adopt a eucharistic prayer. We showed how this prayer, although badly mutilated by subsequent liturgical committees, served later in this denomination as the point of departure for the reconstruction of its order for the Lord's Supper in the twentieth century.

We pointed out that several competent scholars have already investigated these developments, including Howard G. Hageman, Jack M. Maxwell, Daniel M. Meeter, and Gregg A. Mast. Mast concluded his study of the liturgical renewals in the Reformed churches of the nineteenth century with the assertion that this history prepared the soil in which the liturgical and ecumenical movements of the twentieth century could germinate in them.[1] Our contribution to the historical research into the liturgical thought and practice of the RCA was to extend the narrative to the twentieth century. We showed how these movements that influenced the major ecclesial traditions—Protestant, Roman Catholic, and Orthodox—created a climate for liturgical study and reform never before seen in the history of the Christian churches. Ecumenical dialogue, informed by the critical research into the origins and development of liturgical traditions, succeeded in achieving a broad consensus among the Reformed churches concerning the form of eucharistic celebrations. Under the leadership of Howard G. Hageman, the RCA was prompted by the changes in the churches worldwide to reflect more deeply about the formulation of its own liturgy and an understanding of its use. This process led to the composition and adoption of the Communion Prayer, which in our estimation marks a high point in the tradition of its celebration of the Lord's Supper.

We did not limit our investigation, however, to a survey of this history. We also set the more ambitious goal of showing how the "transformation in tradition" has consequences for the meaning itself of the Lord's Supper. In the path that we followed we diverged from an approach favored generally among Reformed theologians and historians. These scholars have tended to regard liturgy rather restrictively as a constellation of theological themes that may or may not be suitable for expression in Reformed worship. They have conceived as their project the testing of these themes against the theological doctrines that can be derived from texts in Scripture and in the Reformed confessions. On the basis of new exegetical and historical research into these texts, theological insights are reclaimed and introduced into revised liturgies, which in any case are intended to remain in the trajectory of an authentically Reformed tradition.

We considered this approach to be probematic because it regards the world of the celebration itself as a secondary concern. In this approach scholars have recourse first to theological doctrines, which they formulate apart from the liturgical celebration, and then apply them to the celebration in order to illuminate its meaning. "The theology of the liturgy" then becomes "the theology of the sacraments," which is itself elaborated without reference to the "ordo" of worship or the structure of the liturgy.[2] We have already seen in the third chapter how the didactic "Instruction" that precedes the Communion Prayer reflects and perpetuates this approach.

In contrast, we approached the Communion Prayer on the basis of the principles that emerged from our study of the structure and dynamic of early eucharistic praying. Our decision in this regard was guided by the conviction that liturgy is not a theological discourse about God, Christ, the Spirit, the Church and the world; rather it is a symbolic and ritual action in words and gestures that expresses its meaning in its performance. The theology of the liturgy is second order reflection on what faith discerns about the meaning of the celebration as it is enacted. Thus it must be attentive to the entire liturgical action, its structure and expression, in order to draw the theology from the world of the celebration itself. For this reason, the theological doctrines connected with the traditional Reformed Lord's Supper—real presence, mystical union with Christ in the Holy Spirit, *Christus in circumscriptio loco*, and eschatological banquet—received less attention in this study than the categories of *anamnesis*, *epiclesis*, *eucharistia*, and the *pasch* of Jesus Christ.

Whether or not we succeeded in uncovering the underlying meaning-intention of the Communion Prayer by means of our approach, we must leave the reader to decide. No doubt many will object that there is no consensus on the relationship between the *lex orandi* and *lex credendi* among the Reformed churches. In contrast to the Roman Catholic, Orthodox, and even the Anglican churches, the Reformed churches, at least in practice, have never been bound to their liturgical forms. The Reformed churches have served traditionally as examples of "orthodox" societies in which more emphasis is placed on doctrinal beliefs, rather than of "orthopraxic" societies in which more emphasis is placed on proper performance of rites. And, as we have already observed, these doctrinal beliefs are achieved independently of liturgical practice. Consequently, those who are interested in learning what the Reformed churches believe concerning the Lord's Supper will naturally turn to someone thoroughly catechized in the Reformed confessions. Yet the student of liturgy may ask whether even in Reformed churches a view of God, human beings, and the world is at least as transparent through a reflective observation of the actual expressions of worship as through a careful hearing of discursive speech about what these worshippers believe.

If this is true, then Reformed theologians cannot afford to neglect a direct analysis of liturgical expressions in their churches, that is, if they still desire that their churches maintain their identity as specifically Christian and Reformed. For their part, the members appointed to the Committee on the Revision of The Liturgy by the RCA Synod in 1950 were aware that the theological integrity of their ecclesial tradition depended on the consistency between the theology of the Reformed confessions and that expressed in worship. The work we have done has perhaps shown us to be even more sensitive to this relationship, insofar as we have been more concerned about the reciprocity between the *lex credendi* and *lex orandi*. Our insight into sacramental celebrations as linguistic mediations of the "real" have taught us that liturgical practice does not merely give expression to prior theological formulae; it also acts on them by creating and reinforcing in the worshippers attitudes and orientations that are activated when the sacraments are celebrated. As a renowned scholar in the psychology of religion has explained:

> the expression of religious convictions in worship are not of the order of constative language. In giving expressive form to his attitude toward God the believer at the same time completes the attitude by making it his own, confirming its truth both for himself and towards God. His statement is therefore both expressive and performative. These terms designate the dual function of religious practice: the assumption of religious attitude and its achievement. Religious acts may arise from a religious orientation, and in that context may be called consequences. But they also bring about that orientation, and in that perspective they constitute the religion itself in act and the process of becoming, and not merely its effects. Understanding theology therefore also means understanding how the theology emerges through the performative practices.[3]

If this phenomenological insight into the efficacy of performative practices is valid, then the method that we have employed to uncover the meaning of the Communion Prayer is certainly legitimate. In the performance of the Eucharist as it is determined by the Communion

Prayer, we have seen that the Lord's Supper is no mere *verbum visibile*, an appendix to the proclamation of the satisfaction made by Christ and of the gift of Christ's righteousness. It is a dynamic ecclesial event of a transformative interaction with the triune God. The grace of the covenant from the Father through the Son in the Spirit is expressed and actualized through the participation of the community in the self-offering of the incarnate Son to the Father in the Spirit.

Appendix A

The Unabridged Form for the Sacrament of the Lord's Supper

Beloved in the Lord Jesus Christ, attend to the words of institution of the holy Supper of our Lord Jesus Christ, as they are delivered by the Apostle Paul:

1. "For I have received of the Lord that which I also delivered unto you, That the Lord Jesus, the same night in which he was betrayed, took bread; and when he had given thanks, he brake it, and said, Take, eat: this is my body, which is broken for you: this do in remembrance of me. After the same manner also he took the cup, when he had supped, saying, This cup is the new testament in my blood: this do ye, as oft as ye drink it, in remembrance of me. For as often as ye eat this bread, and drink this cup, ye do show the Lord's death until he come. Wherefore, whosoever shall eat this bread, and drink this cup of the Lord unworthily, shall be guilty of the body and blood of the Lord. But let a man examine himself, and so let him eat of that bread and drink of that cup; for he that eats and drinks unworthily, eats and drinks damnation to himself, not discerning the Lord's body."

   That we may now celebrate the Supper of our Lord to our comfort, it is above all things necessary:

   I. Rightly to examine ourselves.
   II. To direct the Supper to that end for which Christ has ordained and instituted the same, namely, to his remembrance.

2. The true examination of ourselves consists of these three parts:

   a. *First.* That everyone consider by himself his sins and the curse due to him for them, to the end that he may abhor and humble himself before God; considering that the wrath of God against sin is so great, that, rather than it should go unpunished, he has punished the same in his beloved Son Jesus Christ, with the bitter and shameful death of the cross.

   b. *Secondly.* That everyone should examine his own heart, whether he believes this faithful promise of God, that all his sins are forgiven him only for the sake of the passion and death of Jesus Christ; and that the perfect righteousness of Christ is imputed and freely given him as his own, yea, so perfectly as if he had satisfied in his own person for all his sins, and fulfilled all righteousness.

c. *Thirdly.* That everyone should examine his own conscience, whether he purposes henceforth to show true thankfulness to God in his whole life, and to walk uprightly before him; as also, whether he has laid aside unfeignedly all enmity, hatred, and envy, and does firmly resolve henceforth to walk in true love and peace with his neighbor.

All those, then, who are thus disposed God will certainly receive in mercy, and count them worthy partakers of the Table of his Son Jesus Christ. On the contrary, those who do not feel this testimony in their hearts eat and drink judgment to themselves.

3. Therefore, we also, according to the command of Christ and the Apostle Paul, admonish all those who are defiled with following sins to keep themselves from the Table of the Lord, and declare to them that they have no part of the kingdom of Christ: such as all idolators; all those who invoke deceased saints, angels, or other creatures; all those who worship images: all enchanters, diviners, charmers, and those who confide in such enchantments; all despisers of God and his Word, and of the holy Sacraments; all blasphemers; all those who are given to raise discord, sects, and mutiny, in church or state; all perjured persons; all those who are disobedient to their parents and superiors; all murderers, contentious persons, and those who live in hatred and envy against their neighbors; all adulterers, whoremongers, drunkards, thieves, usurers, robbers, gamesters, covetous; and all those who lead offensive lives.

All these, while they continue in such sins, shall abstain from this meat, which Christ has ordained only for the faithful, lest their condemnation and judgment be made the heavier.

4. But this is not designed, dearly loved Brethren and Sisters in the Lord, to deject the contrite hearts of the faithful, as if none might come to the Supper of the Lord but those who are without sin. For we do not come to this Supper to testify thereby that we are perfect and righteous in ourselves; but, on the contrary, considering that we seek our life out of ourselves, in Jesus Christ, we acknowledge that we lie in the midst of death. Therefore, notwithstanding we feel many infirmities and miseries in ourselves; as namely, that we have not perfect faith, and that we do not give ourselves to serve God with such zeal as we are bound, but have daily to strive with the weakness of our faith and the evil lusts of our flesh; yet, since we are, by the grace of the

Holy Ghost, sorry for these weaknesses, and earnestly desire to fight against our unbelief, and to live according to all the commandments of God, therefore we rest assured that no sin or infirmity, which still remains against our will in us, can hinder us from being received of God in mercy, and from being made worthy partakers of this heavenly meat and drink.

5. Let us now also consider to what end the Lord has instituted his Supper, namely, that we do it in remembrance of him. Now, after this manner are we to remember him by it.

    a. 1. That we be confidently persuaded in our hearts, that our Lord Jesus Christ, according to the promises made to our forefathers in the Old Testament, was sent of the Father into the world: that he assumed our flesh and blood: that he bore for us the wrath of God, under which we should have perished everlastingly, from the beginning of his incarnation to the end of his life upon earth: that he fulfilled for us all obedience to the divine law, and righteousness, especially when the weight of our sins and the wrath of God pressed out of him the bloody sweat in the garden, where he was bound that we might be freed from our sinss: that he afterward suffered innumerable reproaches, that we might never be confounded; that he, although innocent, was condemned to death, that we might be acquitted at the judgment seat of God: yea, that he suffered his blessed body to be nailed on the cross, that he might affix thereon the handwriting of our sins: that he also took upon himself the curse due to us, that he might fill us with his blessings: that he humbled himself unto the deepest reproach and pains of hell, both in body and soul, on the tree of the cross, when he cried out in a loud voice, "My God, my God, why hast thou forsaken me?" that we might be accepted of God, and never be forsaken of him: and finally that he confirmed, with his death and shedding of his blood, the new and eternal testament, that covenant of grace and reconciliation, when he said, "It is finished."

    b. 2. And, that we might firmly believe that we belong to this covenant of grace, the Lord Jesus Christ, in his last Supper, "took bread, and when he had given thanks, he brake it, and gave it to his disciples, and said, Take, eat, this is my body which is broken for you, this do in remembrance of me. In like manner also, after supper, he took the cup, gave thanks and said, Drink ye all of it; this cup is the new testament in my blood, which is shed for you and for many for the remission of sins; this do ye, as often as ye drink it, in remembrance of me." That is: as often as you eat of this bread and drink of this cup, you shall thereby, as by a sure remembrance and pledge, be admonished and assured of this my hearty love and faithfulness toward you: that whereas you should have otherwise have suffered eternal death, I have given my body to the death of the cross, and shed my blood for you; and as certainly feed and nourish your hungry and thirsty soul with my crucified body and shed blood to everlasting life, as this bread is broken before your eyes, and this cup is given to you, and you eat and drink the same with your mouth in remembrance of me.From this institution of the holy Supper of our Lord Jesus Christ, we see that he directs our faith and trust to his perfect sacrifice, once offered on the cross, as to the only ground and foundation of our salvation; wherein he is become to our hungry and thirsty souls the true meat and drink of life eternal. For by his death he has taken away the cause of our eternal death and misery, namely, sin; and obtained for us the quickening Spirit, that we by the same, which dwells in Christ as the Head and in us as his members, might have true communion with him, and be made partakers of all his blessings, of life eternal, righteousness, and glory.

c. Besides, that we, by the same Spirit, may also be united as members of one body, in true brotherly love; as the holy Apostle says, "For we, being many, are one bread and one body; for we are all partakers of one that one bread." For as out of many grains one meal is ground and one bread baked, and out of many berries being pressed together one wine flows and mixes itself together; so shall we all, who by a true faith are ingrafted into Christ, through brotherly love be all together one body, for the sake of Christ, our beloved Savior, who has so exceedingly loved us; and shall show this, not only in word, but also in very deed toward one another.

Hereto assist us, the almighty God and Father of our Lord Jesus Christ, through his Holy Spirit. AMEN.

That we may obtain all this, let us humble ourselves before God, and with true faith implore his grace.

6. O most merciful God and Father, we beseech thee that thou wilt be pleased, in this Supper, in which we celebrate the glorious remembrance of the bitter death of thy beloved Son Jesus Christ, to work in our hearts through the Holy Spirit, that we may daily, more and more, with true confidence, give ourselves up unto thy Son Jesus Christ, so that our afflicted and contrite hearts, through the power of the Holy Ghost, may be fed and comforted with his true body and blood; yea, with him, true God and true Man, that only heavenly bread: and that we may no longer live in our sins, but he in us, and we in him; and thus truly be made partakers of the new and everlasting testament and covenant of grace: that we may not doubt that thou wilt for ever be our gracious Father, never more imputing our sins unto us, and providing us, as thy beloved children and heirs, with all things neces-

sary, as well for the body as the soul. Grant us also thy grace, that we may take upon us our cross cheerfully, deny ourselves, confess our Savior, and in all tribulations with uplifted heads expect our Lord Jesus Christ from heaven, where he will make our mortal bodies like unto his most glorious body and take us unto himself in eternity.

OUR FATHER, WHO ART IN HEAVEN, HALLOWED BE THY NAME, THY KINGDOM COME, THY WILL BE DONE ON EARTH AS IT IS IN HEAVEN. GIVE US THIS DAY OUR DAILY BREAD. AND FORGIVE US OUR DEBTS, AS WE FORGIVE OUR DEBTORS. AND LEAD US NOT INTO TEMPTATION, BUT DELIVER US FROM EVIL; FOR THINE IS THE KINGDOM, AND THE POWER, AND THE GLORY, FOREVER. AMEN.

7. Strengthen us also by this holy Supper in the Catholic undoubted Christian Faith, whereof we make confession with our mouths and hearts, saying:

I BELIEVE IN GOD THE FATHER ALMIGHTY, MAKER OF HEAVEN AND EARTH; AND IN JESUS CHRIST HIS ONLY SON, OUR LORD; WHO WAS CONCEIVED BY THE HOLY GHOST, BORN OF THE VIRGIN MARY; SUFFERED UNDER PONTIUS PILATE, WAS CRUCIFIED, DEAD, AND BURIED; HE DESCENDED INTO HELL; THE THIRD DAY HE ROSE AGAIN FROM THE DEAD; HE ASCENDED INTO HEAVEN, AND SITTETH ON THE RIGHT HAND OF GOD THE FATHER ALMIGHTY; FROM THENCE HE SHALL COME TO JUDGE THE QUICK AND THE DEAD. I BELIEVE IN THE HOLY GHOST; THE HOLY CATHOLIC CHURCH; THE COMMUNION OF SAINTS; THE FORGIVENESS OF SINS; THE RESURRECTION OF THE BODY; AND THE LIFE EVERLASTING. AMEN.

8. That we may be now fed with the true heavenly bread, Christ Jesus, let us not cleave with our hearts unto the external bread and wine, but lift them on high in heaven, where Christ Jesus is our Advocate, at the right hand of his heavenly Father, whither all the Articles of our Faith lead us; not doubting that, through the working of the Holy Ghost, we shall as certainly be fed and refreshed in our souls with his body and blood, as we receive the holy bread and wine in remembrance of him.

9. *In breaking and distributing the bread, the minister shall say:*

The Bread which we break is the communion of the Body of Christ.

And when he gives the cup:

The Cup of Blessing which we bless is the communion of the Blood of Christ.

During the Communion, a Psalm shall or may be devoutly sung, or some chapter read, in remembrance of the death of Christ, as Isaiah 53, John 13, 14, 15, 16, 17, 18, or the like.

After the Communion the minister shall say:

10. Beloved in the Lord, since the Lord has now fed our souls at his Table, let us therefore jointly praise his holy name with thanksgiving, and every one say in his heart thus:

Bless the Lord, O my soul:
AND ALL THAT IS WITHIN ME, BLESS HIS HOLY NAME.
Bless the Lord, O my soul,
AND FORGET NOT ALL HIS BENEFITS:
Who forgiveth all thine iniquities,
WHO HEALETH ALL THY DISEASES;
Who redeemeth thy life from destruction;
WHO CROWNETH THEE WITH LOVINGKINDNESS
AND TENDER MERCIES.
The Lord is merciful and gracious,
SLOW TO ANGER, AND PLENTEOUS IN MERCY.
He hath not dealt with us after our sins;
NOR REWARDED US ACCORDING TO OUR INIQUITIES.
For as the heaven is high above the earth,
SO GREAT IS HIS MERCY TOWARD THEM THAT FEAR HIM.
As far as the east is from the west.
SO FAR HATH HE REMOVED OUR TRANSGRESSIONS FROM US.
Like as a father pitieth his children.
SO THE LORD PITIETH THEM THAT FEAR HIM.

Who hath not spared his own Son, but delivered him up for us all, and given us all things with him. Therefore God commends therewith his love toward us, in that while we were yet sinners, Christ died for us; much more then, being now justified by his blood, we shall be saved from wrath through him. For, if, when we were enemies, we were reconciled to God by the death of his Son; much more, being reconciled, we shall be saved by his life. Therefore shall my mouth and heart show forth the praise of the Lord from this time forth for evermore.

Let everyone say with an attentive heart:

ALMIGHTY, MERCIFUL GOD AND FATHER, WE RENDER THEE MOST HUMBLE AND HEARTY THANKS, THAT THOU HAS, OF THINE INFINITE MERCY, GIVEN US THIINE ONLY BEGOTTEN SON, FOR A MEDIATOR AND A SACRIFICE FOR OUR SINS, AND TO BE OUR MEAT AND DRINK UNTO LIFE ETERNAL; AND THAT THOU GIVEST US LIVELY FAITH, WHEREBY WE ARE MADE PARTAKERS OF THESE THY BENEFITS. THOU HAST ALSO BEEN PLEASED, THAT THY BELOVED SON JESUS CHRIST SHOULD INSTITUTE AND ORDAIN HIS HOLY SUPPER FOR THE CONFIRMATION OF THE SAME. GRANT, WE BESEECH THEE, O FAITHFUL GOD AND FATHER, THAT, THROUGH THE OPERATION OF THY HOLY SPIRIT, THE COMMEMORATION OF THE DEATH OF OUR LORD JESUS CHRIST MAY TEND TO THE DAILY INCREASE OF OUR FAITH, AND OF OUR SAVING FELLOWSHIP WITH HIM; THROUGH JESUS CHRIST THY SON, OUR LORD.AMEN.

Appendix B

Eucharistic Prayer

The Constitution of the Church directs that in the administration of the Lord's Supper, "after the sermon and usual prayers are ended, the Form for the administration of the Lord's Supper shall be read, and a prayer suited to the occasion shall be offered, before the members participate of the ordinance."

The following is submitted as suitable prayer, which may be used in compliance with this direction.

It is very meet and right, above all things, to give thanks unto Thee, O Eternal God: Who by Thy word didst create heaven and earth, and all things therein. For all Thy bounties known to us, for all unknown, we give Thee thanks: but chiefly, that when, through disobedience, we had fallen from Thee, Thou didst not suffer us to depart from Thee forever, but hast ransomed us from eternal death, and given us the joyful hope of everlasting life, through Jesus Christ Thy Son; Who, being Very and Eternal God, became Man for us men, and for our salvation.

Not as we are ought, but as we are able, we bless Thee for His holy incarnation; for His life on earth; for His precious sufferings and death upon the cross; for His resurrection from the dead; and His glorious ascension to Thy right hand.

We bless Thee for the giving of the Holy Ghost; for the sacraments and ordinances of the Church; for the communion of Christ's Body and Blood; for the great hope of everlasting life, and of an eternal weight of glory.

Thee, Mighty God, Heavenly King, we magnify and praise. With angels and archangels, and all the hosts of heaven, we worship and adore Thy glorious name, joining in the song of the Cherubim and Seraphim, and saying:

HOLY, HOLY, HOLY, LORD GOD OF SABAOTH, HEAVEN AND EARTH ARE FULL OF THY GLORY. HOSANNA IN THE HIGHEST. BLESSED IS HE THAT COMETH IN THE NAME OF THE LORD. HOSANNA IN THE HIGHEST.

And we most humbly beseech Thee, O Merciful Father, to vouchsafe unto us Thy gracious presence, as we commemorate in this Supper the most blessed sacrifice of Thy Son; and to bless and sanctify with Thy Word and Spirit these Thine own gifts of bread and wine which we set before Thee; that we receiving them, according to our

Saviour's institution, in thankful remembrance of His death and passion, may, through the power of the Holy Ghost, be very partakers of His body and blood, with all His benefits, to our salvation and the glory of Thy Most Holy Name.

And here we offer and present to Thee, O Lord, ourselves, our souls and bodies, to be a reasonable, holy, and living sacrifice unto Thee; humbly beseeching Thee that all who are partakers of this Holy Communion, may be filled with Thy grace and heavenly benediction. And although we may be unworthy, through our manifold sins, to offer unto Thee any sacrifice, yet we beseech Thee to accept this our bounden duty and service; not weighing our merits, but pardoning our offences through Jesus Christ our Lord.

And rejoicing in the communion of Thy saints, we bless Thy Holy Name for all Thy servants who have departed in the faith, and who, having accomplished their warfare, are at rest with Thee; beseeching Thee to enable us so to follow their faith and good example, that we with them may finally be partakers of Thy heavenly Kingdom — when, made like unto Christ, we shall behold Him with unveiled face, rejoicing in His glory, and by Him we, with all Thy Church, holy and unspotted, shall be presented with exceeding joy before the presence of Thy glory. Hear us, O Heavenly Father, for His sake: to Whom, with Thee and the Holy Ghost, be glory for ever and ever. Amen.

Appendix C

The Abridged Form for the Sacrament of the Lord's Supper

Prayer

1. EP. It is very meet and right, above all things, to give thanks unto thee, O eternal God. For all thy bounties known to us, for all unknown, we give thee thanks; but chiefly, that when, through disobedience, we had fallen from thee, thou didst not suffer us to depart from thee forever, but hast ransomed us from eternal death, and given us the joyful hope of everlasting life, through Jesus Christ thy Son; who being true and eternal God, became Man for us men, and for our salvation. Not as we ought but as we are able, we bless thee for his holy incarnation; for his life on earth; for his precious sufferings and death upon the cross; for his resurrection from the dead; and for his glorious ascension to thy right hand. We bless thee for the giving of the Holy Spirit; for the sacraments and ordinances of the Church; for the communion of Christ's body and blood; for the great hope of everlasting life, and of an eternal weight of glory.

    Thee, mighty God, heavenly King, we magnify and praise. With angels and archangels, and all the hosts of heaven, we worship and adore thy glorious name.

2. EP. We most humbly beseech thee, O merciful Father, to vouchsafe unto us thy gracious presence, as we commemorate in this Supper the most blessed sacrifice of thy Son; and to bless and sanctify with thy Word and Spirit these thine own gifts of bread and wine, which we set before thee; that we, receiving them, according to our Savior's institution, in thankful remembrance of his death and passion, may, through the power of the Holy Spirit, be made true partakers of his body and blood, with all his benefits, to our salvation and the glory of thy most holy name. AMEN.

Words of Institution

Beloved in the Lord Jesus Christ, attend to the words of the institution of the holy Supper of our Lord Jesus Christ, as they are delivered by the Apostle Paul:

1. "For I have received of the Lord that which also I delivered unto you, That the Lord Jesus, the same night in which he was betrayed, took bread; and when he had given thanks, he brake it, and said, Take, eat: this is my body, which is broken for you: this do in remembrance of me. After the same manner also he took the cup, when he had supped, saying, This cup is the new testament in my blood: this do ye, as oft as ye drink it, in remembrance of me. For as often as ye eat this bread, and drink this cup, ye do show the Lord's death till he come."

Exhortation to Self-Examination

2. That we may now celebrate the Supper of the Lord to our comfort, it is necessary, first, rightly to examine ourselves, and, secondly, to direct the Supper to that end for which it was instituted by our Lord Jesus Christ.

   Let everyone, therefore, first consider his sins and the curse due to him for them, that he may truly humble himself before God. Let everyone also examine his own heart, whether he believes this faithful promise of God, that all his sins are forgiven him only for the sake of the passion and death of Jesus Christ; and that the perfect righteousness of Christ is imputed and freely given to him as his own, even as perfectly as if he had satisfied in his own person for all his sins and fulfilled all righteousness. Finally, let everyone examine his conscience, whether he purposes henceforth to show true thankfulness to God in his whole life, to walk uprightly before him, and to live in love and peace with his neighbor.

   All those who are thus minded God will certainly receive in mercy, and count them worthy partakers of the Table of his Son Jesus Christ. On the contrary, according to the command of Christ and the Apostle Paul, we admonish all those who are continuing in unrepented sin to keep themselves from the Lord's Table.

3. But this is not designed, dearly beloved Brethren and Sisters in the Lord, to distress the contrite hearts of his people, as if none might come to his Table but those who are without sin. For we do not come to this Supper to testify that we are righteous in ourselves, but rather that we are conscious of our sinfulness and trust in Jesus Christ alone for our salvation. Therefore, notwithstanding we feel that we have not perfect faith, and that we do not serve God with such zeal as we are bound, but have daily to strive with the weakness of our faith and the evil lusts of our flesh; yet since we are, by the grace of the Holy Spirit, sorry for these weaknesses, and eanestly desirous to fight against our unbelief and to live according to all the commandments of God, therefore we rest assured that no sin or infirmity, which still remains

against our will in us, can hinder us from being received of God in mercy, and from being made worthy partakers of this heavenly food.

Meaning of the Sacrament

4. Let us also consider to what end the Lord has instituted his Supper: "This do," he said, "in remembrance of me."

    a. We are, therefore, to remember that our Lord Jesus Christ, according to the promises made in the Old Testament, was sent of the Father into the world; that he assumed our flesh and blood; that he bore for us the wrath of God, under which we should have perished everlastingly; that he fulfilled for us all obedience to the divine law; that he, although innocent, was condemned to death that we might be acquitted at the judgment seat of God; that he took upon himself the curse due to us, that he might fill us with his blessings; that he humbled himself unto death, even the bitter and shameful death of the cross, when he cried out with a loud voice, "My God, my God, why hast thou forsaken me?" that we might be accepted of God and never be forsaken of him; and finally, that he confirmed with the shedding of his blood the new and eternal covenant of grace and reconciliation, when he said, "It is finished."

    b. That we might firmly believe that we belong to this covenant of grace, the Lord Jesus, the same night he was betrayed, instituted the holy Supper, thus teaching us that as often as we eat of this bread and drink of this cup, we are thereby, as by a sure remembrance and pledge, admonished and assured of his hearty love and faithfulness toward us; that, whereas we should otherwise have suffered eternal death, he has given his body to the death of the cross, and shed his blood for us; and will as certainly feed and nourish our hungry and thirsty souls with his crucified body and shed blood to everlasting life, as this bread is broken before our eyes, and this cup is given to us, and we eat and drink in remembrance of him. From this institution of the holy Supper of our Lord Jesus Christ, we see that he directs our faith and trust to his perfect sacrifice, once offered on the cross, as the only ground of our salvation; wherein he is become to our hungry and thirsty souls the true meat and drink of life eternal. For by this death he has taken away the cause of our eternal death and misery, namely sin; and obtained for us the quickening Spirit, that we by the same Spirit, which dwells in Christ as the Head and in us as his members, may have true communion with him, and be made partakers of all his blessings, of life eternal, righteousness and glory.

c.   So also are we, by the Holy Spirit, to be united as members of one body, in true brotherly love; as the holy Apostle saith, "For we, being many, are one bread and one body; for we are all partakers of that one bread."

Hereto assist us the almighty God and Father of our Lord Jesus Christ, through his Holy Spirit. AMEN.

Prayer

3.   EP. Let us pray.

We here present ourselves to thee, O Lord, our souls and bodies, to be a holy and living sacrifice unto thee; humbly beseeching thee that all who are partakers of this holy Communion may be filled with thy grace and heavenly benediction. And though we are unworthy, through our manifold sins, to offer to thee any sacrifice, yet we beseech thee to accept this our bounden duty and service; not weighing our merits but pardoning our offences; through Jesus Christ our Lord. AMEN

Or,

5.   O most merciful God and Father, we beseech thee that thou wilt be pleased, in this Supper, in which we celebrate the glorious remembrance of the bitter death of thy beloved Son Jesus Christ, to work in our hearts through the Holy Spirit, that we may daily, more and more, with true confidence, give ourselves up unto thy Son Jesus Christ, so that our afflicted and contrite hearts, through the power of the Holy Ghost, may be fed and comforted with his true body and blood; yea, with him, true God and true Man, that only heavenly bread: and that we may no longer live in our sins, but he in us, and we in him; and thus truly be made partakers of the new and everlasting testament and covenant of grace: that we may not doubt that thou wilt for ever be our gracious Father, never more imputing our sins unto us, and providing us, as thy beloved children and heirs, with all things necessary, as well for the body as the soul. Grant us also thy grace, that we may take upon us our cross cheerfully, deny ourselves, confess our Savior, and in all tribulations with uplifted heads expect our Lord Jesus Christ from heaven, where he will make our mortal bodies like unto his most glorious body and take us unto himself in eternity.

Confession of Faith

6.   Strengthen us also by this holy Supper in the Christian Faith, whereof we make confession with our mouths and hearts, saying:

I BELIEVE IN GOD THE FATHER ALMIGHTY, MAKER OF HEAVEN
AND EARTH;

AND IN JESUS CHRIST HIS ONLY SON, OUR LORD; WHO WAS
CONCEIVED BY THE HOLY GHOST, BORN OF THE VIRGIN MARY;
SUFFERED UNDER PONTIUS PILATE, WAS CRUCIFIED, DEAD, AND
BURIED; HE DESCENDED INTO HELL; THE THIRD DAY HE ROSE
AGAIN FROM THE DEAD; HE ASCENDED INTO HEAVEN, AND
SITTETH ON THE RIGHT HAND OF GOD THE FATHER ALMIGHTY;
FROM THENCE HE SHALL COME TO JUDGE THE QUICK AND THE
DEAD.

I BELIEVE IN THE HOLY GHOST; THE HOLY CATHOLIC CHURCH;
THE COMMUNION OF SAINTS; THE FORGIVENESS OF SINS; THE
RESURRECTION OF THE BODY; AND THE LIFE EVERLASTING. AMEN.

Communion

7. That we may be now fed with the true heavenly bread, Christ Jesus, let us
    not cleave with our hearts unto the external bread and wine, but lift them on
    high in heaven, where Christ Jesus is our Advocate, at the right hand of his
    heavenly Father, whither all the Articles of our Faith lead us; not doubting
    that, through the working of the Holy Ghost, we shall as certainly be fed
    and refreshed in our souls with his body and blood, as we receive the holy
    bread and wine in remembrance of him.

8. *In breaking and distributing the bread, the minister shall say:*

    The Bread which we break is the communion of the Body of Christ.

    And when he gives the cup:

    The Cup of Blessing which we bless is the communion of the Blood of
    Christ.

Communion Thanksgiving

9. Beloved in the Lord, since the Lord has now fed our souls at his Table, let us
    therefore jointly praise his holy name with thanksgiving, and every one say
    with mouth and heart thus:

    Bless the Lord, O my soul:
      AND ALL THAT IS WITHIN ME, BLESS HIS HOLY NAME.
    Bless the Lord, O my soul,

AND FORGET NOT ALL HIS BENEFITS:
Who forgiveth all thine iniquities;
    WHO HEALETH ALL THY DISEASES;
Who redeemeth thy life from destruction;
    WHO CROWNETH THEE WITH LOVINGKINDNESS
    AND TENDER MERCIES.
The Lord is merciful and gracious,
    SLOW TO ANGER, AND PLENTEOUS IN MERCY.
He hath not dealt with us after our sins;
    NOR REWARDED US ACCORDING TO OUR INIQUITIES.
For as the heaven is high above the earth
    SO GREAT IS HIS MERCY TOWARD THEM THAT FEAR HIM.
As far as the east is from the west,
    SO FAR HATH HE REMOVED OUR TRANSGRESSIONS FROM US.
Like as a father pitieth his children,
    SO THE LORD PITIETH THEM THAT FEAR HIM.

Who hath not spared his own Son, but delivered him up for us all, and given us all things with him.
    THEREFORE SHALL MY MOUTH AND HEART SHOW FORTH THE PRAISE OF THE LORD FROM THIS TIME FORTH FOREVERMORE. AMEN.

Prayer

O almighty, merciful God and Father, we render thee most humble and hearty thanks, that thou hast, of thine infinite mercy, given us thine only begotten Son, for a mediator and a sacrifice for our sins, and to be our meat and drink unto life eternal. Grant, we beseech thee, O faithful God and Father, that through the operation of the Holy Spirit, the commemoration of the death of our Lord Jesus Christ may tend to the daily increase of our faith, and of our saving fellowship with him; through Jesus Christ thy Son, in whose name we conclude our prayers, saying:

OUR FATHER, WHO ART IN HEAVEN, HALLOWED BE THY NAME, THY KINGDOM COME, THY WILL BE DONE ON EARTH AS IT IS IN HEAVEN. GIVE US THIS DAY OUR DAILY BREAD. AND FORGIVE US OUR DEBTS, AS WE FORGIVE OUR DEBTORS. AND LEAD US NOT INTO TEMPTATION, BUT DELIVER US FROM EVIL; FOR THINE IS THE KINGDOM, AND THE POWER, AND THE GLORY, FOREVER. AMEN.

Notes

Introduction

1. Gerrit T. Vander Lugt, ed. *The Liturgy of the Reformed Church in America together with the Psalter selected and arranged for responsive reading* (New York: The Board of Education of the Reformed Church in America, 1968). Hereafter *Liturgy and Psalms*.
2. *Ibid.*, 63-70.
3. *Ibid.*, 66-68.
4. *Ibid.*, 66.
5. *Ibid.*
6. Howard G. Hageman, "The Order for the Sacrament of the Lord's Supper," in *A Companion to the Liturgy: A Guide to Worship in the Reformed Church in America*, ed. Garrett C. Roorda (New York: Half Moon Press, 1971), 35-36.
7. Gregory Dix, *The Shape of the Liturgy* (London: A & C Black, 1945), 48.
8. For a critical edition of Luther's 1523 *Formula Missae*, as well as of his 1526 *Deutsche Messe* see Hans-Christian Drömann, "Das Abendmahl nach den Ordnungen Martin Luthers," in *Coena Domini I: Die Abendmahlsliturgie der Reformationskirchen im 16./17. Jahrhundert*, ed. by Irmgard Pahl (Freiburg, Switzerland: Universitätsverlag, 1983), 25-39. ET in Bard Thompson, *Liturgies of the Western Church* (New York: World Publishing, 1961), 95-137 and R.C.D. Jasper and G.J. Cuming, *Prayers of the Eucharist: Early and Reformed* (Collegeville: The Liturgical Press, 1992), 189-199.
9. John Calvin, *La Forme des Prieres et Chants ecclesiastiques, avec la maniere d'adminstrer les Sacramens, et consacrer le Mariage: selon la coustume de l'Eglise ancienne* in Petrus Barth, Wilhelm Niesel, and Dora Scheuner (eds.), *Joannis Calvini Opera selecta*, volume II (München, 1926-1952), 11-58. For a critical edition of the French *La maniere de celebrer la cene*, see Bruno Bürki, *Coena Domini I*, 347-367. ET in Thompson, *Liturgies of the Western Church*, 197-210 and Jasper and Cuming, *Prayers of the Eucharist*, 213-218.
10. Markus Jenny, *Die Einheit des Abendmahlsgottesdienstes bei den elsässischen und schweizerischen Reformatoren* (Zwingli Verlag: Zürich-Stuttgart, 1968), 108.
11. Hageman, "The Order for the Sacrament of the Lord's Supper," 36, 39.
12. *Liturgy and Psalms*, 75-93. (They also can be found in Appendix A and C.)

Chapter One

1. For a critical edition of the Dutch *Forme om dat Heylige Avendtmael te Houden*, see A.C. Honders, "Das Abendmahl nach der Ordnung des Petrus Dathenus 1566," *Coena Domini I*, 525-535. For a detailed historical account of the reception and transmission of this form for the Lord's Supper, as well as the rest of the liturgical prayers and forms used in the Reformed Church in the Netherlands and in its colonial churches in North America, see Daniel James Meeter, *"Bless the Lord, O My Soul:" The New-York Liturgy of the Dutch Reformed Church, 1767* (Lanham, MD and London: The Scarecrow Press, Inc., 1998): 1-91.

2. *Ibid.*, 8,9. For the origin of the Reformed refugee communities in London, see Andrew Pettegree, *Foreign Protestant Communities in Sixteenth-Century London* (New York: Oxford University Press, 1986), 23-76. For the career of John a Lasco, see Dirk W. Rodgers, *John a Lasco in England* (New York: Peter Lang, 1994).

3. *Kirchenordnung, wie es mit der christlichen lehre, heiligen sacramenten und ceremonien in des durchleuchtigsten, hochgebornen fürsten und herren, herrn Friderichs, pfaltzgraven bey Rhein, des heiligen römischen reichs ertzdruchsessen und churfürsten, hertzogen in Bayrn etc. churfürstenthumb bey Rhein gehalten wirdt [vom 15. November 1563]* in Emil Sehling, *Die evangelischen Kirchenordnungen des XVI. Jahrhunderts, Vierzehnter Band, Kurpfalz,* (Tübingen: J.C.B. Mohr (Paul Siebeck), 1969), 333-408. See also Wilhelm Niesel, ed., *Bekenntnisschriften und Kirchenordnungnen der nach Gottes Wort reformierten Kirche* 3rd ed. (Zurich: Evangelischer Verlag, 1938), 136-218. From the Niesel edition, Bard Thompson has translated into English three sections ("of Common Prayer;" "of the Preparation for the Holy Supper; and "of the Lord's Holy Supper") in "The Palatinate Liturgy Heidelberg 1563" *Theology and Life* 6/1 (Spring 1963): 49-67. For a critical edition of the German *Form, das Heilige Abendmal zu halten*, see also Frieder Schulz, *"Das Abendmahl nach der Kurpfälzischen Ordnung"* in *Coena Domini I*, 495-523.

4. For the text of the Heidelberg Catechism, see Sehling, *Die evangelischen Kirchenordnungen des XVI. Jahrhunderts, Vierzehnter Band*, 342-368; Niesel, *Bekenntnisschriften und Kirchenordnungnen*, 149-181. Standard English edition for the RCA is the translation of Miller-Osterhaven, approved in 1967 and contained in *Liturgy and Psalms*, 461-491. Citations from the Catechism will be taken from this translation.

5. Robert M. Kingdon, "International Calvinism" in *Handbook of European History 1400-1600: Late Middle Ages, Renaissance, and Reformation,* Vol. 2, eds. Thomas A. Brady, Jr., Heiko Oberman, and James D. Tracy (Grand Rapids: Eerdmans, 1995), 243.

6. Lyle D. Bierma, *The Doctrine of the Sacraments in the Heidelberg Catechism: Melanchthonian, Calvinist, or Zwinglian?*, (Princeton: Princeton Theological Seminary, 1999), 32.

7. Philip Schaff, *The Creeds of Christendom, III*, (New York: Harper, 1931), 13. Cited in Bard Thompson, "Historical Background of the Catechism" in *Essays on the*

Heidelberg Catechism, eds. Bard Thompson et al. (Philadelphia: United Church Press), 12.

8. Frank C. Senn, *Christian Liturgy: Evangelical and Catholic*, (Minneapolis: Augsburg Fortress Press, 1997), 325.

9. *Ibid.*

10. *Sacrae Caesura Maiestatis Declaratio, Quomodo in Negocio Religionis Per Imperium usque ad definitionem Concilii generalis vivendum sit, in Comitiis Augustanis. Maii, Anno 1548, proposita & ab omnibus imperii ordinibus recepta.* Augsburg: Philipp Ulhard, 1548. Text in Joachim Melhausen (ed.), *Das Augsburger Interim von 1548* (Neukirchen-Vluyn: Neukirchener Verlag, 1970.) For a more detailed description of the Interim, see Martin Brecht, "Luther's Reformation," in *Handbook of European History 1400-1600, Vol. 2*, 148, and Oliver K. Olson, *Matthias Flacius and the Survival of Luther's Reform* (Wiesbaden: Harrassowitz Verlag, 2002), 84-85.

11. *Corpus Reformatorum* 6:865-74. Cited in Senn, *Christian Liturgy*, 325.

12. Brecht, "Luther's Reformation," 149.

13. Senn, *Christian Liturgy*, 325.

14. *Ibid.*

15. *Ibid.*, 328.

16. *Ibid.*

17. *Reformationsmandat an die Amleute, betreffend die Abschaffung des katholischen Gottesdiensts und vorläufige Ordnung des Gottesdiensts im evangelischen Sinne, vom 16. April 1556.* Critical edition of this text, as well as the 1556 Church Order, in Sehling, *Die evangelischen Kirchenordnungen des XVI. Jahrhunderts, Vierzehnter Band, Kurpfalz*, 111-220.

18. *Erneuerung des Bildermandats vom 14. December 1557, ibid.*, 255.

19. Thompson, "Historical Background of the Catechism," 16-17.

20. Bierma, *The Doctrine of the Sacraments in the Heidelberg Catechism*, 32.

21. Sehling, *Die evangelischen Kirchenordnungen des XVI. Jahrhunderts, Vierzehnter Band, Kurpfalz*, 38.

22. ET in Fred H. Klooster, *The Heidelberg Catechism: Origin and History* (Grand Rapids: Calvin Theological Seminary, 1982), 87.

23. *Ibid.*

24. Bard Thompson, "Reformed Liturgies: An Historical and Doctrinal Interpretation of the Palatinate Liturgy of 1563, Mercersburg Provisional Liturgy of 1858, Evangelical and Reformed Order of 1944, and their Sources," B.D. Thesis, (New York: Union Theological Seminary, 1949), 7.

25. Sehling, *Die evangelischen Kirchenordnungen des XVI. Jahrhunderts, Vierzehnter Band, Kurpfalz*, 38

26. Cited in Thompson, "Historical Background of the Catechism," 19-20.

27. Sehling, *Die evangelischen Kirchenordnungen des XVI. Jahrhunderts, Vierzehnter Band, Kurpfalz*, 39.

28. Klooster, *The Heidelberg Catechism*, 99.

29. Cited in Thompson, "Historical Background of the Catechism," 21.

30. Klooster, *The Heidelberg Catechism*, 102.

31. Bierma, *The Doctrine of the Sacraments in the Heidelberg Catechism*, 33.
32. Klooster, *The Heidelberg Catechism*, 103.
33. Thompson, "Historical Background of the Catechism," 22.
34. Klooster, *The Heidelberg Catechism*, 110.
35. Thompson, "Historical Background of the Catechism," 24-25.
36. Sehling, *Die evangelischen Kirchenordnungen des XVI. Jahrhunderts, Vierzehnter Band, Kurpfalz*, 39.
37. Thompson, "Historical Background of the Catechism," 23.
38. Bierma, *The Doctrine of the Sacraments in the Heidelberg Catechism*, 34
39. *Ibid.*
40. *"Deinde etiam cupiebat optimus sanctissimus Princeps, ut Praxis quam maxime et ad methodum et ad puritatem Catechismi accederet."* Letter to Bullinger (October 25 1563) in Karl Sudhoff, *C. Olevianus und Z. Ursinus: Leben und ausgewählte Schriften*, vol. 8 of *Leben und ausgewählte Schriften der Väter und Begründer der reformierten Kirche* (Elberfeld: R.L. Friderichs, 1857), 483-484.
41. Thompson, "The Palatinate Liturgy," 54.
42. *Ibid.*
43. Thompson, "The Reformed Church in the Palatinate," 40.
44. *Von der vorbereitung zum H. Abendmahl* in Niesel, *Bekenntnisschriften und Kirchenordnungen*, 187-189. ET in Thompson, "The Palatinate Liturgy," 57-58.
45. *Ibid.*, 57.
46. To demonstrate this dependence, Frieder Schulz has set in parallel columns the texts of the three examination questions and the corresponding questions and answers from the Heidelberg Catechism in his article "Die Vorbereitung zum Abendmahl in der Kirchenordnung der Kurpfalz von 1563" *Jahrbuch für Liturgik und Hymnologie* 7 (1962): 11-14.
47. Thompson, "The Palatinate Liturgy," 58.
48. The corresponding sections in the form included in Appendix A are numbered for easy reference.
49. *La Forme des Prieres et Chants ecclesiastiques, avec la maniere d'adminstrer les Sacramens, et consacrer le Mariage: selon la coustume de l'Eglise ancienne* in P. Barth et al. (eds.), *Joannis Calvini Opera selecta* volume II, 11-58. For a critical edition of the French *La maniere de celebrer la cene*, see Bürki, *Coena Domini I*, 347-367. ET in Thompson, *Liturgies of the Western Church*, 197-210 and Jasper and Cuming, *Prayers of the Eucharist*, 213-218.
50. The form draws here also on Marten Micron's *De christlicke Ordinancien der Nederlantscher Ghemeinten te London*, an important source for its drafters. See Willem Frederik Dankbaar (ed.). *Marten Micron, De christlicke Ordinancien der Nederlantscher Ghemeinten te London (1554)*, Kerkhistorische Studien behorende bij het Nederlands Archief voor Kerkgeshiedenis, Deel VII, 's-Gravenhage 1956. For a critical edition of the Dutch form for the Supper, see A. Casper Honders "Das Abendmahl nach den Ordnungen Johannes a Lascos (1550) 1555 und Marten Microns 1554," *Coena Domini I*, 431-460. The extent of Micron's own dependence on

Calvin is demonstrated in Elise Sprengler-Ruppenthal's, *Mysterium und Riten nach der Londoner Kirchenordnung der Niederlander* (Cologne: Graz, 1967), 144-176.

51. Sehling, *Die evangelischen Kirchenordnungen des XVI. Jahrhunderts, Vierzehnter Band, Kurpfalz,* 149.

52. The three stages of self-examination are, however, already to be found in Calvin and Micron.

53. Verbal parallels between this section of the form and the Catechism can be found in qq. 19, 35, 37, 38, 39, and 44.

54. See qq. 75-79.

55. *Liturgy and Psalms*, 461.

56. *Ibid.*

57. For a translation of the texts of prayers and rubrical directions for the ordinary Sunday service, see Thompson, "The Palatinate Liturgy" 49-56.

58. Meeter's judgment is even more severe: "[This] service was bereft of any liturgical celebration of guilt-grace-gratitude, even though that is manifestly the structure of the Catechism that always accompanies the Liturgy. See Meeter,"*Bless the Lord, O My Soul,*" 201. For a translation of the prayers, see 98-104; for extensive commentary on their sources and themes, see 183-217.

59. Concerning the ideal order of Reformed worship Hageman reported a conversation that he had had with the Dutch Reformed theologian Hendrikus Berkhof: "Reformed liturgy, said [Berkhof], should follow the order of the Reformed confession—guilt, grace, and gratitude, as in the Heidelberg Catechism. In the opening part of the liturgy, we express our guilt; in the central section we hear again the good news of our salvation through the grace of God; in response to that we offer ourselves in gratitude and service." *The Church Herald* (June 27, 1980): 30.

60. Howard Hageman, "Liturgical Origins of the Reformed Churches" in *The Heritage of John Calvin,* ed. John H. Bratt (Grand Rapids: William B. Eerdmans Publishing Company, 1973), 132.

61. Sehling, *Die evangelischen Kirchenordnungen des XVI. Jahrhunderts, Fünfzehnter Band, Württemberg I,* 70; *Vierzehnter Band, Kurpfalz,* 148.

62. Hageman, "Liturgical Origins of the Reformed Churches," 131-132.

63. Among the most thorough studies of the eucharistic doctrine of Calvin include Ronald S. Wallace, *Calvin's Doctrine of Word and Sacrament* (London: Oliver and Boyd, 1953), esp. 197-233; Kilian McDonnell, *John Calvin, the Church, and the Eucharist* (Princeton: Princeton University Press, 1967), 156-293; and Brian A. Gerrish, *Grace and Gratitude: The Eucharistic Theology of John Calvin* (Minneapolis: Augsburg Press, 1993).

64. For an overview of the problem as it relates to the Reformed churches in the Palatinate, see Bierma, *The Doctrine of the Sacraments in the Heidelberg Catechism.*

65. *Liturgy and Psalms*, 476-477.

66. Paul Rorem, "The Consensus Tigurinus (1549): Did Calvin Compromise?" In *Calvinus Sacrae Scripturae Professor: Calvin as Confessor of Holy Scripture,* ed. William H. Neusner (Grand Rapids: Eerdmans, 1994), 90.

67. John Calvin, *Instistutes of the Christian Religion,* ed. John T. McNeill, trans. Ford Lewis Battles (Philadelphia: Westminster, 1960), 1439 [4.18.11].

68. Wallace, *Calvin's Doctrine of Word and Sacrament,* 140

69. *Liturgy and Psalms,* 479.

70. *Ibid.,* 477.

71. Howard G. Hageman, *Pulpit and Table* (Richmond: John Knox Press, 1962), 13-35.

72. Sprengler-Ruppenthal, *Mysterium und Riten nach der Londoner Kirchenordnung der Niederlander,* 62.

73. Honders, "Das Abendmahl nach den Ordnungen Johannes a Lasco (1550) 1555 und Marten Microns 1554," 452.

74. Resolutions of the Synod concerning the use of Dathenus' order of worship are found in *De Kercken-Ordeninghen der Ghereformeerder Nederlandtscher kercken in de vier Nationale Synoden ghemaeckt ende ghearresteert. Mitsgaders Eenige anderen in den Provincialen Synoden van Hollandt ende Zeelandt gheconcipieert ende besloten waerby noch anderen in bysondere vergaderinghen goet-ghevonden, by ghevoeght zyn,* ed. I. Andriesz, Delft, 1622, 13ff. Cited in Bryan D. Spinks, *From the Lord and "The Best Reformed Churches: A Study of the Eucharistic Liturgy in the English Puritan and Separatist Traditions 1550-1563* (Rome: C.L.V. Edizioni Liturgiche, 1984), 138. See also Meeter, *"Bless the Lord, O My Soul,"* 10-11.

75. Frederik Lodewijk Rutgers, *Acta van de Nederlandsche Synoden der zestiende eeuw* (s'-Gravenhage, 1889), 147. (The translation of this formula, known as the *London aanhangsel* [London appendix], is my own.)

76. Meeter, *"Bless the Lord, O My Soul,"* 14.

77. According to Meeter, among all the Protestant churches only the Dutch Reformed have consistently used the term "liturgy" to designate the forms of worship in their service books, anticipating the modern use of the term by several centuries. See Daniel James Meeter, "Is the Reformed Church in America a Liturgical Church?" in Heather Murray Elkins, ed. *Pulpit, Table, and Song: Essays in Celebration of Howard G. Hageman* (Lanham, MD: The Scarecrow Press, 1996), 199.

78. *Ibid.,* 17-18.

79. Gerald F. De Jong, *The Dutch Reformed Church in the American Colonies* (Grand Rapids: Eerdmans, 1978), 7.

80. *Ibid.,* 49.

81. Meeter, *"Bless the Lord, O My Soul,"* 30.

82. Arie C. Brouwer, *Reformed Church Roots: Thirty-Five Formative Events* (New York: RCA Press, 1977), 18. The stages in the history of the Anglicization of the Dutch American Reformed churches in New York and New Jersey, which necessitated the English version of the Netherlands Liturgy, are recounted by De Jong, *The Dutch Reformed Church in the American Colonies,* 211-227, and by Meeter in *"Bless the Lord, O My Soul,"* 37-75.

83. For the annotated critical edition of *The Liturgy of the Reformed Church in Netherland. Or The Forms used therein in Publick Worship* (1767), see Meeter, *"Bless the Lord, O My Soul,"* 98-180. Curiously, the *London aanhangsel* is not attested in the form for the administration of the Lord's Supper.

84. "Until 1772, the Dutch Reformed Churches in America were subject, at least theoretically, to the Classis of Amsterdam. After achieving their independence in 1772, the new denomination became known as the "Dutch Reformed Church in North America" and as the "Reformed Dutch Church in the United States of America." In 1819, it was incorporated as the "Reformed Protestant Dutch Church in North America." An attempt was made about 1840 to drop the term "Dutch" from the official title, but the proposal failed. It was not until 1867 that the present name of "Reformed Church in America" came into use." See De Jong, *The Dutch Reformed Church in the American Colonies*, 236. In the following chapter we will employ the term "DRC" to refer to the Dutch Reformed Church in America. In narrating the events that occurred after 1867, we will naturally refer to this denomination as the "RCA."

Chapter Two

1. *The Liturgy of the Reformed Church in America Together with the Psalter Arranged for Responsive Reading* (New York: The Board of Education, 1907).
2. *The Liturgy of the Reformed Church in America as Reported to the General Synod of 1873 by the Committee on Revision* (New York: Reformed Church in America, 1873).
3. *The Liturgy of the Reformed Church in America Together with the Book of Psalms, for use in Public Worship* (New York: Board of Publication, RCA, 1882).
4. *Ibid.*, 45.
5. See Hageman, *Pulpit and Table*, esp. 60-108; "Liturgical Development in the Reformed Church of America: 1868-1947," *Journal of Presbyterian History* 47 (1969), 262-289. Jack Martin Maxwell, *Worship and Theology: The Liturgical Lessons of Mercersburg* (Pittsburgh: Pickwick Press, 1976); and Gregg Alan Mast, *The Eucharistic Service of the Catholic Apostolic Church and its Influence on Reformed Liturgical Renewals of the Nineteenth Century* (Lanham, MD: Scarecrow Press, Inc., 1999).
6. Louis H. Gunneman, *The Shaping of the United Church of Christ: An Essay in the History of American Christianity* (Cleveland: United Church Press, 1977), 168.
7. *Ibid.*, 169-170.
8. *Ibid.*, 170.
9. James I. Good, *History of the Reformed Church in the United States, 1725-1792* (Reading: n.p., 1899), 295-309.
10. Nathan D. Mitchell, "Church, Eucharist, and Liturgical Reform at Mercersburg: 1843-1857" (Ph.D dissertation, University of Notre Dame, 1978), 17.
11. James I. Good, *History of the Reformed Church in the United States in the Nineteenth Century* (New York: the Board of Publications of the Reformed Church in America, 1911), 4-5.
12. Mitchell, "Church, Eucharist, and Liturgical Reform at Mercersburg," 17.
13. Good, *History of the Reformed Church in the United States in the Nineteenth Century*, 178-188.

14. Mast, *The Eucharistic Service of the Catholic Apostolic Church*, 116.

15. Good, *History of the Reformed Church in the United States in the Nineteenth Century*, 180.

16. Herman Harmelink, III, *Ecumenism and the Reformed Church* (Grand Rapids: Eerdmans, 1968), 32.

17. *Ibid.*, 33.

18. John W. Nevin, *The Anxious Bench* (Chambersburg, PA: Office of the "Weekly Messenger," 1843) .

19. William G. McLoughlin, *Revivals, Awakenings, and Reform: An Essay on Religion and Social Change in America, 1607-1977* (Chicago: The University of Chicago Press, 1978), 124. See Maxwell's critical observations in this connection: "The means of grace became the conversion experience itself with its public testimony to a sinful life set free by the blood of Christ. Objectivity in worship yielded to the maudlin sentimentality of revivalistic hymns, and the liturgy lost its historic sense of a corporate oblation in response to God's gift in Christ." *Worship and Theology*, 56.

20. John W. Nevin, *The Anxious Bench* 2nd ed. (Chambersburg, Pa.: Publication Office of the German Reformed Church, 1844) in *Catholic and Reformed: Selected Theological Writings of John Williamson Nevin*, ed. Charles Yrigoyen, Jr. and George H. Bricker (Pittsburgh: Pickwick Press, 1978), 112.

21. *Ibid.*, 115.

22. *Ibid.*, 111.

23. For the text of the sermon, see the anthology *The Mercersburg Theology*, ed. James Hastings Nichols (New York: Oxford University Press, 1966), 33-55.

24. *Ibid.*, 38.

25. *Ibid.*, 39.

26. *Ibid.*, 39.

27. *Ibid.*, 39.

28. *Ibid.*, 39.

29. *Ibid.*, 39-40. Heidlelberg Catechism Q and A 76.

30. *Ibid.*, 40.

31. *Ibid.*, 42.

32. *Ibid.*, 47.

33. *Ibid.*, 49.

34. *Ibid.*, 34 (Editor's Introduction).

35. For these proposals, see Harmelink, *Ecumenism and the Reformed Church*, 33.

36. For a general introduction to the life and thought of Philip Schaff, see George H. Shriver, *Philip Schaff: Christian Scholar and Ecumenical Prophet* (Macon: Mercer University Press, 1987); and Gary K. Pranger, *Philip Schaff (1819-1893): Portrait of an Immigrant Theologian* (New York: Peter Lang, 1997). For an anthology with informative introductions, see Klaus Penzel, *Philip Schaff: Historian and Ambassador of the Universal Church* (Macon: Mercer University Press, 1991).

37. See Philip Schaf, *The Principle of Protestantism*, trans. John W. Nevin (Chambersburg, PA: Publication Office of the German Reformed Church, 1845; reprint, *The*

Principle of Protestantism and *What is Church History* ed. Bruce Kuklick (New York: Garland Publishing, Inc., 1987).

38. *Ibid.*, 49.

39. *Ibid.*, 173-74.

40. Stephen R. Graham, *Cosmos in the Chaos: Philip Schaff's Interpretation of Nineteenth-Century American Religion* (Grand Rapids: Eerdmans, 1995), 53-54.

41. Theodore Appel, *The Life and Work of John Williamson Nevin* (Philadelphia: Reformed Church Publication House, 1889; reprinted New York: Arno Press, 1969), 415. But see John Payne's discussion of the eventual departure of Nevin from Schaff as the former became increasingly disillusioned with contemporary Protestantism. "Schaff and Nevin, Colleagues at Mercersburg: The Church Question," *Church History* 61 (1991): 169-190.

42. The most helpful introduction to the theological partnership of Nevin and Schaff at Mercersburg remains James Hasting Nichols, *Romanticism in American Theology: Nevin and Schaff at Mercersburg* (Chicago: University of Chicago Press, 1961).

43. For a brief historical overview of the relations between Protestants and Catholics in America, see Graham, *Cosmos in the Chaos*, 45-50

44. *Ibid.*, 50.

45. For a summary of the attacks of the denominational presses against Nevin and Schaff, see Good, *History of the Reformed Church in the United States in the Nineteenth Century*, 221-222. See also Nichols, *Romanticism in American Theology*, 86.

46. See *The Christian Intelligencer*, IV (Aug. 7, 1845), 14. See also (Aug. 28, 1845), 26, and *passim*.

47. James W. Van Hoeven, "Dort and Albany: Reformed Theology Engages a New Culture," in *Word and World: Reformed Theology in America*, ed. James W. Van Hoeven (Grand Rapids: Eerdmans, 1986), 25.

48. *Ibid.*

49. Nevin's replies are summarized in Good, *History of the Reformed Church in the United States*, 224-25.

50. Nevin, "The Mystical Union" *The Weekly Messenger*, October 8, 1545. Cited in *The Mercersburg Theology*, 197.

51. For the resolutions, see Nichols, *Romanticism in American Theology*, 312.

52. *Reformed Confessionalism in Nineteenth-Century America: Essays on the Thought of John Williamson Nevin*, ed. by Sam Hamstra, Jr. and Arie J. Griffioen (Lanham, MD: Scarecrow Press, 1995), xvi.

53. Nevin, *Mystical Presence*, 1846; reprinted in *The Anxious Bench* and *The Mystical Presence* (New York: Garland Publishing, Inc., 1987), 3.

54. Harmelink, *Ecumenism in the Reformed Church*, 34.

55. John W. Nevin, "Doctrine of the Reformed Church on the Lord's Supper," *Mercersburg Review* 2 (1850), 372-3. For Nevin's case that the German Reformed tradition is Melanchthonian on the decrees and Calvinist on the sacraments, see Nichols, *Romanticism in American Theology*, 98-100; and William Borden Evans, "Imputation and Impartation: The Problem of Union with Christ in Nineteenth-

Century American Reformed Theology" (Ph.D. diss., Vanderbilt University, 1996), 304-307.

56. *Minutes*, General Synod, 1846, 30.

57. *Ibid.*, 30-1.

58. *Ibid.*, 1847, 139.

59. Cited in Mast, *The Eucharistic Service of the Apostolic Church*, 116.

60. Paul H. Conkin, *The Uneasy Center: Reformed Christianity in Antebellum America* (Chapel Hill: The University of North Carolina Press, 1995), 195.

61. Cited in a lecture Howard Hageman delivered in 1966, published in Gregg Mast, *In Remembrance and Hope: The Ministry and Vision of Howard G. Hageman* (Grand Rapids: Eerdmans, 1998), 122.

62. *The Christian Intelligencer*, XXIII (April 28, 1853), 1.

63. Hageman has observed that the original constitution (1793) did not require that the forms for the sacraments be read. With regard to the Supper, the revised constitution (1833), however, made the reading of the form mandatory: "Every Church shall observe such a mode in the administration of the Lord's Supper as shall be judged most conducive to edification; provided, however, that after the sermon and usual public prayers are ended, the form for the administration of the Lord's Supper shall be read, and a prayer suited to the occasion shall be offered before the members participate of the ordinance." *A Digest of Constitutional and Synodical Legislation of the Reformed Church in America* ed. Edward T. Corwin (New York, 1906), lxix. Cited by Hageman in "Liturgical Development in the Reformed Church of America," 267.

64. *Minutes*, General Synod, 1847, 330.

65. Philip Schaff, "The New Liturgy," *Mercersburg Review* 10 (1858), 204-205.

66. *Ibid.*, 205.

67. For a discussion of the Mayer Liturgy, see Maxwell, *Worship and Reformed Theology*, 78-88.

68. Thompson, "Reformed Liturgies: An Historical and Doctrinal Interpretation of the Palatinate Liturgy of 1563, Mercersburg Provisional Liturgy of 1858, Evangelical and Reformed Order of 1944, and their Sources," 27-29.

69. Thompson has counted twenty-nine articles on the Heidelberg Catechism which came from the pen of Nevin between 1840 and 1842. See "The Catechism and Mercersburg Theology" in *Essays on the Heidelberg Catechism*, 60. In 1847 Nevin adapted them in book form, *The History and Genius of the Heidelberg Catechism* (Chambersburg: Publication Office of the German Reformed Church, 1847).

70. Bomberger's report is reprinted in Philip Schaff, "The New Liturgy," 209-212.

71. For this debate, *ibid.*, 212-13.

72. John H.A. Bomberger, "The Old Palatinate Liturgy of 1563," *Mercersburg Review* 2 (1850) 81-96, 265-286; and 3 (1851) 97-128.

73. *Ibid.*, 269-274

74. Nevin, "Early Christianity" is reprinted in *Catholic and Reformed: Selected Theological Writings of John Williamson Nevin*, eds. Charles Yrigoyen, Jr. and George H. Bricker (Pittsburgh: Pickwick Press, 1978), 175-310.

75. *Ibid.*, 291.

76. Schaff, "The New Liturgy," 218-20. For a summary of these principles, from which we have adapted above, see Michael A. Farley, "The Liturgical Theology of John Williamson Nevin," *Studia Liturgica* 33 (2003), 208.

77. Luther J. Binkley, *The Mercersburg Theology* (Manheim, PA: Sentinel Printing House, 1953), 109.

78. Mast, *The Eucharistic Service of the Apostolic Church*, 64.

79. George H. Shriver, *Philip Schaff: Christian Scholar and Ecumenical Prophet* (Macon, GA: Mercer University Press, 1987), 40.

80. This sectarian movement originated in Albury, England under the leadership of Henry Drummond (1786-1860) and the influence of Edward Irving (1792-1834), a controversial preacher of premillenarianism and champion of the renewal of the charismatic gifts of the early church. In 1826 Drummond convened about fifty men to discuss what the Scriptures taught concerning the Second Coming of Christ. It was later revealed that the Second Coming would not occur until the spiritual preparation of the church. The Irvingites held that the sole authority in the church belonged to the twelve apostles. This apostolate died out after the first century, but in 1835 the movement sought to restore the apostolate by delegating twelve men to go out on an ecumenical mission to the churches in Europe and Russia. They were instructed to represent the Catholic Apostolic Church as the spiritual center to which all churches were to turn in order that the Bride of Christ might be ready for the imminent return of the Bridegroom. In doctrine the Catholic Apostolic Church subscribed to the Apostles, Nicene, and Athanasian Creeds. In worship it sought to return to the undivided Church as understood from a study of the early liturgies and writings of the Fathers. See Columba Graham Flegg, *'Gathered Under Apostles:' A Study of the Catholic Apostolic Church* (Oxford: Clarendon Press, 1992). For the central role of the liturgical study and publications of this movement in the Reformed liturgical renewals in the nineteenth century, see Mast, *The Eucharistic Service of the Catholic Apostolic Church*. For a general introduction, see Kenneth W. Stevenson, "The Catholic Apostolic Church—its History and its Eucharist," *Studia Liturgica* 13 (1979), 21-43.

81. Cited in Mast, *The Eucharistic Service of the Catholic Apostolic Church*, 65.

82. *Ibid.*, 66.

83. Nevin, *Vindication of the Revised Liturgy* in *Catholic and Reformed: Selected Theological Writings of John Williamson Nevin*, 331.

84. This liturgy was published under the title, *A Liturgy: or,Order of Christian Worship* (Philadelphia: Lindsay and Blakiston, 1857). The table of contents, including the lectionary of Scripture lessons for the church year, is reproduced in Maxwell, *Worship and Reformed Theology*, 425-433, 467-468

85. For the complete text, see *A Liturgy: or, Order of Christian Worship*, 129-136.

86. *Ibid.*, 190-202.

87. For an English translation of the Liturgy of St. James, see Jasper and Cuming, *Prayers of the Eucharist*, 60-69. For an analysis of Schaff's eucharistic prayer, see Maxwell, *Worship and Reformed Theology*, 227-236.

88. John W. Nevin, *The Liturgical Question with Reference to the Provisional Liturgy of the German Reformed Church: A Report by the "Liturgical Committee"* (Philadelphia: Lindsay & Blakiston, 1862), 27.

89. Hageman, *Pulpit and Table*, 91.

90. Cited in *Ibid.*

91. Maxwell, *Worship and Reformed Theology*, 258.

92. See his able two-part defense of Nevin and his theology in "Dr. Nevin and his Antagonists," *Mercersburg Review* 5 (1853), 89-124; 145-181.

93. For an attempt to clarify the reasons for Bomberger's defection and subsequent controversy, see Maxwell, *Worship and Reformed Theology*, 262-282

94. Thompson, "Reformed Liturgies," 37.

95. John W. Nevin *The Liturgical Question with Reference to the Provisional Liturgy of the German Reformed Church: A Report by the "Liturgical Committee"* (Philadelphia: Lindsay & Blakiston, 1862).

96. *Ibid.*, 6.

97. *Ibid.*, 23.

98. *Ibid.*, 25.

99. *Ibid.*, 40-42.

100. *Ibid.*, 61.

101. *Ibid.*, 62.

102. *An Order of Worship for the Reformed Church* (Philadelphia: S.R. Fisher, 1867).

103. See Maxwell, *Worship and Reformed Theology*, 323-334.

104. Hageman, *Pulpit and Table*, 97-98.

105. Andrew A. Bonar, *Presbyterian Liturgies with Specimens of Forms of Prayer for Worship as Used in the Continental Reformed, and American Churches; with the Directory for Public Worship of God agreed upon by the Assembly of Divines at Westminster; and Forms of Prayer for Ordinary and Communion Sabbaths, and for other Services of the Church* (Edinburgh: Myles MacPhail, 1858).

106. *Euchologion or Book of Prayers* (Edinburgh and London: William Blackwood and Sons, 1867).

107. George W. Sprott, *The Worship and Offices of the Church of Scotland* (Edinburgh and London, 1882), 118.

108. Hageman, "Liturgical Development in the Reformed Church of America," 262.

109. *Ibid.*, 262-63.

110. *The Liturgy of the Reformed Church in America as Reported to the General Synod of 1873.*

111. *A Digest of Constitutional and Synodical Legislation of the Reformed Church in America*, ed. Edwin Corwin (New York, 1906), 373.

112. *The Liturgy of the Reformed Church in America as Reported to the General Synod of 1873*, 109-111. For the text of this prayer, see Appendix B.

113. *A Digest of Constitutional and Synodical Legislation*, lxix.

114. Hageman, "Liturgical Development in the Reformed Church of America," 280.

115. See Appendix C. Again I have numbered the sections of the form, indicating the sections drawn from the eucharistic prayer with "EP," for easy reference.

116. Hageman, "Liturgical Development in the Reformed Church of America," 283.

Chapter Three

1. *Minutes of the General Synod*, Volume XXXXVIII, 1968.
2. Robert Hotz, "Sacrament," *Dictionary of the Ecumenical Movement*, ed. Nicholas Lossky et al. (Grand Rapids: Eerdmans, 1991), 885-889.
3. R.W. Franklin, *Nineteenth-Century Churches: The History of a New Catholicism in Württemberg, England, and France* (New York and London: Garland Publishing, Inc., 1987), 3.
4. *Institutions liturgique*, Vol. 3 (Paris: Julien, Lanier et Ce, Editeurs, 1851), 170-71; cited in Robert L. Tuzik, *How Firm a Foundation: Leaders of the Liturgical Movement* (Chicago: Liturgy Training Publications, 1990), 17.
5. For the text, see *Worship and Liturgy: Official Catholic Teachings*, ed. James J. Megivern (Wilmington, NC: McGrath Publishing Company, 1978), 16-26.
6. Sacra Tridentina: Decree on Frequent and Daily Reception of Holy Communion (December 20, 1905) in *Worship and Liturgy: Official Catholic Teachings*, 27-32.
7. See, e.g., Bernard Botte, *From Silence to Participation: An Insider's View of Liturgical Renewal*, trans. John Sullivan (Washington, D.C.: The Pastoral Press, 1988), 10.
8. *Tra Le Sollecitudini* in *ibid.*, 17-18.
9. For a summary of the paper, see Raymond Loonbeek and Jacques Mortiau, *Un Pionnier Dom Lambert Beauduin (1873-1960): Liturgie et Unité des chrétiens*, vol. 1 (Louvain-La-Neuve: Editions de Chevetogne, 2001), 79-81.
10. Senn, *Christian Liturgy*, 613.
11. Ibid., 611. In the informative first chapter, "The Continental Liturgical Movement and its Influence," in his *Worship and Theology in England: The Ecumenical Century 1900-1965, Vol. 5* (Princeton: Princeton University Press, 1965), Horton Davies characterizes Beauduin as a "man who knew the supreme importance of worship, but also the extraordinary difficulty of maintaining the life of devotion in the crowded tenements of the industrial cities of present-day Europe, and with the apparent lack of any nexus between worship and daily work" (24).
12. Lambert Beauduin, "La Piété de L'Eglise," *Mélanges liturgiques* (Louvain, 1954), 17-18.
13. Gerrit T. VanderLugt, "Principles of Reformed Worship," *The Church Herald* (May 11, 1951), 8.
14. Edward J. Kilmartin, *The Eucharist in the West: History and Theology* (Collegeville: The Liturgical Press, 1998), 268.
15. Odo Casel, *The Mystery of Christian Worship and Other Writings*, ed. Burkhard Neunheuser, O.S.B. (Westminster, MD: The Newman Press; and London, Darton, Longman & Todd, 1932 for Part I, 1959 for Part II, 1962 for this English translation), 9.
16. In addition to texts from Ephesians and Colossians, Casel also often cites Heb. 1:1ff.; Jn. 1:14ff; 1 Jn. 1:2; Rom. 16:25; 1 Cor. 2:8ff. in support of his concept of the Christian mystery.

17. Casel, *The Mystery of Christian Worship*, 58.
18. Odo Casel, "Mysteriengegenwart," *Jahrbuch für Liturgiewissenschaft 8* (1928), 145.
19. Casel, *The Mystery of Christian Worship*, 104.
20. For a critical reflection on Casel's understanding of the relation of the Hellenistic mystery cults to Christian worship, see Louis Bouyer, *Life and Liturgy* (London: Sheed and Ward, 1956), 86-98.
21. Casel, *The Mystery of Christian Worship*, 53. For a succinct summary of Casel's description of the mystery rites, see Kilmartin, *Eucharist in the West*, 273.
22. Casel, *The Mystery of Christian Worship*, 53.
23. Kilmartin, *Eucharist in the West*, 273-4; I.H. Dalmais, "Theology of the Liturgical Celebration," in *The Church at Prayer: Principles of the Liturgy*, ed. Aimé Georges Martimort, trans. Matthew J. O'Connell (Collegeville: The Liturgical Press, 1987), 269.
24. *Ibid.*
25. For brief comparison of the Casel's theory and the statements of the Council of Trent on the sacrifice of the Mass, see Gerhard Karl Schäfer, *Eucharistie im ökumenischen Kontext: Zur Diskussion um das Herrenmahl in Glauben und Kirchenverfassung von Lausanne 1927 bis Lima 1982* (Göttingen: Vandenhoeck & Ruprecht, 1988), 90.
26. A.G. Hebert was himself a pioneer in the liturgical movement in the Anglican Church. His contribution to the movement was his widely read, *Liturgy and Society: The Function of the Church in the Modern World* (London: Faber & Faber, 1935).
27. *Ways of Worship: The Report of a Theological Commission on Faith and Order*, eds. Pehr Edwall, Eric Hayman, William D. Maxwell (London: SCM Press LTD, 1951), 77.
28. Yngve Brilioth, *Eucharistic Faith and Practice, Evangelical and Catholic*, trans. A.G. Hebert (London: SPCK, 1930).
29. For a favorable review of Brilioth's schematization, see Bouyer, *Life and Liturgy*, 75-85.
30. Brilioth, *Eucharistic Faith and Practice*, 278.
31. *Ibid.*, 279.
32. *Ibid.*, 284.
33. *Ibid.*, 286.
34. *Ibid.*
35. Frank C. Senn, "Introduction," in *New Eucharistic Prayers: An Ecumenical Study of Their Development and Structure*, ed. Frank Senn (New York: Paulist Press, 1987), 3.
36. *Ibid.*
37. Brilioth, *Eucharistic Faith and Practice*, 278.
38. London: A & C Black, 1945.
39. *Ibid.*, 48.
40. *Ibid.*
41. "The Order for the Sacrament of the Lord's Supper," in *A Companion to the Liturgy*, 35.

42. *Ibid.*, 36.

43. *Ibid.*

44. Dix, *Shape of the Liturgy*, 245.

45. Ibid., 751.

46. Garrett C. Roorda, "Worship and Liturgy in the Reformed Church in America," in *A Companion to the Liturgy*, 1.

47. Tissington Tatlow, "The World Conference on Faith and Order," in *A History of the Ecumenical Movement: 1517-1948 vol. 1* (eds.) Ruth Rouse and Stephen Charles Neill, (Geneva: WCC, 1954), 407.

48. Lukas Vischer (ed.), *A Documentary History of the Faith and Order Movement 1927-1963* (St. Louis: The Bethany Press, 1963), 199-201. ("Joint Commission Appointed to Arrange for a World Conference on Faith and Order. Report on Plan and Scope (1911)")

49. The World Conference for the Consideration of Questions touching Faith and Order: Report of the Joint Commission to the General Convention of the Protestant Episcopal Church 1916 Gardiner 1916, 10. Cited in Martien E. Brinkman, *Progress in Unity? Fifty Years of Theology within the World Council of Churches: 1945-1995: A Study Guide* (Grand Rapids: Eerdmans, 1995), 8. For the history of the use of the terms "faith" and "order," see Günther Gassman, *Konzeptionen der Einheit in der Bewegung für Glauben und Kirchenverfassung 1910-1937* (Göttingen: Vandenhoeck & Ruprecht, 1979), 49-50.

50. Brinkman, *Progress in Unity?*, 8.

51. The participants at both conferences restricted their theological considerations to the sacraments of baptism and the Lord's Supper, since it was on these two sacraments that all the churches represented could agree. The statements on the sacraments are contained in the final report ("Sacraments") of the sixth section at Lausanne; those at Edinburgh are found in the final report ("The Church of Christ: Ministry and Sacraments") of the fifth section. See resp. *Faith and Order: Proceedings of the World Conference Lausanne, August 3-21, 1927*, ed. H.N. Bate (London: Student Christian Movement, 1927), 390-91; *The Second World Conference on Faith and Order Held at Edinburgh, August 3-18, 1937*, ed. Leonard Hodgson (New York: The Macmillan Company, 1938), 239-249. See also *A Documentary History of the Faith and Order Movement 1927-1963*, 38-39; 52-61. For an analysis of the content of the preparatory materials, working papers, conference addresses, and reports related to the Lord's Supper at these two Conferences, see Schäfer, *Eucharistie im ökumenischen Kontext*, 1-75.

52. *The Third World Conference on Faith and Order Held at Lund August 15 to 28, 1952*, ed. Oliver S. Tomkins (London: SCM Press LTD, 1953), 70.

53. The Reformed contributors include W.D. Maxwell, J. Schweizer, A. Graf, R. Paquier, G. van der Leeuw, and M. Thurian.

54. *Ways of Worship*, 20-21.

55. *Ibid.*, 30.

56. *Ibid.*, 21.

57. *Ibid.*, 21.

58. *Ibid.,* 23.

59. *Ibid.,* 31.

60. No doubt the report has in view here Dix's *Shape of the Liturgy,* and Dekkers' *Inleiding tot de liturgiek* (Antwerpen, Brussels: N.v. Standaard-boekhandel, 1942).

61. *Ibid.,* 33.

62. *Ibid.*

63. *Ibid.,* 34.

64. *Ibid.*

65. *Ibid.,* 35.

66. *Ibid.*

67. *Ibid.*

68. Gerardus van der Leeuw, *Sacramentstheologie* (Nijkerk: G.F. Callenbach, 1949), 239. Compare this assertion to his optimistic assessment of the potential of Casel's theology in *Ways of Worship,* 229: "The idea of representation as it is advocated in many circles nowadays, Roman Catholic as well as Anglican and Lutheran, seems to present some perspectives for a future development of sacramental theology for the Reformed Churches also."

69. *Dienstboek voor de Nederlandse Hervormde Kerk: in Ontwerp* ('s-Gravenhage: Boekencentrum N.V., 1955). For an overview of its contents, see Howard Hageman, "Three Reformed Liturgies," *Theology Today XV, no. 4* (January 1959): 508-510.

70. Davies, *Worship and Theology in England, 1900-1965,* 36.

71. *Ways of Worship,* 225.

72. *Ibid.,* 226.

73. *Ibid.,* 229.

74. Thompson, "The Palatinate Liturgy," 59.

75. Among his works include *Zur Ordnung des Gottesdienst in den nach Gottes Wort reformierten Gemeinden der deutschsprachigen Schweiz* (Zürich, n.p. 1944); *Reformierte Abendmahlsgestaltung in der Schau Zwinglis* (Basel: Friedrich Reinhardt, 1950).

76. *Ways of Worship,* 132.

77. Bruno Bürki, "Reformed Worship in Continental Europe since the Seventeenth Century," in *Christian Worship in Reformed Churches Past and Present,* ed. by Lukas Vischer (Grand Rapids: Eerdmans, 2003), 49. For a biographical sketch of Paquier, see also Bruno Bürki, *Cène du Seigneur—eucharistie de l'Eglise: Le cheminement des Eglises réformées romandes et françqises depuis le XVIIIe siécle, d'après leurs textes liturgiques: Volume B: Commentaire* (Fribourg Suisse: Editions Universitaires, 1985), 46-56.

78. *Ibid.,* 51.

79. Bürki, "Reformed Worship in Continental Europe since the Seventeenth Century," 49.

80. For complete texts of the 1931 and 1952 eucharistic liturgies , see Bürki, *Cene du Seigneur: Volume A,* 127-145.

81. Ways of Worship., 242.

82. *Ibid*. In this connection, see the statement of John Calvin: "[O]ur merciful Lord, according to this infinite kindness, so tempers himself to our capacity that, since we are creatures who always creep on the ground, cleave to the flesh, and, do not think about or even conceive of anything spiritual, he condescends to lead us to himself even by these earthly elements, and to set before us in the flesh a mirror of spiritual blessings." *Institutes of the Christian Religion*, 1278 [4.14.3]. There evidently is a basis here for the criticisms that Paquier makes in his essay.

83. *Ways of Worship*, 242. In this connection, see also Calvin here: "Therefore let it be regarded as a settled principle that the sacraments have the same office as the Word of God: to offer and set forth Christ to us, and in him the treasures of heavenly grace. *Institutes of the Christian Religion*, 1292 [4.14.17].

84. *Ways of Worship*, 243.

85. *Ibid*.

86. *Ibid*., 244.

87. *Ibid*., 245.

88. *Ibid*., 232.

89. *Ibid*., 233.

90. *Ibid*., 234.

91. *Ibid*., 233.

92. *Ibid*.

93. *Ibid*.

94. *Ibid*.

95. *Ibid*., 235.

96. *Ibid*., 239.

97. Howard Hageman "The Liturgical Revival," *Theology Today VI, no. 4* (January 1950): 490-505.

98. Minutes of the General Synod, Vol. XXXIX, 1951, 287.

99. Howard Hageman, "Our Liturgical History," (May 4, 1951): 12-13; Gerrit T. VanderLugt, "Principles of Reformed Worship," (May 11, 1951), 8,17; Robert C. Oudersluys, "The Place and Need of a Formulated Liturgy in the Reformed Church," (May 18, 1951), 7; M. Stephen James, "The Needed Scope of Liturgical Revision," (May 25, 1951), 8-9. Hageman had already begun to familiarize the denomination with the liturgical tradition of the Reformed Churches by a series of articles that appeared in a featured column in the Church Herald during the preceding year. "The Romance of the Liturgy" was the first (February 3), followed by "The Liturgy of John Calvin" (April 21), "The Liturgy of the Heidelberg Catechism" (May 5), "The Dutch Liturgy" (May 12), and a concluding article entitled "A Reformed Service" (May 19), in which he attempted to describe what a Lord's Day service might have been like in Geneva, Heidelberg, or Frankenthal in the middle sixteenth-century.

100. For the text, see Appendix II.

101. Hageman, "Our Liturgical History," 12.

102. Liturgical Orders and Forms As Revised from the Liturgy of the Reformed Church in America Submitted by Direction of General Synod June, 1952 For study and Permissive use by the Churches, 34-53.

103. *Minutes of the General Synod,* Vol. XXXIX, 279.

104. *Ibid.,* Vol. XLI, 217-218.

105. *Ibid.,* Vol XLII, 319.

106. The Provisional Liturgy Orders and Forms of Worship as revised from The Liturgy of the Reformed Church in America and approved by General Synod for study and permissive use, June 1958, 18.

107. *Ibid.,* 20.

108. Oscar Cullman and F.J. Leenhardt, *Essays on the Lord's Supper,* trans. J.G. Davies (London: Lutterworth Press, 1958).

109. *Ibid.,* 23.

110. *Minutes of the General Synod,* Vol. XLII, 319.

111. *Ibid.,* Vol. XLIII, 323.

112. *Ibid.,* Vol XLIII, 299.

113. Mast, *In Remembrance and Hope,* 27.

114. *Minutes of the General Synod,* Vol XLIV, 367.

115. Mast, *In Remembrance and Hope,* 27.

116. The Provisional Liturgy Orders and Forms of Worship as proposed by the Committee on Revision of the Liturgy of the Reformed Church in America and approved by General Synod for study and permissive use June, 1963, 27.

117. Bürki, *Cène du Seigneur—eucharistie de l'Eglise, Volume B: Commentaire,* 165.

118. *Ibid., Volume A: Textes,* 156-159.

119. The Provisional Liturgy, June, 1963, 27-28.

120. We draw here on a copy of The Liturgy of the Church of South India Celebrated during the Second Assembly of the World Council of Churches, at the First Methodist Church in Evanston, Illinois on Sunday, August 29, 1954. We found this liturgy among the committees' papers and reports archived in the Gardner Sage Library, New Brunswick Theological Seminary, New Brunswick, New Jersey.

121. The Order for the Sacrament of the Lord's Supper," in *A Companion to the Liturgy,* 39.

122. *The Liturgy of the Reformed Church in America together with the Psalter Selected and arranged for responsive reading,* ed. Gerrit T. Vander Lugt =Liturgy and Psalms.

123. *Ibid.,* 63-65. Two options are provided. The first is the one that appears in the 1958 Provisional Liturgy; the second is one that appears in the 1963 version.

124. *Ibid.,* 65.

Chapter Four

1.   Hageman, *Pulpit and Table,* 110-116.

2. Louis Bouyer, *Eucharist: Theology and Spirituality of the Eucharistic Prayer*, trans. Charles Underhill Quinn (Notre Dame: University of Notre Dame Press, 1968), 100.

3. John Reumann, *The Supper of the Lord: The New Testament, Ecumenical Dialogue, and Faith and Order on Eucharist* (Philadelphia: Fortress Press, 1985), 49.

4. See, e.g., Rudolph Bultmann, *Theology of the New Testament* (New York: Scribners 1951-1955), I, 144-151; Eduard Schweizer, *The Lord's Supper according to the New Testament* (Philadelphia: Westminster Press, 1967); Willi Marxsen, *The Lord's Supper as a Christological Problem*, trans. Lorenz Nietig, (Philadelphia: Fortress Press, 1970).

5. Joachim Jeremias, *The Eucharistic Words of Jesus*, trans. Norman Perrin (New York: Charles Scribner's Sons, 1966), 79-83.

6. See, *inter alia*, Annie Jaubert, *The Date of the Last Supper* (Staten Island, NY: Alba House, 1965); and I. Howard Marshall, *The Last Supper and the Lord's Supper* (Grand Rapids: Eerdmans, 1981).

7. Cesare Giraudo, *Eucaristia per la Chiesa: Prospettive teologiche sull'eucaristia a partire dalla "lex orandi"* (Rome: Editrice Pontificia Università Gregoriana, 1989). For a concise summary of the themes we delineate here see "The Eucharist as Re-Presentation," *Religious Studies Bulletin* 4 (1984): 154-159.

8. Bouyer, *Eucharist*, 79, 99; Enrico Mazza, *The Eucharistic Prayers of the Roman Rite*, trans. Matthew J. O'Connell (New York: Pueblo, 1986), 17.

9. This table is adapted from that of Jeremias, *The Eucharistic Words of Jesus*, 111-12.

10. Bouyer, *Eucharist*, 79-80; Robert Cabie, *The Church at Prayer: An Introduction to the Liturgy: Volume II: The Eucharist*, trans. Matthew J. O'Connell (Collegeville: The Liturgical Press, 1986), 8; Senn, *Christian Liturgy*, 55-56; Enrico Mazza, *The Origins of the Eucharistic Prayer*, trans. Ronald E. Lane (Collegeville: The Liturgical Press, 1995), 82-83.

11. For a critical Latin edition of the *Kiddush* prayer formulae, see Anton Hänggi and Irmgard Pahl, *Prex Eucharistica: Textus E Variis Liturgiis Antiquoribus Selecti*, Spicilegium Friburgense 12 (Fribourg: Editions Universitaires, 1968), 6-7. English translations of several Jewish prayer texts are found in most recent edition of Ronald C. Jasper and Geoffrey J. Cuming, *Prayers of the Eucharist: Early and Reformed* (Collegeville: The Liturgical Press, 1992), 10-12.

12. Joseph Heinemann, *Prayer in the Talmud: Forms and Patterns* (Berlin: Walter De Gruyter, 1977), 18.

13. Xavier Léon-Dufour, *Sharing the Eucharistic Bread: The Witness of the New Testament*, trans. Matthew J. O'Connell (New York: Paulist Press, 1987), 22. For an explanation of this ancient near Eastern concept, see also Jeremias, *The Eucharistic Words of Jesus*, 232-236.

14. *Ibid.*

15. Richard Schaeffler, "Therefore we remember..." The Connection between Remembrance and Hope in the Present of the Liturgical Celebration. Religious-Philosophical Reflections on a Religious Understanding of Time," in *The Meaning*

of the Liturgy, ed. Angelus A. Häussling, trans. Linda M. Maloney (Collegeville: The Liturgical Press, 1994), 18.

16. David N. Power, *The Eucharistic Mystery: Revitalizing the Tradition* (New York: Crossroad, 1995), 37

17. Mazza, *The Eucharistic Prayers of the Roman Rite*, 267.

18. Ithamar Gruenwald, *Rituals and Ritual Theory in Ancient Israel* (Leiden: Brill, 2003), 218.

19. Jacob Neusner, "Introduction" in *The Mishna: A New Translation* (New Haven: Yale University Press, 1988), xvi.

20. Bouyer, *Eucharist*, 79-80.

21. The texts of this invitation vary according to the number of participants, and pose a number of problems. For a discussion of these problems, see Heinemann, *Prayer in the Talmud*, 113-122. The rules are stipulated in m*Ber*. 7.3.

22. m.*Ber*. 6.8.

23. Talmudic tradition attributes it to Rabbi Gamaliel, who composed it at Jamnia after the revolt of Bar Kochba in 135. The first three, according to the same tradition, are considerably older. The first *berakah* is attributed to Moses, the second to Joshua, and third to David and Solomon. Thus "the order of grace after meals is as follows: The first benediction is that of "Who feeds." The second is the benediction is of the land. The third is "Who builds Jerusalem." The fourth is "Who is good and bestows good." (b.*Ber* 48b). For commentary, see Carmine Di Sante, *Jewish Prayer: The Origins of Christian Liturgy*, trans. Matthew J. O'Connell (New York: Paulist Press, 1991), 145-148.

24. See Thomas J. Talley, "From *Berakah* to *Eucharistia*: A Reopening Question," in *Living Bread, Saving Cup: Readings on the Eucharist*, ed. R. Kevin Seasoltz (Collegeville: The Liturgical Press, 1982), 85-86. For a critical Latin edition of the two texts of the *Birkat ha-mazon*, see Hänggi and Pahl, *Prex Eucharistica*, 10-11.

25. Louis Finkelstein, "The Birkhat Ha-Mazon," *Jewish Quarterly Review*, vol. XIX (1928-29), 211-262.

26. For a critical Latin edition of the text that Finkelstein proposed, see Hänggi and Pahl, *Prex Eucharistica*, 9-10. For an English translation, see Jasper and Cuming, *Prayers of the Eucharist*, 10. The translation from the Latin is mine.

27. Léon-Dufour, *Sharing the Eucharistic Bread*, 53.

28. bBer 48b.

29. The rubrics indicate embolisms for the feasts of Hanuka and Purim, specifically. See Hänggi and Pahl, *Prex Eucharistica*, 11 and 52. (The translation from the Latin is mine.) Louis Ligier has sought to demonstrate that the practice of embolisms in the *Birkat ha-mazon* goes back at least to the second century C.E. See his "The Origins of the Eucharistic Prayer: From the Last Supper to the Eucharist," *Studia Liturgica* 9:4 (1973): 172-75.

30. Hänggi and Pahl, *Prex Eucharistica*, 11-12 (translation mine.) .

31. *Ibid.*, 27. We use here Jeremias' translation in *Eucharistic Words*, 252. Jeremias argued that this embolism goes back to the time of Jesus.

32. *Ibid.*

33. *The Book of the Jubilees*, trans. James C. VanderKam (Corpus Scriptorum Christianorum Orientalium 511, Lovanii: In aedibus E. Peeters, 1989).
34. Talley, "From *Berakah* to *Eucharistia*," 85.
35. Heinemann, *Prayer in the Talmud*, 63-64.
36. Hans Bernhard Meyer, *Eucharistie: Geschichte, Theologie, Pastoral* (Regensburg: Verlag Friedrich Pustet, 1989), 67.
37. Enrico Mazza, "Didache 9-10: Elements of a Eucharistic Interpretation" in *The Didache in Modern Research*, ed. Jonathan A. Draper (Leiden: E.J. Brill, 1996), 296.
38. Mazza, *The Eucharistic Prayers of the Roman Rite*, 25.
39. For the Greek text and a Latin recension, see Hänggi and Pahl, *Prex Eucharistica*, 66-68. (The translation from the Greek is mine.) For an English translation, see Jasper and Cuming, *Prayers of the Eucharist*, 23-24.
40. R.H. Connolly, "Agape and Eucharist in the Didache," *Downside Review* 55 (1937), 477-489; Dix, *Shape of the Liturgy*, 48 n.2; 90-93.
41. J.P. Audet, *La Didachè. Instructions des Apotres* (Paris: Gabalda, 1958), 405-407.
42. See, *inter alia*, Martin Dibelius, "Die Mahl-Gebete der Didache," *Zeitschrift für die neutestamentliche Wissenschaft* 37 (1938), 32-41; Jeremias, *Eucharistic Words*, 117-18, 134; Bultmann, *Theology of the New Testament*; Willy Rordorf, "The Didache" in *The Eucharist of the Early Christians*, trans. Matthew J. O'Connell (New York: Pueblo, 1978), 1-23; Kurt Niederwimmer, *The Didache: A Commentary*, trans. Linda M. Maloney (Minneapolis: Fortress Press, 1998). For a useful summary of the various hypotheses proposed, see this last work, 141-143.
43. This is the hypothesis proposed by H. Lietzmann in his celebrated study, *Messe und Herrenmahl: Eine Studie zur Geschichte der Liturgie* (Bonn: Marcus and Weber), 230-238. Cited in Geoffrey Wainwright, *Eucharist and Eschatology* (New York: Oxford University Press, 1981), 68. Lietzmann, however, suggested that the invitational formula in 10.6 was misplaced. It originally followed the prayers in chapter 9, which he considered to be those that accompanied the community's Eucharist. The agape meal followed, to which he assigned the prayers in 10.2-5. The texts therefore relate an agape introduced by a eucharistic celebration.
44. Wainwright, *Eucharist and Eschatology*, 68.
45. For the following, we depend on the exegetical insights found in Huub van de Sandt and David Flusser, *The Didache: Its Jewish Sources and its Place in Early Judaism and Christianity* (Assen: Royal Van Gorcum, 2002), 302-304.
46. Jonathan A. Draper, "Ritual Process and Ritual Symbol in Didache 7-10 *Vigiliae Christianae* 54 (2000): 142.
47. *Ibid.*
48. van de Sandt and Flusser, *The Didache*, 302-3.
49. *Ibid.*, 303
50. *Ibid.*
51. For a recent criticism of the comparative approach that liturgical historians have generally adopted since Finkelstein's article, see Paul F. Bradshaw, *Eucharistic Origins* (Oxford: Oxford University Press, 2004), 32-35.

52. For an argument against the hypothesis of Finkelstein, see the recent work of Aaron Milavec, *The Didache: Faith, Hope, and Life of the Earliest Christian Communities, 50-70 C.E.* (New York: The Newman Press, 2003), 416-421.

53. Mazza, *Origins of the Eucharistic Prayer*, 23.

54. Hänggi and I. Pahl, *Prex Eucharistica*, 11. Here the *siddur Rav Saadja* has according to the Latin recension, "*Et propter haec omnia gratias agimus.*"

55. Talley, "From *Berakah* to *Eucharistia*," 123.

56. van de Sandt and Flusser, *The Didache*, 314 (note 130).

57. *Ibid.*, 315. See also Talley, "From *Berakah* to *Eucharistia*," 126.

58. For the early Jewish-Christian theology of the name, see Basil Studer, *Trinity and Incarnation: Faith of the Early Church*, trans. Matthias Westerhoff (Collegeville: The Liturgical Press, 1993), 36; Jean Daniélou, *The Theology of Jewish Christianity*, trans. John A. Baker (London: Darton, Longman & Todd, 1964), 147-172; Aloys Grillmeier, *Christ in Christian Tradition: From the Apostolic Age to Chalcedon (451)*, trans. J.S. Bowden (New York: Sheed and Ward, 1965), 46-50.

59. Edward J. Kilmartin, "The Eucharistic Prayer: Content and Function of Some Early Eucharistic Prayers," in *The Word in the World: Essays in Honor of Frederick L. Moriarty*, eds. Richard J. Clifford and George W. MacRae (Cambridge, MA: Weston College Press, 1973), 129.

60. Mazza, *Origins of the Eucharistic Prayer*, 20-22.

61. *Ibid.*, 21.

62. *Ibid.*, 22. See also Enrico Mazza, "The Eucharist in the First Four Centuries," in *The Eucharist*, Handbook for Liturgical Studies, Volume III, ed. Anscar J. Chupungco (Collegeville: The Liturgical Press, 1999), 23-24.

63. Mazza, *Origins of the Eucharistic Prayer*, 21.

64. Johannes Betz, "The Eucharist in the *Didache*," in *The* Didache *in Modern Research*, 256-258; Kilmartin, "The Eucharistic Prayer: Content and Function of Some Early Eucharistic Prayers," 127-129.

65. *Ibid.*, 128.

66. Enrico Mazza, "*Didache* 9-10," 291-299; *Origins of the Eucharistic Prayer*, 22-26

67. *Ibid.*, 23.

68. Mazza refers to the *Birkat ha-mazon* of Maimonides, cited by Finkelstein: "O Lord, our God, we praise you and bless your name, as it is written, 'when you have eaten your fill, you must bless the Lord, your God, for the good country he has given you' (Deut. 8:10)." *Ibid.*

69. *Ibid.*, 24.

70. Mazza, "*Didache* 9-10," 299, 294.

71. *Ibid.*, 294.

72. *Ibid.*, 296.

73. Mazza, *Origins of the Eucharistic Prayer*, 25.

74. *Ibid.*

75. For the nature, origin, and content of these liturgical prayers, see Heinemann, *Prayer in the Talmud*, 13-36; 218-250.

76. Hänggi and Pahl, *Prex Eucharistica*, 48-49 (translation is mine).

77. *Ibid.*, 38.
78. Heinemann, *Prayer in the Talmud*, 219.
79. Hageman, "The Order for the Sacrament of the Lord's Supper," in *A Companion to the Liturgy*, 36.
80. For an historical introduction, see Paul F. Bradshaw, et al., *The Apostolic Tradition: A Commentary* (Minneapolis: Fortress Press, 2002), 1-16.
81. For an understanding of the temporal consciousness that structures Israel's worship, we find the remarks of Michael Kunzler to be especially instructive: "Israel's worship is essentially orientated towards the future, and out of the memory of the past, creates the promise of what will come; the great deeds of Yahveh which are "recalled to mind," are "today" a reality which creates life." Michael Kunzler, *The Church's Liturgy*. Trans. Placed Murray OSB, et al. (London: Continuum, 2001), 33:
82. For an account of the historical development of the eucharistic prayer, see Allan Bouley, *From Freedom to Formula: The Evolution of the Eucharistic Prayer from Oral Improvisation to Written Texts* (Washington, D.C.: The Catholic University of America Press, 1981). See also previously mentioned Bouyer, *Eucharist*; Mazza, *Origins of the Eucharistic Prayer*; Bradshaw, *Eucharistic Origins*.
83. For a critical edition of the Latin version of this prayer text, see Hänggi and Pahl, *Prex Eucharistica*, 80-81. (The translation from the Latin is mine.) For an English translation, see Jasper and Cuming, *Prayers of the Eucharist*, 34-35.
84. Mazza, "The Eucharist in the First Four Centuries," 43.
85. On the sources of the narrative, see Mazza, *The Origins of the Eucharistic Prayer*, 102-129.
86. Hänggi and Pahl, *Prex Eucharistica*, 81 (translation mine).
87. *Ibid.*
88. In regard to our claim that the eucharistic prayer has an anamnetic-epicletic structure, a point of clarification is in order here. The term *anamnesis* can designate that section of the eucharistic prayer that recalls God's saving acts; it can also refer in the more restricted sense to that part of the prayer after the institution narrative that begins "remembering (*memores*)," Similarly, *epiclesis* can mean "petition" generally, but it typically refers to the invocation of the Holy Spirit on the bread and wine of the Eucharist and the people who share them.
89. Louis Ligier, "The Origins of the Eucharistic Prayer," *Studia Liturgica* 9 (1973): 161-185. Liturgical historians are aware that the institution narrative is not attested in the structure of the earliest eucharistic prayer texts as it is in later more evolved and complex eucharistic prayer texts. Among the texts Ligier has singled out for mention include the East Syrian litugy of Addai and Mari, and the oldest recenscion of the Alexandrian anaphora of St Mark, that of the Strasbourg Papyrus, as prayers that "constitute a complete and closed euchologia which does not demand to be prolonged by anything at all, either a *Sanctus* or a narrative" (179). For a critical edition of these texts, resp., see Hänggi and Pahl, *Prex Eucharistica*, 375-380; 116-119.
90. *Ibid.*, 180.

91. Cesare Giraudo, *La struttura letteraria della preghiera eucaristica: Saggio sulla genesi letteraria di una forma* (Rome: Biblical Institute Press, 1981). For a distillation of arguments contained in this study salient to our investigation, see "Le récit de l'institution dans la prière eucharistique a-t-il des précédents?," *Nouvelle revue théologique* 106 (1984): 513-535. It is on this article that our discussion here depends.

92. *Ibid.*, 521.

93. *Ibid.*, 532-533.

Chapter Five

1.   This adage is an abbreviation of the original formulation *legem credendi lex statuat supplicandi* ("Let the law of prayer establish the law of belief"), ascribed to Prosper of Aquitane, a fifth century monk. For an interpretation of this formulation in its original context, see Kilmartin, *The Eucharist in the West*, 344-346; and Kevin W. Irwin, *Context and Text: Method in Liturgical Theology* (Collegeville: The Liturgical Press, 1994), 3-10. For an extended discussion on the problem of the relation between the law of prayer and the law of belief in the history of the church, see Geoffrey Wainwright, *Doxology: The Praise of God in Worship, Doctrine, and Life* (New York: Oxford University Press, 1980), 218-274.

2.   Kilmartin, *Eucharist in the West*, 340, 355

3.   *Liturgy and Psalms*, 66-68.

4.   Alasdair I.C. Heron, *Table and Tradition: Toward an Ecumenical Understanding of the Eucharist* (Philadelphia: The Westminster Press, 1983), 170.

5.   For this insight into the meaning of the *sanctus*, we our indebted to Edward J. Kilmartin. See Jerome M. Hall, *We Have the Mind of Christ: The Holy Spirit and Liturgical Memory in the Thought of Edward J. Kilmartin* (Collegeville: The Liturgical Press, 2001), 65.

6.   In his commentary on the 1950 version of the ERF eucharistic prayer, J.D. Benoit did not hesitate to "affirm the necessity of this sacrifice of ourselves in union with the unique sacrifice of Christ," presumably understanding the new French Reformed liturgy to convey exactly this intention. J.D. Benoit, *Liturgical Renewal: Studies in Catholic and Protestant Developments on the Continent*, trans. Edwin Hudson (London: SCM Press LTD, 1958), 40-41.

7.   *Lieben bruder und schwestern, bitten gott den vatter durch unsern herren Jesum Christum, das er uns den heiligen geist, den tröster zuschicke, das er mache unser leib zu eim lebendigen, heiligen, wolgefelligen opfer, das do ist der vernunftig gottesdienst, der gott gefelt, das beschehe uns allen. Amen.* For a critical edition of Scwarz' *Deutsche Messe* 1524, see Hans-Christian Drömann, "Das Abendmahl nach den Strassburger Ordnungen," *Coena Domini I*, 311-329.

8.   The Reformed liturgical theologian Jean-Jacques von Allmen has described the work of the Holy Spirit in the liturgical celebration in similar terms: "[T]he work of the Holy Spirit...consists, on the one hand, in efficaciously applying what God has done *illic et tunc* [there and then] in Jesus Christ to the *hic et nunc* [here and

now] of such and such a man or community (or event)—the Holy Spirit thus mediates Christ to us—and, on the other hand, in efficaciously referring the *hic et nunc* of such and such a man or community (or event) to the *illic et tunc* of what God has done in Jesus Christ at Golgotha and in the garden of Joseph of Arimathea—the Holy Spirit brings us into communion with Christ." *Worship: Its Theology and Practice* (New York: Oxford University Press, 1965), 40.

9. *Ibid.*, 159.
10. Kilmartin, *Eucharist in the West*, 341.
11. Kunzler, *The Church's Liturgy*, 3-4.
12. For the claim that the communication of sacramental grace should be understood in terms of a symbolic communication of the language of faith rather than a metaphysical scheme of cause and effect, we depend here on Louis-Marie Chauvet, *Symbol and Sacrament: A Sacramental Reinterpretation of Christian Existence*, trans. Patrick Madigan and Madeleine Beaumont (Collegeville: The Liturgical Press, 1995), 431. See esp. 409-446.
13. *Ibid.*, 235.
14. *Ibid.*, 236. [Italics author's.]
15. *Ibid.*
16. *Ibid.*, 284.
17. *Ibid.*, 236.
18. F. Dumortier, "Le Dieu de l'histoire devenu le Dieu de la nature: Dt 26, 4-10," *Assemblées du Seigneur* 14 (Paris: Cerf, 1973), 24-25. Cited in Chauvet, *Symbol and Sacrament*, 284-85.
19. For this transformation of temporal consciousness mediated by the liturgical recitation of the institution narrative, see the illuminating remarks of liturgical theologian Angelus A. Häussling: "[Memorial] has a linguistic form and expresses in words the fact that people who remember have become something different; they can and must understand themselves as different...They...identify themselves as contemporaries, which they are through the power of sacramental reality; *they do so by using textual quotations to put themselves in the roles of the historical contemporaries: as they were, so are we* [italics added]." Angelus Haussling, OSB, "Liturgy: Memorial of the Past and Liberation in the Present," in *The Meaning of the Liturgy*, ed. Angelus Haussling, OSB, trans. Linda M. Maloney (Collegeville: The Liturgical Press, 1991), 111.
20. Ligier, "The Origins of the Eucharistic Prayer," 180.
21. See F.J. Leenhardt, "This is My Body" in *Essays on the Lord's Supper*, 53-55.
22. Bodo Nischan, "The '*Fractio Panis*': A Reformed Communion Practice in Late Reformation Germany" *Church History* 53 (1984), 26. .
23. *Liturgy and Psalms*, 476-77.
24. The complete title of Erastus' work is *Erzelung Etlicher ursachen, warumb das hochwirdige Sacrament des Nachtmals unsers Herrn und Heylandts Jesu Christi, nicht solle ohne das brodbrechen gehalten werden* [*An Account of the Various Reasons Why the Holy Sacrament of the Supper of our Lord and Savior Jesus Christ Should Not Be*

Celebrated without the Breaking of the Bread] (Heidelberg, 1563, 1565). Cited in Nischan, "The 'Fractio Panis'," 20.

25. Oliver K. Olson, "Lutheran-Reformed Confrontation and the Revolt of the Netherlands" in *Controversy and Conciliation: The Reformation and the Palatinate 1559-1583*, ed. Derk Visser (Allison Park, PA: Pickwick Publications, 1986), 148.

26. For this summary of the content of Erastus' work, we depend here on Nischan, "The 'Fractio Panis'," 20 and Olson, "Lutheran-Reformed Confrontation," 148-150.

27. *Liturgy and Psalms*, 67.

Conclusion

1. Mast, *The Eucharistic Service of the Catholic Apostolic Church*, 153.

2. Alan D. Falconer, "Word, Sacrament, and Communion: New Emphases in Reformed Worship in the Twentieth Century" in *Christian Worship in Reformed Churches Past and Present*, 143.

3. Antoine Vergote, *Religion, Belief and Unbelief: A Psychological Study* (Leuven: Leuven University Press, 1996), 279, 280

Bibliography

Primary Sources

Bürki, Bruno. *Cène du seigneur – eucharistie de l'église: Le cheminement des Eglises réformées romandes et françaises depuis le XVIIIe siècle, d'après leurs textes liturgiques: Volume A: Textes.* Cahiers oecuméniques 17A. Fribourg Suisse: Editions Universitaires, 1985.

Calvin, John. *La Forme des Prieres et Chantz ecclesiastiques, anec la maniere d'adminstrer les Sacramens, et consacrer le Mariage: selon la coustume de l'Eglise ancienne.* In *Joannis Calvini Opera Selecta.* Vol. 2. Ed. by Petrus Barth, Wilhelm Niesel, and Dora Scheuner. Munich: Kaiser, 1952.

The Church of South India. *The Service of the Lord's Supper or The Holy Eucharist.* 2nd ed. London: Oxford University Press, 1950.

_____. *The Liturgy of the Church of South India.* Celebrated during the Second Assembly of the World Council of Churches. First Methodist Church, Evanston, Illinois, USA, 29 August 1954.

Committee appointed by the General Synod of 1902 of the Reformed Church in America. *Revision of the Liturgical Forms of the Reformed Church in America.* New York: Styles & Cash, 1903.

Committee on Liturgical Form Revision appointed by the Synod of 1957 of the Christian Reformed Church. *Proposed Revisions of the Form for the Lord's Supper.* Grand Rapids: Christian Reformed Publishing House, 1959.

Committee on Revision of the *Book of Common Order*, The Presbyterian Church in Canada. *Basic Principles of Worship and Commentary on the Great Service of Word and Sacrament*, 1957.

Committee on Revision of the *Book of Church Order*, The Presbyterian Church in the United States. *Study Draft of the Directory for the Worship and Work of the Church*, 1961.

Dienstboek voor de Nederlandse Hervormde Kerk: in Ontwerp. 's-Gravenhage: Boekencentrum N.V., 1955.

Hanggi, Anton. and Pahl, Irmgard. *Prex eucharistica. Textus e variis liturgiis antiquioribus selecti.* Spicilegium friburgense 12. Fribourg, 1968.

Jasper, R.C.D. and G.J. Cuming, eds. *Prayers of the Eucharist: Early and Reformed*. New York: Oxford University Press, 1992.

Liturgical Orders and Forms As Revised from the Liturgy of the Reformed Church in America Submitted by Direction of General Synod June, 1952 For study and Permissive use by the Churches.

Liturgy and Confessions. Reformed Church in America: Reformed Church Press, 1990.

The Liturgy of the Reformed Church in America Together with the Psalter Arranged for Responsive Reading. New York: The Board of Education, 1907. Reprint, 1945.

The Liturgy of the Reformed Church in America together with the Psalter Selected and Arranged for Responsive Reading. New York: The Board of Education of the Reformed Church in America, 1968.

A Liturgy: or,Order of Christian Worship. Philadelphia: Lindsay and Blakiston, 1857.

Minutes of the General Synod, Vol.XXXIX-XLIV. New York: Reformed Church in America, 1951.

Niesel, Wilhelm, ed. *Kirchenordnung der Kurpfalz*. 1563. In *Bekenntnisschriften und Kirchenordnungen der nach Gottes Wort reformierten Kirche*. 3rd ed. Zurich: Evangelischer Verlag, 1938.

Office of the General Assembly, The United Presbyterian Church in the United States in America. *On Amending the Directory of Worship and the Form of Government Chapter VIII, Sections 4, 5 and 6, and Chapter XI, Sections 15–23*. 1961.

Pahl, Irmgard, ed. *Coena Domini I. Die Abendmahlsliturgie der Reformationskirchen im 16./17. Jahrhundert*. Spicilegium Friburgense 29. Universitatsverlag Freiberg Schweiz, 1983.

The Provisional Liturgy Orders and Forms of Worship as proposed by the Committee on Revision of the Liturgy of the Reformed Church in America and approved by General Synod for study and permissive use, June, 1963.

The Provisional Liturgy Orders and Forms of Worship as revised from The Liturgy of the Reformed Church in America and approved by General Synod for study and permissive use, June 1958.

Sehling, Emil, ed. *Die evangelischen Kirchenordnungen des XVI. Jahrhunderts, Vierzehnter Band, Kurpfälz*. Tübingen: J.C.B. Mohr (Paul Siebeck), 1969.

Thompson, Bard. *Liturgies of the Western Church*. New York: World Publishing, 1962.

_____, trans. "The Palatinate Liturgy Heidelberg, 1563." *Theology and Life* 6, no. 1 (Spring 1963): 49-67.

Secondary Sources

Appel, Theodore. *The Life and Work of John Williamson Nevin*. Philadelphia: Reformed Church Publication House, 1889. Reprint, New York: Arno Press and the New York Times, 1969.

Audet, J.P. *La Didachè. Instructions des Apotres*. Paris: Gabalda, 1958.

Barkley, John M. "Pleading His Eternal Sacrifice in the Reformed Liturgy." In *The Sacrifice of Praise*, ed. Bryan D. Spinks, 123-142. Rome: Edizioni Liturgiche, 1981.

_____. *The Worship of the Reformed Church*. Ecumenical Studies in Worship No. 15. Richmond: John Knox Press, 1967.

Bate, H.N., ed. *Faith and Order: Proceedings of the World Conference Lausanne, August 3– 21, 1927*. London: Student Christian Movement, 1927.

Beauduin, Lambert. *Mélanges liturgiques*. Louvain: Centre Liturgiques, 1954.

Beardslee III, John W. "Some Implications for Worship in Traditional Reformed Doctrine." *Reformed Review* 30 (Spring 1977): 210-215.

Benoit, J.D. *Liturgical Renewal: Studies in Catholic and Protestant Developments on the Continent*. Translated by Edwin Hudson. London: SCM Press LTD, 1958.

Bergsma, Joop. "The Eucharistic Prayer in the Non-Roman Catholic Churches of the West Today." *Studia Liturgica* 11 (1976): 177-185.

Betz, Johannes. "The Eucharist in the *Didache*." In *The* Didache *in Modern Research*, ed. Jonathan Draper, 244-275. Leiden: Brill, 1996.

Bierma, Lyle D. *The Doctrine of the Sacraments in the Heidelberg Catechism: Melanchthonian, Calvinist, or Zwinglian?* Studies in Reformed Theology and History, No. 4. Princeton: Princeton Theological Seminary, 1999.

Binkley, Luther J. *The Mercersburg Theology*. Mannheim, PA: Sentinel Printing House, 1953.

Bomberger, John H.A. "Dr. Nevin and his Antagonists," *Mercersburg Review* 5 (1853): 89-124; 145-181.

_____. "The Old Palatinate Liturgy of 1563." *Mercersburg Review* 2 (1850): 81-96, 265-286; and 3 (1851: 97-128.

Bornert, René. *La Réforme protestante du culte à Strasbourg au XVIe siècle (1523-1598): approche sociologique et interprétation théologique*. Studies in Medieval and Reformation Thought. Leiden: E.J. Brill, 1981.

Bouley, Allan. *From Freedom to Formula: The Evolution of the Eucharistic Prayer from Oral Improvisation to Written Texts*. Washington, D.C.: The Catholic University Press of America, 1981.

Bouyer, Louis. *Eucharist: Theology and Spirituality of the Eucharistic Prayer.* Notre Dame: Notre Dame University Press, 1968.

_____. *Life and Liturgy.* London: Sheed and Ward, 1956.

Botte, Bernard. *From Silence to Participation: An Insider's View of Liturgical Renewal.* Translated by John Sullivan. Washington, D.C.: The Pastoral Press, 1988.

Bradshaw, Paul F, et al. *The Apostolic Tradition: A Commentary.* Minneapolis: Fortress Press, 2002.

_____. *Eucharistic Origins.* Oxford: Oxford University Press, 2004.

_____. *The Search for the Origins of Christian Worship: Sources and Methods for the Study of Early Liturgy.* Oxford: Oxford University Press, 2002.

Brecht, Martin. "Luther's Reformation." In *Handbook of European History 1400-1600: Late Middle Ages, Renaissance, and Reformation, Vol.* 2, eds. Thomas A. Brady, Jr., Heiko A. Oberman, and James D. Tracy, 129-160. Grand Rapids: Eerdmans, 1995.

Brilioth, Yngve. *Eucharistic Faith and Practice, Evangelical and Catholic.* London: SPCK, 1965.

Brinkman, Martien E. *Progress in Unity? Fifty Years of Theology within the World Council of Churches: 1945-1995: A Study Guide.* Grand Rapids: Eerdmans, 1995

Brouwer, Arie C. *Reformed Church Roots: Thirty-Five Formative Events.* New York: Reformed Church Press, 1977.

Bultmann, Rudolph. *Theology of the New Testament.* New York: Scribners, 1951-1955.

Bürki, Bruno. *Cène du seigneur — eucharistie de l'église: Le cheminement des Eglises réformées romandes et françaises depuis le XVIIIe siècle, d'après leurs textes liturgiques: Volume B: Commentaire.* Cahiers oecuméniques 17B. Fribourg Suisse: Editions Universitaires, 1985.

_____. "Jean-Jacques von Allmen dans le Mouvement Liturgique." *Studia Liturgica* 17 (1987): 52-61.

Cadier, J. "La priere eucharistique de Calvin." In *Eucharisties d'Orient et d'Occidnent.* Semaine liturgique de l'Institut Saint-Serge. 1. Lex Orandi 46, 171-180. Paris: Les editions du Cerf, 1970.

Calvin, John. *Institutes of the Christian Religion* [1559 edition]. Edited by John T. McNeill. Translated by Ford Lewis Battles. 2 vols. Philadelphia: Westminster, 1960.

Casel, Odo. *The Mystery of Christian Worship and Other Writings.* Translated by I.T. Hale. Westminster, MD: Newman Press, 1963.

Chauvet, Louis-Marie. *Symbol and Sacrament.* Translated by Matthew J. O'Connell.

Collegeville: Pueblo, 1995.

Chupungco, Anscar J., ed. *Introduction to the Liturgy*. Handbook for Liturgical Studies. Volume I. Collegeville: The Liturgical Press, 1997.

_____. *Fundamental Liturgy*. Handbook for Liturgical Studies. Volume II. Collegeville: The Liturgical Press, 1998.

_____. *The Eucharist*. Handbook for Liturgical Studies. Volume III. Collegeville: The Liturgical Press, 1999.

Clark, Francis. *Eucharistic Sacrifice and the Reformation*. London: Dartmann, Longman, and Todd LTD, 1960.

Conkin, Paul K. *The Uneasy Center: Reformed Christianity in Antebellum America*. Chapel Hill: The University of North Carolina Press, 1995.

Connolly, R.H. "Agape and Eucharist in the *Didache*." *Downside Review* 55 (1937): 477-489

Corwin, Edward T. ed., *A Digest of Constitutional and Synodical Legislation of the Reformed Church in America*. New York, 1906.

Crumley, Jr., George W. *A People at Worship: Reflections on Worship in the Reformed Church in America*. The Heritage and Hope Series of the Reformed Church in America. Focus Two: Worship. Reformed Church Press, 1979.

Cullmann, Oscar and F.J. Leenhardt. *Essays on the Lord's Supper*. Translated by J.G. Davies. Ecumenical Studies in Worship no. 1. London: Lutterworth Press, 1958.

Cuming, Geoffrey. *He Gave Thanks: An Introduction to the Eucharistic Prayer*. Nottingham: Grove Books, 1981.

Danielou, Jean. *The Theology of Jewish Christianity*. Translated by John A. Baker. London: Darton, Longmann & Todd, 1964.

Dankbaar, Willem Frederik, ed. *Marten Micron, De christlicke Ordinancien der Nederlantscher Ghemeinten te London (1554)*. Kerkhistorische Studien behorende bij het Nederlands Archief voor Kerkgeshiedenis, Deel VII. 's-Gravenhage, 1956.

Davies, Horton. *Bread of Life & Cup of Joy: Newer Ecumenical Perspectives on the Eucharist*. Grand Rapids: Eerdmans, 1993.

_____. *Worship and Theology in England: From Newman to Martineau, 1850-1900*. Volume IV. Princeton: Princeton University Press, 1962.

_____. *Worship and Theology in England: The Ecumenical Century, 1900-1965*. Volume V. Princeton: Princeton University Press, 1965.

Davies, J.G., ed. *A Dictionary of Liturgy and Worship*. New York: Macmillan, 1972.

De Jong, Gerald F. *The Dutch Reformed Church in the American Colonies*. Grand Rapids:

Eerdmans, 1978.

Dekkers, Eligius. *Inleiding tot de liturgiek*. Antwerpen, Brussels: N.v. Standaard-boekhandel, 1942.

Dibelius, Martin. "Die Mahl-Gebete der *Didache.*" *Zeitschrift für die neutestamentliche Wissenschaft* 37 (1938): 32-41.

Di Sante, Carmine. *Jewish Prayer: The Origins of the Christian Liturgy*. Translated by Matthew J. O'Connell. New York: Paulist Press, 1985.

Dix, Gregory. *The Shape of the Liturgy*. London: A & C Black, 1945.

Draper, Jonathan, ed. *The* Didache *in Modern Research*. Leiden: Brill, 1996.

_____. "Ritual Process and Ritual Symbol in *Didache* 7-10." *Vigiliae Christianae* 54 (2000): 121-158.

Duba, Arlo D. "Why a Eucharistic Prayer?" *Reformed Liturgy and Music* 22 (Fall 1988): 187-189.

Edwall, Pehr, Eric Hayman, and William D. Maxwell, eds. *Ways of Worship: The Report of a Theological Commission on Faith and Order*. London: SCM Press LTD, 1951.

Elkins, Heather Murray, ed. *Pulpit, Table, and Song: Essays in Celebration of Howard G. Hageman*. Lanham, MD: The Scarecrow Press, 1996.

Elwood, Christopher. *The Body Broken: The Calvinist Doctrine of the Eucharist and the Symbolization of Power in Sixteenth-Century France*. Oxford: Oxford University Press, 1999.

Evans, William Borden. "Imputation and Impartation: The Problem of Union with Christ in Nineteenth-Century American Reformed Theology." Diss. Vanderbilt University, 1996.

Fagerberg, David W. *What is Liturgical Theology? A Study in Methodology*. Collegeville: The Liturgical Press, 1992.

Farley, Michael A. "The Liturgical Theology of John Williamson Nevin." *Studia Liturgica* 33 (2003): 204-222.

Farris, Stephen. "Reformed Identity and Reformed Worship." *Reformed World* 43 (Mr-Je 1993): 69-76.

Fenwick, John R.K., and Bryan D. Spinks. *Worship in Transition: The Liturgical Movement in the Twentieth Century*. New York: Continuum, 1995.

Fey, Harold E. *The Ecumenical Movement: A History of the Ecumenical Movement Volume 2: 1948-1968*. Philadelphia: Westminster Press, 1986.

Fink, Peter E., ed. *The New Dictionary of Sacramental Worship*. Collegeville: The Liturgical Press, 1990.

Finkelstein, Louis. "The Birkhat Ha-Mazon." *Jewish Quarterly Review*, vol. XIX (1928-29): 211-262.

Flegg, Columba Graham. *'Gathered Under Apostles' A Study of the Catholic Apostolic Church*. Oxford: Clarendon Press, 1992.

Franklin, R.W. *Nineteenth-Century Churches: The History of a New Catholicism in Württemberg, England, and France*. New York: Garland Publishing, Inc., 1987.

Fredman, Ruth Gruber. *The Passover Seder: Afikoman in Exile*. Philadelphia: University of Pennsylvania Press, 1981.

Frishman, Judith, Willemien Otten, and Gerard Rouwhorst, eds. *Religious Identity and the Problem of Historical Foundation: The Foundational Character of Authoritative Sources in the History of Judaism and Christianity*. Leiden: Brill, 2004.

Gassman, Günther. *Konzeptionen der Einheit in der Bewegung für Glauben und Kirchenverfassung 1910-1937*. Göttingen: Vandenhoeck & Ruprecht, 1979.

Gerhards, Albert and Klemens Richter, eds. *Das Opfer: Biblischer Anspruch und liturgische Gestalt*. Quaestiones disputatae, 186. Freiburg im Breisgau: Herder, 2000.

Gerrish, B.A. *Grace & Gratitude: The Eucharistic Theology of John Calvin*. Minneapolis: Fortress Press, 1993.

_____. *Tradition and the Modern World: Reformed Theology in the Nineteenth Century*. Chicago: The University of Chicago Press, 1978.

Gibbard, S.M. "Liturgical Life in the Church of South India: The Book of Common Worship in Practice." *Studia Liturgica* 3 (1964): 193-209.

Giraudo, Cesare. "The Eucharist as Re-Presentation." *Religious Studies Bulletin* 4 (1984): 154-159.

_____. *Eucaristia per la Chiesa: Prospettive teologiche sull'eucaristia a partire dalla "lex orandi"* Rome: Editrice Pontificia Università Gregoriana, 1989.

_____. "Le récit de l'institution dans la prière eucharistique a-t-il des antécédents?" *Nouvelle Revue Theologique* 106 (1984): 513-536.

_____. *La struttura letteraria della preghiera eucaristica: Saggio sulla genesi letteraria di una forma*. Rome: Biblical Institute Press, 1981.

Good, James I. *History of the Reformed Church in the United States, 1725-1792*. Reading, 1899.

Graham, Stephen R. *Cosmos in the Chaos: Philip Schaff's Interpretation of Nineteenth-Century American Religion*. Grand Rapids: Eerdmans, 1995.

Grillmeier, Aloys. *Christ in Christian Tradition: From the Apostolic Age to Chalcedon (451)*. Translated by J.S. Bowden. New York: Sheed and Ward, 1965.

Gruenwald, Ithamar. *Rituals and Ritual Theory in Ancient Israel.* Leiden: Brill, 2003.

Gunnemann, Louis H. *The Shaping of the United Church of Christ: An Essay in the History of American Christianity.* Cleveland: United Church Press, 1977.

Hageman, Howard G. "Changing Understandings of Reformed Corporate Worship." *Reformed Liturgy and Music* 18 (Fall 1984): 155-158.

_____. "The Coming-of-Age of the Liturgical Movement: Report on Section IV of the Montreal Conference." *Studia Liturgica* 2 (1963): 256-265.

_____. "Discerning the Body of the Lord." *The Church Herald,* 12 September 1952, 9, 22-23.

_____. "The Dutch Liturgy." *The Church Herald,* 12 May 1950, 5.

_____. "The Eucharistic Prayer in the Reformed Church in America." *Reformed Review* 30, no.3 (Spring 1977): 166-179.

_____. "Liturgical Activities in the Reformed Church in America." *Studia Liturgica* 3 (Winter 1964): 190-92.

_____. "Liturgical Development in the Reformed Church of America: 1868-1947." *Journal of Presbyterian History* 47 (Sept. 1969): 262-289.

_____. "The Liturgical Origins of the Reformed Churches." In *The Heritage of John Calvin,* ed. John H. Bratt, 110-136. Grand Rapids: Eerdmans, 1973.

_____. "The Liturgical Revival." *Theology Today* VI, no. 4 (January 1950): 490-505.

_____. "The Liturgy of the Heidelberg Catechism." *The Church Herald,* 5 May 1950, 11.

_____. "The Liturgy of John Calvin." *The Church Herald,* 21 April 1950, 13.

_____. "Our Liturgical History." *The Church Herald,* 4 May 1951, 12-13.

_____. "A Preface to the Revision of the Liturgy." *New Brunswick Theological Seminary* (May 1955): 1-6.

_____. *Pulpit and Table.* Richmond: John Knox Press, 1962.

_____. "The Romance of the Liturgy." *The Church Herald,* 3 February 1950, 13.

_____. "A Reformed Service." *The Church Herald,* 19 May 1950, 8.

_____. "Reformed Spirituality." In *Protestant Spiritual Traditions,* ed. Frank C. Senn, 55-79. New York: Paulist Press, 1986.

_____. "Some notes on the Use of the Lectionary in the Reformed Tradition." In *The Divine Drama in History and Liturgy,* ed. John E Booty, 163-177. Allison Park, PA: Pickwick Publications, 1984.

_____. "Three Reformed Liturgies." *Theology Today* XV, no. 4 (January 1959): 507-

520.

Hall, Jerome M. *We Have the Mind of Christ: The Holy Spirit and Liturgical Memory in the Thought of Edward J. Kilmartin.* Collegeville: The Liturgical Press, 2001.

Hamstra, Sam and Arie J. Girffioen. *Reformed Confessionalism in Nineteenth-Century America: Essays on the Thought of John Williamson Nevin.* Lanham, MD: Scarecrow Press, 1995.

Harmelink, Herman III. *Ecumenism and the Reformed Church.* Grand Rapids: Eerdmans, 1968.

Häussling, Angelus A. *The Meaning of the Liturgy.* Translated by Linda M. Maloney. Collegeville: The Liturgical Press, 1994.

Hebert, A.G. *Liturgy and Society: The Function of the Church in the Modern World.* London: Faber & Faber, 1935.

Heinemann, Joseph. *Prayer in the Talmud: Forms and Patterns.* Berlin: Walter de Gruyter, 1977

Heron, Alasdair I.C. *Table and Tradition: Toward an Ecumenical Understanding of the Eucharist.* Philadelphia: The Westminster Press, 1983.

Hilborn, David. "From Performativity to Pedagogy: Jean Ladriere and the Pragmatics of Reformed Worship Discourse." In *The Nature of Religious Language,* ed. Stanley E. Porter, 170-200. Sheffield: Sheffield Academic Press, 1996.

Hodgson, Leonard, ed. *The Second World Conference on Faith and Order Held at Edinburgh, August 3-18, 1937.* New York: The Macmillan Company, 1938.

Honders, A.C. "Remarks on the Postcommunio in Some Reformed Liturgies." In *The Sacrifice of Praise,* ed. Bryan D. Spinks, 143-157. Rome: Edizioni Liturgiche, 1981.

Houssiau, Albert. "The Rediscovery of the Liturgy by Sacramental Theology (1950-1980)." *Studia Liturgica* 15 (1982/1983): 158-177.

Idelsohn, A.Z. *Jewish Liturgy and its Development.* New York: Schocken Books, 1967.

Irwin, Kevin. *Context and Text: Method in Liturgical Theology.* Collegeville: The Liturgical Press, 1994.

_____. *Liturgical Theology.* Collegeville: The Liturgical Press, 1990.

James, M. Stephen. "The Needed Scope of Liturgical Revision." *The Church Herald,* 18 May 1951, 8-9.

Jaubert, Annie. *The Date of the Last Supper.* Staten Island, NY: Alba House, 1965.

Jenny, Markus. *Die Einheit des Abendmahlsgottesdienstes bei den elsassischen und schweiserischen Reformatoren.* Zurich: Zwingli Verlag, 1968.

Jeremias, Joachim. *The Eucharistic Words of Jesus.* Translated by Norman Perrin. New

York: Charles Scribner's Sons, 1966.

Johnson, Daniel L., and Charles Hambrick-Stowe. *Theology and Identity: Traditions, Movements, and Polity in the United Church of Christ.* New York: The Pilgrim Press, 1990.

Jones, Cheslyn, Geoffrey Wainwright, and Edward Yarnold, eds. *The Study of Liturgy.* New York: Oxford University Press, 1978.

Jungmann, Josef A. *The Place of Christ in Liturgical Prayer.* Translated by A. Peeler. Collegeville: The Liturgical Press, 1989.

Kiesling, Christopher and Ross Mackenzie. "The Eucharist as Sacrifice: A Roman Catholic-Reformed Dialogue." *Journal of Ecumenical Studies* (Summer 1978): 416-440.

Kilmartin, Edward J. *Christian Liturgy. I. Systematic Theology of Liturgy.* Kansas City: Sheed & Ward, 1988.

_____. *The Eucharist in the West: History and Theology.* Collegeville: The Liturgical Press, 1998.

_____. "The Eucharistic Prayer: Content and Function of Some Early Eucharistic Prayers." In *The Word in the World: Essays in Honor of Frederick L. Moriarty, S.J.* eds. Richard J. Clifford, S.J. and George W. MacRae, S.J., 117-134. Cambridge: Weston College Press, 1973.

Kingdon, Robert. "International Calvinism." In *Handbook of European History 1400-1600: Late Middle Ages, Renaissance, and Reformation, Vol. 2,* eds. Thomas A. Brady, Jr., Heiko A. Oberman, and James D. Tracy, 229-245. Grand Rapids: Eerdmans, 1995.

Klooster, Fred H. *The Heidelberg Catechism: Origin and History.* Grand Rapids: Calvin Theological Seminary, 1982.

Kunzler, Michael. *The Church's Liturgy.* Translated by Placed Murray OSB, et al. New York: Continuum, 2001.

Leenhardt, F.J. *Parole visible: pour une evaluation nouvelle du sacrement.* Neuchautel: Delachaux and Nestle, 1971.

Léon-Dufour, Xavier. *Sharing the Eucharistic Bread: The Witness of the New Testament.* Translated by Mathhew J. O'Connell. New York: Paulist Press, 1987.

Lies, Lothar. "Trinitatvergessenheit gegenwartiger Sakramententheologie?" *Zeitschrift fur Katholische Theologie* 105 (1983) 290-314.

Lietzmann, Hans. *Messe und Herrenmahl: Eine Studie zur Geschichte der Liturgie.* Bonn: Marcus and Weber, 1926.

Ligier, Louis. "The Origins of the Eucharistic Prayer: From the Last Supper to the

Eucharist." *Studia Liturgica* 9:4 (1973): 161-185.

Lindeboom, J. *Austin Friars: History of the Dutch Reformed Church in London 1550-1950*. Translated by D. De Iongh. The Hague: Martinus Nijhoff, 1950.

Loonbeek, Raymond, and Jacques Mortiau. *Un Pionnier Dom Lambert Beaudin (1873-1960): Liturgie et Unité des chrétiens*. 2 vols. Louvain-La-Neuve: Editions de Chevetogne, 2001.

Lossky, Nicholas, ed. *Dictionary of the Ecumenical Movement*. Grand Rapids: Eerdmans, 1991.

Marshall, I. Howard. *Last Supper and Lord's Supper*. Grand Rapids: Eerdmans, 1980.

Martimort, Aimé Georges, ed. *The Church at Prayer: Principles of the Liturgy*. Translated by Matthew J. O'Connell. Collegeville: The Liturgical Press, 1987.

Marxsen, Willi. *The Lord's Supper as a Christological Problem*. Translated by Lorenz Nieting. Philadelphia: Fortress Press, 1970.

Mast, Gregg A. *The Eucharistic Service of the Catholic Apostolic Church and its Influence on Reformed Liturgical Renewals of the Nineteenth Century*. Drew Studies in Liturgy Series, No. 7. Lanham, MD: The Scarecrow Press, 1999.

_____. *In Remembrance and Hope: The Ministry and Vision of Howard G. Hageman*. The Historical Series of the Reformed Church in America, No. 27. Grand Rapids: Eerdmans, 1998.

Maxwell, Jack M. *Worship and Reformed Theology: The Liturgical Lessons of Mercersburg*. Pittsburgh: Pickwick Press, 1976.

Maxwell, W.D. *The Liturgical Portions of the Genevan Service Book*. Westminster: The Faith Press LTD, 1965.

_____. *An Outline of Christian Worship*. Oxford University Press, 1936.

Mazza, Enrico. *The Celebration of the Eucharist: Origin of the Rite and the Development of its Interpretation*. Translated by Matthew J. O'Connell. Collegeville: The Liturgical Press, 1999.

_____. "Didache 9-10: Elements of a Eucharistic Interpretation." In *The Didache in Modern Research*, ed. Jonathan A. Draper, 276-299. Leiden: Brill, 1996.

_____. *The Eucharistic Prayers of the Roman Rite*. Translated by Matthew J. O'Connell. New York: Pueblo Publishing Company, 1986.

_____. *The Origins of the Eucharistic Prayer*. Translated by Ronald E. Lane. Collegeville: The Liturgical Press, 1995.

McDonnell, Killian. *John Calvin, the Church, and the Eucharist*. Princeton: Princeton University Press, 1967.

McKee, Elsie Anne. "Context, Contours, Contents: Towards a Description of the Classical Reformed Teaching on Worship." *The Princeton Seminary Bulletin* 16 (1995): 172-201.

_____. *John Calvin on the Diaconate and Liturgical Almsgiving.* Genève: Libraire Droz S.A., 1984.

McLoughlin, William G. *Revivals, Awakenings, and Reform: An Essay on Religion and Social Change in America, 1607-1977.* Chicago History of American Religion, ed. Martin E. Marty. Chicago: The University of Chicago Press, 1978.

Macmanus, Frederick R. "Ecumenical Import of the Constitution on the Liturgy." *Studia Liturgica* 4 (1965): 1-8.

Meeter, Daniel James. *"Bless the Lord, O My Soul:" The New-York Liturgy of the Dutch Reformed Church, 1767.* Lanham, MD: The Scarecrow Press, 1998.

Megivern, James J., ed. *Worship and Liturgy: Official Catholic Teachings.* Wilmington, NC: McGrath Publishing Company, 1978.

Meyer, Hans Bernhard. *Eucharistie: Geschichte, Theologie, Pastoral.* Regensburg: Verlag Friedrich Pustet, 1989.

_____. ed. *Liturgie und Gesellschaft.* Innsbruck: Tyrolia-Verlag, 1970.

_____. "Das Werden der literarischen Struktur des Hochbetes." *Zeitschrift fur katholische Theologie* 105 (1983): 184-202.

Milavec, Aaron. *The Didache: Faith, Hope, & Life of the Earliest Christian Communities, 50-70 C.E.* New York: The Newman Press, 2003.

Mitchell, Nathan D. "Church, Eucharist, and Liturgical Reform at Mercersburg: 1843-1857." Ph.D Diss., University of Notre Dame, 1978.

Neusner, Jacob, trans. *The Mishna: A New Translation.* New Haven: Yale University Press, 1988.

Nevin, John W. *The Anxious Bench.* Chambersburg, PA: Office of the "Weekly Messenger," 1843.

_____. *The Anxious Bench.* 2nd edition. In *Catholic and Reformed: Selected Theological Writings of John Williamson Nevin,* eds. Charles Yrigoyen, Jr. and George H. Bricker, 9-126. Pittsburgh: Pickwick Press, 1978.

_____. *The Anxious Bench* and *The Mystical Presence.* Philadelphia: J.B. Lippincott & Co., 1846. Reprint, *The Anxious Bench* and *The Mystical Presence.* New York: Garland Publishing, Inc., 1987.

_____. "Doctrine of the Reformed Church on the Lord's Supper." *Mercersburg Review* 2 (1850): 421-549

_____. "Early Christianity." In *Catholic and Reformed: Selected Theological Writings of*

John Williamson Nevin, eds. Charles Yrigoyen, Jr. and George H. Bricker, 177-310. Pittsburgh: Pickwick Press, 1978.

_____. *The History and Genius of the Heidelberg Catechism*. Chambersburg: Publication Office of the German Reformed Church, 1847.

_____. *The Liturgical Question with Reference to the Provisional Liturgy of the German Reformed Church: A Report by the "Liturgical Committee."* Philadelphia: Lindsay & Blakiston, 1862.

_____. *Vindication of the Revised Liturgy*. In *Catholic and Reformed: Selected Theological Writings of John Williamson Nevin*, eds. Charles Yrigoyen, Jr. and George H. Bricker, 313-403. Pittsburgh: Pickwick Press, 1978.

Nichols, James Hastings. *Corporate Worship in the Reformed Tradition*. Philadelphia: Westminster, 1968.

_____. "The Intent of the Calvinistic Liturgy." In *The Heritage of John Calvin: Heritage Hall Lectures 1960-1970*, ed. John H. Bratt, 87-109. Grand Rapids: Eerdmans, 1973.

_____. "The Liturgical Tradition of the Reformed Churches." *Theology Today* 11 (July 1954): 210-224.

_____, ed. *The Mercersburg Theology*. New York: Oxford University Press, 1966.

_____. *Romanticism in American Theology: Nevin and Schaff at Mercersburg*. Chicago: The University of Chicago Press, 1961.

Niederwimmer, Kurt. *The Didache: A Commentary*. Translated by Linda M. Maloney. Minneapolis: Fortress Press, 1998.

Niesel, Wilhelm. *The Theology of Calvin*. Translated by Harold Knight. London: Lutterworth Press, 1956.

Nischan, Bodo. "The 'Fractio Panis': A Reformed Communion Practice in Late Reformation Germany." *Church History* 53 (1984):17-29.

Oesterley, W.O.E. *The Jewish Background of the Christian Liturgy*. Oxford: Oxford University Press, 1925.

Old, H.O. *The Patristic Roots of Reformed Worship*. Zurich: Theologischer Verlag Zurich, 1975.

Otterness, Richard H. "The *Directory for Worship, 1986* in Reformed Tradition and Contemporary Society." Ph.D Diss. Colgate Rochester Divinity School Bexley Hall Crozer Theological Seminary, 1987.

Oudersluys, Richard C. "The Place and Need of a Formulated Liturgy in the Reformed Church." *The Church Herald*, 18 May 1951, 7.

_____. "The Revision of our Liturgy." *The Western Seminary Bulletin*, Vol. VIII, no. 4

(March 1955): 1-4.

Paquier, Richard. *Dynamics of Worship: Foundations and Uses of Liturgy.* Translated by Donald Macleod. Philadelphia: Fortress Press, 1967.

Pasztor, Janos. "Calvin and the Renewal of the Worship of the Church." *Reformed World* 40:2 (1988): 910-917.

Payne, John. "Schaff and Nevin, Colleagues at Mercersburg: The Church Question." *Church History* 61 (1991): 169-90

Penzel, Klaus, ed. *Philip Schaff: Historian and Ambassador of the Universal Church, Selected Writings.* Macon: Mercer University Press, 1991.

Pettegree, Andrew. *Foreign Protestant Communities in Sixteenth-Century London.* Oxford: Clarendon Press, 1986.

Peterman, Glen O. "Training a Congregation of the Western Synods of the RCA in the "Order of Worship" of the Liturgy as a Means to Equip the Congregation for Mission in the World." Ph.D Diss. San Francisco Theological Seminary, 1971.

Petuchowski, Jacob J., and Michael Brocke, eds. *The Lord's Prayer and Jewish Liturgy.* New York: Seabury Press, 1978.

Phifer, Kenneth G. *A Protestant Case for Liturgical Renewal.* Philadelphia: The Westminster Press, 1965.

Power, David N., Regis A. Duffy, and Kevin W. Irwin. "Current Theology. Sacramental Theology: A Review of the Literature." *Theological Studies* 55 (1994): 657-705.

_____. *The Eucharistic Mystery: Revitalizing the Tradition.* New York: Crossroad, 1992.

Pranger, Gary K. *Philip Schaff (1819-1893): Portrait of an Immigrant Theologian.* Swiss American Historical Society Publications, ed. Leo Schelbert, vol. 11. New York: Peter Lang, 1997.

Quill, Timothy C.J. *The Impact of the Liturgical Movement on American Lutheranism.* Drew Series in Liturgy, No. 3. Lanham, MD: The Scarecrow Press, Inc., 1997.

Reina, Nicholas J. "The Development of the Teaching on Real Presence and on the Notion of the "Sacrament of the Sacrifice" in the Eucharistic Theology of the Anglican, Lutheran, and Roman Catholic Churches and Its Implication for an Ecumenical Eucharistic Service Among These Three Churches." Ph.D Diss. Graduate Theological Union, 1982.

Reumann, John. *The Supper of the Lord: The New Testament, Ecumenical Dialogue, and Faith and Order on Eucharist.* Philadelphia: Fortress Press, 1985

Rice, Howard L., and James C. Huffstutler. *Reformed Worship*. Louisville: Geneva Press, 2001.

Rogers, Dirk W. *John à Lasco in England*. New York: Peter Lang, 1994.

_____. "John à Lasco in London." Ph.D. diss., Drew University, 1991.

Roorda, Garrett C., ed. *A Companion to the Liturgy: A Guide to Worship in the Reformed Church*. New York: Half Moon Press, 1971.

_____. "Confessional Faith and the Liturgy." *The Church Herald*, 23 October 1964, 12-13.

_____. "The Worship of God in the Revised Liturgy." *The Church Herald*, 24 March 1961, 12,22.

Rordorf, Willy, et al. *The Eucharist of the Early Christians*. Translated by Matthew J. O'Connell. New York: Pueblo Publishing Company, 1978.

Rorem, Paul. "The *Consensus Tigurinus* (1549): Did Calvin Compromise?" In *Calvinus Sacrae Scripturae Professor: Calvin as Confessor of Holy Scripture*, edited by Wilhelm H. Neuser, 72-90. Grand Rapids: Eerdmans, 1994.

Rouse, Ruth, and Stephen Charles Neill, eds. *A History of the Ecumenical Movement 1517-1948*. Philadelphia: The Westminster Press, 1986.

Rutgers, Frederik Lodewijk. *Acta van de Nederlandsche Synoden der zestiende eeuw*. 's-Gravenhage, 1889.

Schäfer, Gerhard Karl. *Eucharistie im ökumenischen Kontext: Zur Diskussion um das Herrenmahl in Glauben und Kirchenverfassung von Lausanne 1927 bis Lima 1982*. Göttingen: Vandenhoeck & Ruprecht, 1988.

Schaff, Philip. "The New Liturgy." *The Mercersburg Review* 10 (1858): 199-228.

_____. *The Principle of Protestantism* and *What is Church History*. Reprint. Ed. Bruce Kucklick. New York: Garland Publishing, Inc., 1987.

Schmidt-Lauber, Hans-Christoph. "Das Eucharistiegebet." *Kerygma und Dogma* 48 (2002): 203-237.

Scholl, Hans. *Der Dienst des Gebetes nach Johannes Calvin*. Zurich: Zwingli Verlag, 1968.

Schulz, Frieder. "Die Vorbereitung zum Abendmahl in der Kirchenordnung der Kurpfälz von 1563." *Jahrbuch für Liturgik und Hymnologie* 7 (1962): 1-39.

Schweizer, Eduard. *The Lord's Supper according to the New Testament*. Philadelphia: Westminster Press, 1967.

Schweizer, Julius. *Zur Ordnung des Gottesdienst in den nach Gottes Wort reformierten Gemeinden der deutschsprachigen Schweiz*. Zürich, n.p. 1944.

_____. *Reformierte Abendmahlsgestaltung in der Schau Zwinglis.* Basel: Friedrich Reinhardt, 1950.

Seasoltz, R. Kevin, ed. *Living Bread, Saving Cup: Readings on the Eucharist.* Collegeville: The Liturgical Press, 1987.

Senn, Frank C. *Christian Liturgy: Catholic and Evangelical.* Minneapolis: Fortress Press, 1997.

_____. *New Eucharistic Prayers: An Ecumenical Study of their Development and Structure.* New York: Paulist Press, 1987.

_____. "The Reform of the Mass: Evangelical, but Still Catholic." In *The Catholicity of the Reformation,* eds. Carl E. Braaten and Robert W. Jenson, 35-52. Grand Rapids: Eerdmans, 1996.

Shriver, George H. *Philip Schaff: Christian Scholar and Ecumenical Prophet.* Macon: Mercer University Press, 1987.

Smend, Julius. *Die evangelischen deutschen Messen bis zu Luthers Deutscher Messe.* Nieuwkoop: B. DeGraaf, 1967.

Spinks, Bryan D. *From the Lord and "The Best Reformed Churches:" A Study of the eucharistic liturgy in the English Puritan and Separatist Traditions 1550-1633,* Vol I. Bibliotheca Ephemerides Liturgicae Subsidia, 33. Rome: C.L.V. Edizioni Liturgiche, 1984.

_____, ed. *The Sacrifice of Praise: Studies on the Themes of Thanksgiving and Redemption in the Central Prayers of the Eucharistic and Baptismal Liturgies.* Ephemerides Liturgicae 19. Rome: Edizioni Liturgiche, 1981.

_____, and Iain Torrance, eds. *To Glorify God: Essays on Modern Reformed Liturgy.* Edinburgh: T & T Clark, 1999.

Sprott, George W. *The Worship and Offices of the Church of Scotland.* Edinburgh and London, 1882.

Stevenson, Kenneth W. "The Catholic Apostolic Church—its History and its Eucharist." *Studia Liturgica* 13 (1979): 21-43.

Studer, Basil. *Trinity and Incarnation: The Faith of the Early Church.* Translated by Matthias Westerhoff. Collegeville: The Liturgical Press, 1993.

Swanson, R.N., ed. *Continuity and Change in Christian Worship.* Suffolk, UK: The Boydell Press, 1999.

Talley, Thomas J. "From *Berakah* to *Eucharistia*: A Reopening Question." *Worship* 50 (1976): 115-137.

_____. "The Literary Structure of the Eucharistic Prayer." *Worship* 58 (1984): 404-420.

Tamburello, Dennis E. *Union with Christ: John Calvin and the Mysticism of St. Bernard.* Columbia Series in Reformed Theology. Louisville: Westminster John Knox Press, 1994.

Thompson, Bard. "Historical Background of the Catechism," "The Reformed Church in the Palatinate," and "The Catechism and the Mercersburg Theology." In *Essays on the Heidelberg Catechism,* ed. Bard Thompson et al., Jr., 8-74. Philadelphia: United Church Press, 1963.

_____. "Reformed Liturgies: An Historical and Doctrinal Interpretation of the Palatinate Liturgy of 1563, Mercersburg Provisional Liturgy of 1858, Evangelical and Reformed Order of 1944, and Their Sources." B.D. Thesis, Union Theological Seminary, 1949.

Thurian, Max and Geoffrey Wainwright. *Baptism and Eucharist: Ecumenical Convergence in Celebration.* Faith and Order Paper no. 117. Geneva: World Council of Churches, Grand Rapids: Eerdmans, 1983.

_____. *The Eucharistic Memorial.* (2 Vols.). Translated by J.G. Davies. Ecumenical Studies in Worship no. 7. London: Lutterworth Press, 1960.

_____. *The One Bread.* Translated by Theodore DuBois. New York: Sheed and Ward, 1969.

_____. "The Present Aims of the Liturgical Movement." *Studia Liturgica 3* (1964): 107-114.

Tomkins, Oliver S. *The Third World Conference on Faith and Order Held at Lund August 15 to 28, 1952.* London: SCM Press LTD, 1953.

Torrance, J.B. "The Vicarious Humanity of Christ." In *The Incarnation,* ed. T.F. Torrance, 127-147. Edinburgh: Handsel, 1981.

Torrance, T.F. "The Mind of Christ in Worship. The Problem of Apollinarianism in the Liturgy." In *Theology in Reconciliation.* Ed. T.F. Torrance, 139-214. London: Geoffrey Chapman, 1975.

Tuzik, Robert L. *How Firm a Foundation: Leaders of the Liturgical Movement.* Chicago: Liturgy Training Publications, 1990.

Vanbergen, Paul. "The Constitution on the Liturgy and the Faith and Order Reports on Worship." *Studia Liturgica 5* (1966): 1-19.

VanderKam, James, trans. *The Book of the Jubilees.* Corpus Scriptorum Christianorum Orientalium 511. Louvanii: In aedibus E. Peeters, 1989.

Van der Leeuw, Gerardus. *Sacramentstheologie.* Nijkerk: G.F. Callenbach, 1949.

Vander Lugt, G.T. "Liturgy Means the Work of the People." *The Church Herald,* 28 November 1958, 8.

_____. "Principles of Reformed Worship." *The Church Herald,* 14 May 1951, 8,17.

_____. "Worship the Lord in the Beauty of Holiness." *The Church Herald,* 6 January 1961, 12.

Van de Sandt, Huub and David Flusser. *The Didache: Its Jewish Sources and Its Place in Early Judaism and Christianity.* Assen: Royal Van Gorcum, 2002.

Van Heukelom, Raymond. "Some Comments on the Proposed Revised Liturgy." *The Church Herald,* 6 March 1964, 10,22.

Van Hoeven, James W., ed. *Word and World: Reformed Theology in America.* The Historical Series of the Reformed Church in America No. 16. Grand Rapids: Eerdmans, 1986.

Vischer, Lukas, ed. *Christian Worship in Reformed Churches Past and Present.* Grand Rapids: Eerdmans, 2003.

_____, ed. *A Documentary History of the Faith and Order Movement 1927-1963.* St. Louis: The Bethany Press, 1963.

Visser, Derk, ed. *Controversy and Conciliation: The Reformation and the Palatinate, 1559-1583.* Pittsburgh Theological Monographs New Series, ed. Dikran Y. Hadidian, vol. 18. Allison Park, PA: Pickwick Publications, 1986.

Volker, Alexander. "Eucharistie und Credo: Anmerkung zu einem Problem evangelischer Gottesdienstgestaltung." *Studia Liturgica* 17 (1987): 232-240.

Von Allmen, Jean-Jacques. *The Lord's Supper.* Translated by W. Fletcher Fleet. Ecumenical Studies in Worship no. 19. Richmond: John Knox, 1969.

_____. "Worship and the Holy Spirit" *Studia Liturgica* 2 (1963) 124-135.

_____. *Worship: its Theology and Practice.* London: Lutterworth, 1965.

Vorgrimler, Herbert. *Sacramental Theology.* Translated by Linda S. Maloney. Collegeville: The Liturgical Press, 1992.

Vööbus, Arthur. *Liturgical Traditions in the Didache.* Wetteren, Belgium: Cultura Press, 1968.

Wallace, Ronald S. *Calvin's Doctrine of the Word and Sacrament.* Edinburgh: Oliver and Boyd, 1953.

Wainwright, Geoffery. *Eucharist and Eschatology.* New York: Oxford University Press, 1981.

_____. *For our Salvation: Two Approaches to the Work of Christ.* Grand Rapids: Eerdmans, 1997.

_____. *Doxology: The Praise of God in Worship, Doctrine, and Life.* New York: Oxford University Press, 1980.

Weerda, Jan Remmers. *Der Emder Kirchenrat und seine Gemeinde: Ein Beitrag zur Geschicte reformierter Kirchenordnung in Deutschland, ihrer Grundsatze und ihrer Gestaltung.* Emder Beitrage zum reformierten Protestantismus, Band 3. Wuppertal: Foedus, 2000.

Wegman, Herman A.J. *Christian Worship in East and West: A Study Guide to Liturgical-History.* Translated by Gordon W. Lathrop. New York: Pueblo Publishing Company, 1985.

Wentz, Richard E. *John Williamson Nevin: American Theologian.* Religion in America Series, ed. Harry S. Stout. New York: Oxford University Press, 1997.

White, James F. *Protestant Worship: Traditions in Transition.* Louisville: Westminster/John Knox Press, 1989.

_____. *The Sacraments in Protestant Practice and Faith.* Nashville: Abingdon Press, 1999.

Wolfe, Janet E. "Worship Reformed and Ecumenical: A Comparative History of the Changes in Texts of Worship Resources Developed Since 1961 in the Presbyterian Church (U.S.A.) in Light of Ecumenical Models of Worship." Ph.D Diss. Graduate Theological Union, Berkeley, CA, 1997.

Wolterstorff, Nicholas. "The Reformed Liturgy." In *Major Themes in the Reformed Tradition,* ed. Donald K. McKim, 273-304. Grand Rapids: Eerdmans, 1992.

_____. "Sacrament as Action, not Presence." In *Christ the Sacramental Word: Incarnation, Sacrament, and Poetry,* eds. David Brown and Ann Loades, 103-122. London: SPCK, 1996.

Yrigoyen, Jr., Charles, and George M. Bricker, eds. *Catholic and Reformed: Selected Theological Writings of John Williamson Nevin.* Pittsburgh Original Texts and Translations Series, ed. Dikran Y. Hadidian, no. 3. Pittsburgh: The Pickwick Press, 1978.

_____. *Reformed and Catholic: Selected Historical and Theological Writings of Philip Schaff.* Pittsburgh Original Texts and Translations Series, ed. Dikran Y. Hadidian, no. 4. Pittsburgh: The Pickwick Press, 1979.

Zeeden, Ernst Walter. "Calvinistische Elemente in der kurpfalzischen Kirchenordnung von 1563." In *Existenz und Ordnung: Festschrift fur Erik Wolf zum 60. Geburtstag,* ed. Thomas Wurtenberger, et al., 183-216. Frankfurt am Main: Vittorio Klostermann, 1962.

Zeindler, Matthias. *Gotteserfahrung in der christlichen Gemeinde: Eine systematisch-theologische Untersuchung.* Stuttgart: W. Kohlhammer, 2001.

Index